Experiments in Physics

Colin Siddons

Basil Blackwell

Published by Basil Blackwell Ltd
108 Cowley Road
Oxford OX4 1JF
England

British Library Cataloguing in Publication Data

Siddons, Colin
 Experiments in physics.
 1. Physics–Experiments
 I. Title
 530'.0724   QC33

  ISBN 0–631–90069–1

Typeset in 10pt Rockwell
by Columns of Reading

Printed in Great Britain
by Page Bros. (Norwich) Ltd

Acknowledgements

The author and publishers wish to thank the following
for permission to reproduce photographs:

A & F Pears Ltd/Elida Gibbs Ltd (p. 53);
National Portrait Gallery, London (p. 147)

Contents

Colin Siddons demonstrating at Kettering High School for Girls

Introduction

I STARTED MY career as a science teacher at Kingsbridge in South Devon in 1935. Chance played a part in my choice of science teaching. If it hadn't been for Tolstoi, I might have become a meteorologist.

When I came down from Cambridge, jobs for graduates (even science jobs) were hard to find. Choice was limited. I applied for a post as a meteorologist at the Air Ministry, and was called for an interview. A dozen or so old men sat round a table. The questions began with science – with physics. The old men began to doze as I gave routine answers to routine questions. Then a question was put to me: 'Who is your favourite author?' A trap, perhaps, and if it was I walked straight into it. 'It used to be Dickens but now it's Tolstoi'.

The old men woke up. 'Tolstoi!', they shrieked. 'He's a pacifist isn't he?' Had I known more about Tolstoi I might have been able to allay their fears. In his youth, Tolstoi had a distinguished record fighting with the Tsarist Cavalry in the Caucasian mountains, and was decorated for bravery. But this I did not know at the time. I did not become a meteorologist: I became a science teacher.

When I retired from full-time teaching in 1973, I thought that my teaching days were over: I had a few lecture demonstrations still to do and that would be that. But, instead of becoming fewer, the invitations to lecture multiplied. Fortunately we live in a large terraced house with a big attic and a large cellar. I used the space and the facilities that these provided to try out new experiments or (more accurately) new variations of old experiments.

While you are still teaching, time for trying things out is limited. Lesson 1 with its experiment has to be done in Week 1 and then the apparatus for it has to be put away for a year. Lesson 2 with its experiment and its apparatus takes over. Retirement changes all this: I could and did try different variations on the same experiment for days on end.

When I began teaching, I thought that I had come in rather late in the day. Surely by then (1935) all the interesting experiments in school physics must already have been discovered. Could there be anything left to do? There was, and I came across a number of things while I was still teaching. The stimulus of invitations to give demonstrations ensured that new experiments continued to appear. Many of them have been written up in the pages of *The School Science Review* and other journals. This book includes a selection of ideas from these writings. It also includes reminiscences – mainly of my experiences over more than 50 years as a science teacher, but also from my five years in the army.

My career as a science teacher did not come to an end with my retirement in 1973; it simply changed course.

Chapter 1
Air and Water

Figure 1

NOT LONG AFTER I retired, I was invited to a local first school to 'show some experiments'. Six year olds were quite outside my experience as a science teacher, so when I accepted the invitation I was not quite sure how things would go. I need not have worried: there is no shortage of experiments with air and water which appeal to young children and every experiment was followed with wide-eyed wonder.

After I had gone, the children were asked to *draw* what they had seen. Figure 1 shows the drawing by Steven Robinson, aged $6\frac{1}{2}$. On the right, table-tennis balls and a balloon are held up by Bernoulli. In the centre, soap bubbles are being blown in a bowl. Radio Rex is on the left; I shall explain him later.

From one hole to two holes

Bore a fine hole in the stopper of a wine bottle. Fill the wine bottle with water and put the stopper in. Turn the bottle upside down. Nothing happens: no water comes out. To prove that there is a hole, shake the bottle: water will come out a drop at a time.

Figure 2

Next, use a jam jar (or a fat little onion jar). Make two holes in the lid, a long way apart. Fill the jar with water. Then turn the jar upside down, keeping the two holes at the same level. Nothing happens. Turn the jar slowly so that one hole becomes lower than the other (Figure 2). At first nothing happens, but eventually water drips out of the lower hole while air bubbles into the upper hole. The smaller the holes are and the closer they are together, the more the jar has to be tilted.

Water can get out only *if air can get in*. If the holes are on different levels, the water (being heavier than the air) comes out of the lower hole and is replaced by air bubbling in higher up. If the two holes are on the same level, the water can't make up its mind (so to speak) which hole to come out of.

If a bottle such as a milk bottle is filled with water and then inverted, there is room in the neck of the bottle for water to pour out as air rushes in. In the absence of something to direct the traffic, clumsy gurgling takes place as the descending water argues with the ascending air.

Fit a small rubber hot-water bottle with a stopper which has been bored with a fine hole. Fill the bottle with water and then turn it upside down. The water will come out in a smooth fine stream, making a pleasant contrast with the gurgling water from the milk bottle.

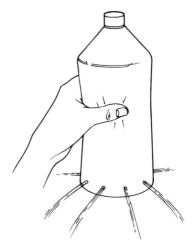

Figure 3

From two holes to eight holes

Drill eight fine holes at the same depth in a plastic bottle (Figure 3) and fill (or half-fill) the bottle with water. Then, standing in an appropriate position, ask in an appropriate tone of voice whether it is possible for a bottle to be full of holes and full of water. If someone says (or is persuaded to say) 'No', then squeeze the bottle.

When I first did this with young children, I wondered if it would distress any of them. It never has yet: after all, the teacher (being nearest) gets wettest.

What does this little entertainment show? One thing is that holes can be bored in plastic bottles; another is that when such bottles are squeezed they shrink in volume. It shows too that plastic bottles really are plastic; a glass bottle would be of no use at all.

From eight holes to hundreds of holes: a sponge

Hold a big rectangular sponge under water. When it has had time to fill up, take it out and support it on two rods. If the bottom face of the sponge is horizontal, no water flows out. Tilt the sponge: water flows out of the bottom edge. Tilt it about a second axis: water flows out of the bottom corner.

I came across another example of the sponge effect in a Hungarian book of experiments (fortunately, the book was illustrated).

Cover a jam jar with a piece of loosely woven cloth (Figure 4) and fasten the cloth round the neck of the jar with string. Pour water through the cloth to fill the jar. Then cover the jar with cardboard and turn it upside down.

Keeping the bottom face of the jar horizontal, push the cardboard off sideways. In spite of the many holes, the water stays in. As soon as the jar is tilted enough to let air in, the water is shot out noisily.

Since holes can be bored in plastic bottles, a spouting jar is easy to make (Figure 5). Start with two holes only. Find out where the jets cross and how the meeting point depends on the head of water. Then try with three or more holes.

Figure 4

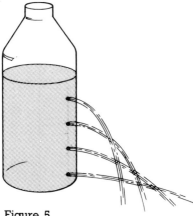

Figure 5

A jet of water shooting out horizontally is parabolic in shape but describes only half a parabola. If a hole is bored in the base of a plastic bottle and a short length of narrow tubing is inserted, a full parabola can be seen (Figure 6).

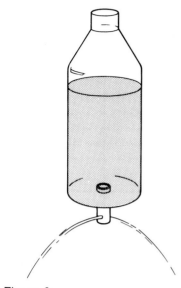

Figure 6

The card and the jam jar

This is one of the best known of all air-and-water demonstrations. A jam jar is filled with water – to the very top, the instructions say. It is covered with a card and turned upside down; the water stays in. The atmosphere pressing upwards is more than a match for the water pressing down (Figure 7). Instead of a card, thin paper (for example, newsprint) can be used.

In another variation, the jam jar is replaced with a tall gas jar. The demonstration then becomes more dramatic, particularly if the jar is held over a head (your own especially). Before turning the gas jar upside down, I used to tell the tale of the schoolgirl who was asked by her parents what the difference was between biology, chemistry and physics. She replied:

If it wriggles it's biology
If it stinks it's chemistry
If it doesn't work it's physics

The reputation that physics experiments have for not 'working' is widespread. I fancy that it is based on psychology rather than on fact. The many experiments that work are forgotten – the one that doesn't is remembered. It gives pupils satisfaction to see that, after all, teachers are not infallible.

In this case, if the experiment doesn't work, somebody gets wet. I did once. The reason why it didn't work involved more physics. Instead of topping the gas jar with a *plain* card I used one which had an advertisement printed on metal foil on one side. Confident in the success of the experiment, I watched the audience – a large group of sixth formers – instead of the gas jar. Too late I realised why they were staring spellbound. The card had curled: off it came, down poured the water on to me.

The moral of this story is that even the slightest modification to any experiment – in this case the use of a fancy card – should be checked beforehand.

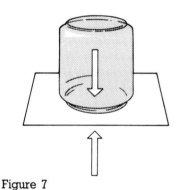

Figure 7

To the very top

The instructions for the jar-and-card experiment stress that the jar must be filled to the very top. However, the card stays on just as well if the jar is three-quarters full, half full or only one-quarter full. So why do the instructions stress that it must be full? To avoid an awkward explanation!

When the jar is full, the situation is simple. The atmosphere is pressing up. Only a small head of water is pressing down. The card is held up by the superior upward pressure (Figure 7). When the jar is half full, air is trapped in the top half. Is not this air pressing down? Will it not press down with atmospheric pressure? Why does the card stay on now?

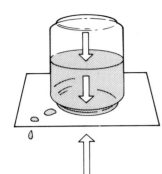

Figure 8

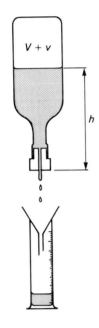

$V + v$

h

Figure 9

The answer may be obvious to an experienced physicist but if a vessel as small as a jam jar is used it is not easy to demonstrate the answer convincingly.

When the jar is inverted, part of the card is pushed down for a moment allowing a little water to leak away. The remaining air expands with a consequent decrease in its pressure. The leakage is short lived; the card is pushed up again (Figure 8).

The leakage from the jam jar is very small – too small to measure accurately. I tried measuring the leakage from a gas jar of 300 cm^3 capacity, half filled with water. The leakage was only about 1 cm^3 – still not really measurable. Calculation showed that the leakage was proportional to the square of the volume of trapped air. Not having anything bigger available, I used a 1 litre wine bottle.

I drilled a fine hole in a plastic stopper and put it into the bottle half filled with water. When the bottle was inverted, water came out – first as a jet, then in drops and then, quite definitely, the last and final drop. I collected and measured the leakage (Figure 9).

The calculation

1 Isothermal   If we assume that the leakage takes place isothermally, we can apply Boyle's law.

Let
   V be the initial volume of air
   v the volume of the leakage
   A the atmospheric pressure in metres of water and
   h the head of water in metres.

Then

$$VA = (V + v)(A - h)$$

and

$$v = \frac{Vh}{A - h}$$

The barometric height corresponded to a column of water 10.5 m long, V was 540 cm^3, h was 0.22 m. Had the change been isothermal, v would have been 12.0 cm^3; actually it was only 10.5 cm^3. The leakage was too quick to be truly isothermal.

2 Adiabatic   If the leakage is adiabatic, then gamma (γ) comes in. Gamma is the ratio

$$\frac{\text{the specific heat capacity of air at constant pressure}}{\text{the specific heat capacity of air at constant volume}}$$

The equation now becomes

$$AV^\gamma = (A - h)(V + v)^\gamma$$

γ is 1.4. Substituting, we find that v is only 8.6 cm^3, not 10.5 cm^3. The leakage was too slow to be truly adiabatic. Thus the leakage was too fast for isothermal conditions, and too slow for adiabatic conditions.

Application of calculus to the equation for v shows that for a given wine bottle the maximum leakage takes place when the bottle is half full.

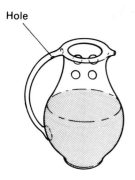

Hole

Figure 10

Bevi se puoi

On holiday in Italy we found in a gift shop a trick jug that I had long searched for in England. It has an attractive pattern on its body but there are holes in its neck (Figure 10). The thick rim bears the legend *'Bevi se puoi'* – 'Drink if you can'. Eighteenth century noblemen in England entertained their guests with such toys. The jug was filled with a tempting inducement to drink and a volunteer had to drink the jar dry without spilling a drop. A heavy forfeit had to be paid if he did not succeed.

The trick is in the hole in the underside of the handle. If you are in the know, you block this with your finger, suck through the spout and empty the jug. If you are not in the know, sucking is of no avail.

The size of the jug is important. The jug has to be large for the trick to work satisfactorily. My jug (which has a capacity of 150 ml) is not really big enough. With a strong sustained suck a little liquid is carried up by the Bernoulli effect. The result of imbibing a *big* jug of strong liquor can be imagined.

100 × 5, not 50 × 10

As part of Children's Book Week, I was invited by a librarian to show some experiments. He advertised the occasion by putting notices in nearby shops. 'I expect we will get about 50 ten year olds', he said. I got the experiments ready and we went off for a fish-and-chip lunch. When we returned, we found the room full. But instead of 50 ten year olds, there were more like 100 five year olds. 50 × 10 may in the abstract equal 100 × 5 but not as an audience.

The children were there squatting on the floor: there was no going back. The show had to go on. I did an experiment – it worked. A plump little boy sprang to his feet and clapped. I reckon that he saved the day. Every time an experiment worked, it was clapped. I used the time taken for the clapping to die down to get the next experiment ready.

The demonstration was a success, but I would advise anybody called on to do a similar lecture to make sure that the age range is more suitable.

Balloons and bladders

An open-ended balloon

Is it possible for a balloon to be blown up with its neck still open? In 1978 the Minister of Education, Shirley Williams, visited the ASE meeting in Liverpool. I had the pleasure of demonstrating to her the blowing up of a balloon with its neck open. Here is how it can be done.

Drill a hole near the bottom of a transparent plastic bottle. Using a rubbery glue, fit in and fix a conical connector. Push a balloon of suitable shape into the mouth of the bottle (Figure 1). When air is sucked out of the bottle, the balloon blows up even though its neck is still wide open. Look into the balloon through the open neck. Who has blown up the balloon: you or the atmosphere?

Next, instead of sucking air out of the bottle, blow in through the tube. For a moment there is instability as the balloon is turned inside out. Any words printed on the balloon will now appear the wrong way round – that is, laterally inverted.

If you have a suitable face, you can do this experiment without the bottle or the balloon. Your face is suitable if it has plenty of cheek. Keep your mouth shut. First blow your cheeks hard, then suck in hard.

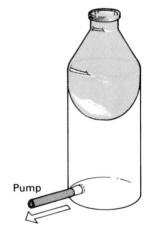

Pump

Figure 1

A squawker

A well-known party toy works on the principle of the Bourdon gauge: if the pressure is increased inside a flexible tube of elliptical cross-section curved into a spiral, the tube straightens. The toy is fitted with a squawker to add to the fun.

Remove the squawker from the tube and fix a balloon on to the squawker. Blow the balloon up through the squawker. Let the balloon down: squawking will be heard. Listen carefully at the end. Instead of dying with a whimper, the note rises both in pitch and in volume. If any member of the class thinks that this is too childish for words, ask them to draw (roughly) the graph of pressure against volume for the balloon.

A powerful blow

Stand a brick on the table and ask the smallest member of the class to blow the brick over. She (for it is generally a girl) tries but does not succeed. Then place the brick on a piece of stiff cardboard

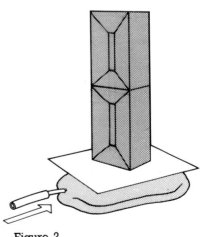

Figure 2

resting on a football bladder to which a plastic tube has been fitted. Position yourself to catch the brick as it topples and ask the girl to blow. The brick falls over. Indeed, two bricks can be blown over in this way (Figure 2).

A pin-pricked balloon

Blow a balloon up and stick a short length of sealing tape on it. Then prick the tape with a pin. The balloon does not burst. Remove the pin. If the balloon is blown up more, the size of the pinhole increases; if the balloon is let down, the size decreases.

The stream of air through the pin-pricked hole has a pleasant cooling effect even though the balloon has been blown up with one's own breath.

A boy at a first school once put this question to me: why is it that if you blow through your mouth when it is nearly shut the air will cool your fingers and yet, if you open your mouth wide and blow out, the air warms your fingers? How does one answer a question like that?

The Magdeburg hemispheres

I have heard the Magdeburg hemispheres denounced as obsolete physics but there are two stories too good to miss about Otto von Guericke, Burgomaster of Magdeburg. First there is the story of the hemispheres themselves, and the twelve horses that could not pull them apart. This prompts the question: were twelve horses really necessary? Would not six horses on one side and a sturdy rock or tree on the other side have done just as well?

The second story is of von Guericke's attempt to measure atmospheric pressure using a water barometer. The 32 ft (10 m) required was about the height of his house. The top of the barometer poked just above the roof, and on the surface of the water von Guericke floated a little red manikin. The superstitious Magdeburgers mistook the manikin for a devil. Noticing that it disappeared during stormy weather, they concluded that von Guericke was in league with the devil, and burned his house down ... or so the story goes.

I thought of these stories one day in 1945 when I was in Madgeburg. Magdeburg was in the British occupied zone before it was transferred to the Soviet zone and, to our astonishment, as we pulled out in *trucks* the Red Army marched in on *foot*. I tried to interest my REME comrades in the tale of the disappearance of Guericke's red devil, but they were more interested in the appearance of the Red Army.

Obsolete physics or not, if a school has the Magdeburg hemispheres it is a pity not to use them. A rough estimate can be made of the atmospheric pressure, not in centimetres of mercury but in newtons per square metre. Pump the air out of the hemispheres and hang them up with a strong S-hook (Figure 3). Find the maximum load that can be held without separation, using a sand bucket to break the fall. Measure the internal diameter. Then divide the maximum load in newtons by the internal area in square metres to get the atmospheric pressure in newtons per square metre.

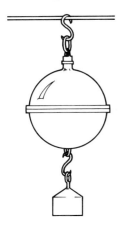

Figure 3

On one occasion when I did this, my young daughter happened to be a member of the class. I held her up by Magdeburg, so to speak. But the seal did not hold. She and one hemisphere fell off ignominiously. While the rest of the class enjoyed it, she gave me a look of withering scorn.

If the maximum load for 5, 10 and 15 strokes is measured in turn, it will be found that the effectiveness of the strokes falls off as their number increases. This is of course to be expected, yet juvenile pumpers don't think so. They argue that if 10 strokes produce a good vacuum, 20 strokes will produce one twice as good.

As a variation, try using the plungers that plumbers use in place of the Magdeburg hemispheres. Two plungers pushed together to force air out will hold substantial loads for a limited time. Alternatively, some types of plastic dustbin lid or plastic washing-up bowl if pressed vigorously on to the flat surface of a light table will then be able to lift the table up (*Take care!*).

Does air have a density?

Ask the class to suggest a method of finding out whether air weighs anything: does it have a density? Somebody may suggest weighing a balloon, first empty and then full of air. Try this. In an actual experiment a spherical balloon with a diameter of 30 cm increased in 'weight' by 1.2 g on being blown up. The volume of air contained was roughly 15 litres. The air therefore apparently had a density of 0.08 g/litre.

Next, in place of the balloon we used a football bladder. There was no increase in weight, although the balance used was sufficiently sensitive to measure an increase in weight of 0.01 g. The volume of air was measured by displacing water from gas jars. It was 1.2 litres. Thus the density of air appeared to be less than 0.01/1.2, i.e. 0.008 g/litre.

The air in the balloon and the air in the bladder both displace air. This displaced air exerts an upthrust. For the bladder (which, being gusseted, can be blown up by a very slight pressure), the weight of the displaced air is practically equal to the weight of the contained air. So there is no apparent gain in weight. Air had to be forced into the balloon, so the air inside the balloon was compressed and therefore denser than the outside air.

The real density of air was found by weighing a suitable stoppered $\frac{1}{2}$ litre flask – first full of air and then after evacuation. The drop in weight was 0.60 g. It was not necessary to assume that all the air had been pumped out. The evacuated flask was opened under water – an exciting part of the experiment – and so the effective volume of air removed was measured. It was 0.50 litres. Thus the density of air by this experiment was 1.2 g/litre.

(It is surprising how few people – even science teachers – know, without having to think, that water is roughly a thousand times denser than the air around us.)

The balloon had actually contained no less than 18 g of air but had increased in weight by only 1.2 g. The pressure inside the balloon therefore exceeded that outside by (roughly) 1.2/18 – that is, by 0.07 atmospheres.

Bell-jars and pumps

Vacuum sealing

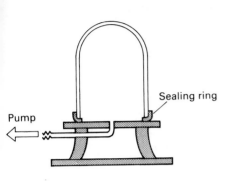

Figure 4

Place an empty bell-jar and its sealing ring on a stand and set up the pump as shown in Figure 4. Make 20 strokes with the pump, then with due caution lift the stand by lifting the bell-jar. This impresses the class. You can then suggest starting from the beginning again making only 10 strokes, and then 5 strokes. I found that even one stroke was sufficient, though I only lifted the stand a short distance for a short time.

If a single stroke has been sufficient, a calculation can be slipped in here. From the capacity of the pump cylinder and the volume of air in the bell-jar, the fractional decrease in pressure brought about by one stroke can be calculated. This decrease multiplied by the area of the base of the bell-jar gives a force. If this force is greater than the weight of the stand, then a lower limit to the atmospheric pressure (N/m^2) can be estimated.

From Ben Nevis to Mount Everest

After the 1945 war there was a flourishing of 'ex-Gov' shops where the army sold off at bargain prices such things as resistors, huge capacitors, ammeters, magnets small, magnets large and even cathode-ray tubes. Fourth-form boys kept me informed. One day they reported that ex-RAF altimeters were on sale. I bought a couple – I should have bought up the whole stock.

Placed in the bell-jar with the pump set to work, the altimeter would record breath-taking ascents: Ben Nevis took a few strokes; Mount Everest needed a lot more. If, when at the top of Mount Everest, we let air in suddenly, the altimeter needle spun round dizzily – the descent was almost frightening.

The increase in 'height' is roughly proportional to the number of strokes of the pump. The reduction of pressure in the bell-jar takes place exponentially but so too does the reduction in atmospheric pressure with increase in height.

No bang in a vacuum

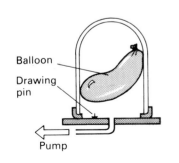

Figure 5

One well-known method of showing that sound will not travel through a vacuum is to hang an electric bell in a bell-jar and to pump the air out. The bell can be seen vibrating but is not heard. In my experience the demonstration is sometimes not very convincing. If it is not, try this method.

Place in the bell-jar a thin-walled balloon, half blown up. Position the balloon a little way above the point of a drawing pin (Figure 5). Pump the air out – the balloon expands and gets nearer the pin point. Those children who can't bear bangs put their hands over their ears, fearing one. The balloon bursts: not a sound is heard.

It is now possible to buy small electronic key finders which you fasten to your keys. If you cannot locate your keys, you clap your hands and a squeaky noise can lead you to them – provided, of course, that they are not too far away. Lay one of these key finders on a soft sound-absorbing base in a bell-jar. Test that it is working, and then pump out the air – the squeak can no longer be produced by clapping hands.

Mercury barometer

The setting up of a mercury barometer is now known to be a health hazard so I will write in the past tense: not about its setting up but about its dismantling. (It is not often that the dismantling of an experiment reveals a point of interest.)

A finger was placed across the end of the tube, and a vessel positioned to catch the falling mercury. (Before you read on, try to think what happened when the finger was removed.) For a moment, nothing happened: then a short length of mercury at the bottom broke away. The remaining column was not long enough to equal the atmospheric pressure: it was pushed up quickly to the top of the tube which it hit with a loud metallic clang. This convincingly demonstrated that there was indeed a vacuum on top. A stream of air then made its way upwards past the descending mercury.

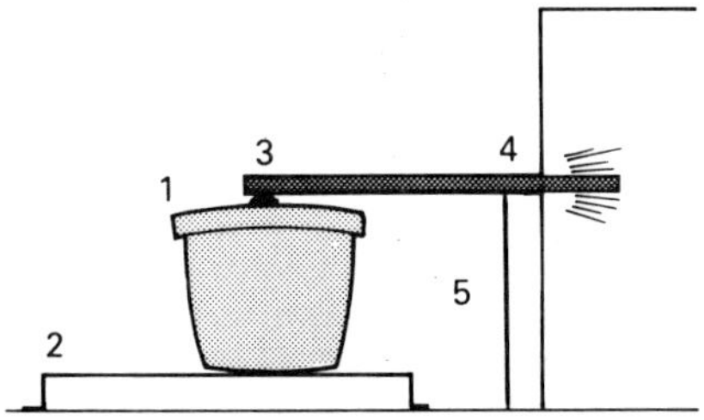

1 A sealed cup
2 Lunch tray
3 Blob of jam to hold
   the end of the pointer
4 Aluminium pointer
5 Toothpick

Figure 6

A lunch-tray altimeter

In 1983 I went as an observer to the International Physics Olympiad which that year was held in Romania. There I had the good fortune to meet a Finnish physics teacher, Jukka Mattila. He told me of an altimeter that he had improvised from materials on his lunch tray on a flight back to Helsinki from Hungary. He had noticed that both ends of his sealed water cup bulged out at high altitudes. This showed that the pressure inside the plane was below that at ground level. When the plane was 11 900 m high the pressure inside it corresponded to a height of 2400 m.

Figure 6 shows the lunch-tray altimeter. The pointer moved 60 mm during the descent. At ground zero, Jukka crushed the altimeter and drank the water.

Radio Rex

Whatever the age of my audience, I have always ended my lecture demonstrations with Radio Rex (Figure 7). The celluloid bulldog 3 cm by 4 cm is pushed into the kennel. I stand back and shout 'Cats' – out jumps the fierce dog. I put him back and, after I have given a signal, the audience shouts 'Cats'. A juvenile audience (though possessed of smaller lungs) never fails to get Rex out. Has not a teacher given them permission to *shout*? Adult audiences often fail the first time – a matter of psychology, not of physics.

Radio Rex originated in the USA earlier this century when 'radio' still had a magic sound about it. It has nothing to do with radio of course. Inside the kennel is a 1.5 V battery, an electromagnet and a steel tongue. When Rex is pushed in, the tongue is pushed back so that it completes the circuit through the electromagnet. This then holds the tongue in position.

On the wall of the kennel a loosely hanging brass amulet straddles and touches two copper wires. This amulet is therefore a second switch. Sound waves passing through the air momentarily break the circuit (if they are sufficiently strong) and release the tongue which then ejects Rex.

It is necessary to stand the kennel on a shock absorber:

Figure 7

members of the class sitting by the demonstration table soon find out that a gentle unobservable tap of the table will bring Rex out. In contrast, if the kennel roof is taken off, a much louder shout is required.

The drawing shown in Chapter 1 (Figure 1) was done by Steven. While the other children were still laughing at Rex, I heard Steven say, 'Vibrations. It's done by vibrations.'

Chapter 3

Floating and Sinking

AFTER I HAD been asked to give a talk to seven year olds on 'things to do with air and water' I worked out some experiments on floating. This made me realise that there was more, much more, to floating than Archimedes principle.

Floaters can be divided into two main classes, 'real floaters' and 'maybe floaters'. Real floaters are such things as table-tennis balls and ice-cubes. If real floaters are pushed down beneath the surface they rise again – in the case of table-tennis balls, very briskly. Maybe floaters are such things as pins which, with a little knowhow, can be floated but which once pushed down stay down.

Real floaters

These can be subdivided into two classes: one-way floaters and two-way floaters. A long candle will always float with its axis horizontal; an empty custard powder tin can float with its axis horizontal and it can float with its axis vertical. Cylindrical containers rescued from the scrap bin can be tested and then assigned to their subclass.

Short broad cylinders such as draughts pieces will (experience tells us) only float with their axis vertical. Long narrow cylinders such as pencils will only float with their axis horizontal. But what about long broad cylinders?

Theory

The conditions for stability of floating cylinders can be predicted. The stability depends on two ratios:

L/d, the ratio of the length L to the diameter d
Δ, the ratio of the density of the solid to the density of the liquid.

Consider the curve shown in Figure 1. Any cylinder for which (L/d, Δ) is in the shaded area will float with its axis vertical. In Figure 2 any cylinder for which (L/d, Δ) is in the shaded area will float with its axis horizontal. Figure 3 combines the two curves. It has five regions:

- In region A the axis will be horizontal.
- In region B the axis will be vertical.
- In regions C_1 and C_2 the axis is stable either in the horizontal position or in the vertical position.
- In region D the cylinder is stable neither in the horizontal position nor in the vertical position. The axis must therefore be tilted.

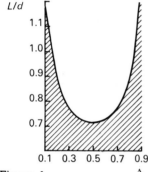

Figure 1

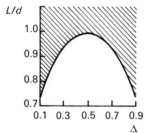

Figure 2

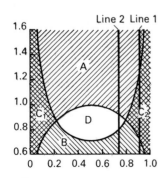

Figure 3

Figure 4

Practice

1 *Kitchen scrap* To test the predictions, I began with kitchen scrap. Two polystyrene drinking cups glued together as shown in Figure 4 had an L/d value of 2.0 and a ratio of effective densities of only 0.012. They made an imposing sight floating on water with only 1/80th of their length below the surface. Theory predicted that they should float both horizontally and vertically and this they did. A custard 'tin' with $L/d = 1.0$, $\Delta = 0.11$, bore out the prediction that it too should float both horizontally and vertically. A bean tin with the top replaced and $L/d = 0.76$, $\Delta = 0.22$, was predicted to be in the B class and it did indeed only float vertically.

2 *Wood* Next I turned to wooden cylinders. Here it was possible to get a wide range of L/d values and, using paraffin as well as water, two values for Δ. Agreement with prediction was poor. The wood was not homogeneous. The centre of mass of the cylinder was not on the geometrical axis.

This reminded me of a wartime experience while at sea. The convoy of troopships on which I sailed from Glasgow to South Africa in 1942 was escorted by HMS Orion. When the Orion was about to depart, its duty done, we were asked to give it a goodbye cheer but, in order not to upset the navigation of the ships, one half of us had to cheer from starboard and the other half from port. At that time (but now no more) I was surprised, because even on our densely packed troopship the ratio of mass of men to mass of boat must have been very small.

3 *Wax candles* In search of homogeneity, I turned from wooden dowels to wax candles, using candles of diameter 3.0 cm and relative density 0.94. With a heated knife, I cut them into sections, ranging in L/d value from 1.63 down to 0.47. Line 1 on Figure 3 indicates that within this L/d range the candles should float horizontally, then either horizontally or vertically, then vertically. This they did, verifying the theory and showing the homogeneity of the candles.

Next I used strong brine in place of water, the relative density now becoming 0.78. Line 2 on Figure 3 shows that the candle sections should be horizontal, then perhaps tilted, then vertical. This was what happened.

There is thus a marked difference between the behaviour of the wax cylinder in water and in brine. This difference can be demonstrated dramatically. Float a wax cylinder ($L/d = 1.5$) in water. Its axis will be vertical. Add brine slowly to the water. Eventually, and suddenly, the cylinder turns through 90° so that its axis is horizontal.

Elementary physics textbooks mention the possibility of a vessel which floats safely in buoyant sea water sinking when moving into less buoyant fresh water. There is another danger, however: the possibility of a vessel turning on to its side when moving from fresh water into the more buoyant sea.

A prediction that I have not so far been able to confirm can be made from Figure 3. A cylinder with an L/d value of 0.875 and a relative density of 0.80 should float in any position.

4 *Taper in a jam jar* Another person whom I met at the 1983 International Physics Olympiad in Romania was Waldemar Gorzkowski. He organises a Polish Physics Olympiad. Problems are set for different age groups. There is no difficulty in thinking up new numerical problems but practical problems are themselves a problem. Waldemar wrote to me: could I suggest a practical problem using only objects that could be found in the kitchen? I suggested 'the taper in the jam jar'.

The wax taper hangs from a cotton thread held in the hand. It is lowered into the water in the jam jar. At first the taper stays upright but, as the length submerged increases, it eventually reaches a critical depth at which it begins to tilt. If the cotton is lowered further, no more taper is submerged – it simply tilts more.

This simple situation produces a quadratic equation (there are not many such in physics). If x is the fraction of the total length of the taper submerged and Δ is the ratio of the density of the taper wax to the density of the submerging liquid, then application of the law of moments brings the equation

$$x^2 - 2x + \Delta = 0$$

This yields a rational solution

$$x = 1 - \sqrt{(1 - \Delta)}$$

It is possible to do the experiment as simply as this, but it is difficult to measure the critical length accurately. It is better to hang the taper by a thread wrapped round a rod (Figure 5). To lower the taper, the rod is turned. In this way x can be measured more accurately.

As an alternative to tapers, thin wooden rods could be used; paraffin, meths or brine could be used instead of water.

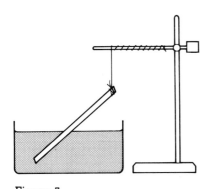

Figure 5

Maybe floaters

My interest in maybe floaters began by accident. To find relative densities by the weighing-in-air and weighing-in-water method, I used besides metals more domestic objects such as potatoes, carrots and lumps of coal. (These last, once washed, are clean to handle.) One day it happened that I had ready to hand some flat rods of solid polystyrene which I had obtained for electrostatics experiments. The density of polystyrene is 1.07 g/cm^3, and so the rods 'should' sink. A fine hole was bored near the end of each rod so that it could be held up by cotton. The rod was weighed first in air and then in water. The fourth-formers were doing the experiment. One girl came up to me. She was puzzled – the rod did not sink.

It did not sink because it was flat in shape and had been put down gently in a horizontal position. I knew, of course, that steel pins could be floated. Vaguely, I knew the reason – surface tension. But I had not realised that flat objects could be floated when they were made of materials denser than water. Quick tests with microscope slides, aluminium discs, steel diaphragms, 'tin' lids and gramophone records showed that all these could be floated if laid flat on water.

Discs

For electrostatics experiments I had obtained an aluminium disc 14 cm in diameter, 0.42 mm thick and of mass 17 g. I found it to be a superb maybe floater. Launched in a large glass trough, it makes a pleasing sight (Figure 6). Around the perimeter, a wall of water comes down smoothly, making a large flat circular depression.

The following experiment was in my list of experiments with air and water suitable for first schools, which shows its popularity. I fixed a rod in the centre of the disc and slipped light annular rings over the rod, one at a time. Each new ring pushed the disc further down into the water. Surely the next ring would sink the disc – but no, it didn't. Perhaps the next, or the next. Eventually, to the great joy of the beholders, the disc would gracefully sink.

More sophisticatedly, I measured the mass that could be added without sinking the disc. Nearly always, it would take a load of 30 g wt. Once it took 32 g wt. If we take 31 g wt as the critical extra load, this makes the total load borne 48 g wt (17 + 31).

Why does this disc float, since it is heavier than water? Where does the upward force of 48 g wt come from? Surface tension?

The surface tension round the edge of a 14 cm diameter disc cannot be greater than 3 g wt. But the surface tension does allow the wall of water to be formed. In consequence, the total volume of water displaced is greater than the volume of the disc.

The effective weight of water displaced is 48 − 3, that is 45 g wt. On a 14 cm disc, such an upthrust will be produced at a depth of 0.29 cm. The disc was 0.04 cm thick. When it was on the point of sinking, its top surface was 0.29 − 0.04, that is 0.25 cm, below the water level. The critical height of the water wall is thus 0.25 cm. What decides this height?

Figure 7 shows a section of the wall. The curvature AB in the horizontal plane can be neglected. Consider the equilibrium of the section. There are two surface tension pulls in the horizontal plane. One is along CD; the other (in the opposite direction) is the horizontal component of the pull on AB. The resultant of these two forces equals the upthrust due to water pressure on the face CDEF. This leads to the equation

$$\sigma(1 - \cos \theta) = \tfrac{1}{2}g\rho h^2$$

Substituting 7.4×10^{-2} N m^{-1} for the surface tension σ and 2.5×10^{-3} m for the height h of the wall, we find that the angle θ of contact is 54°. When the disc is only lightly loaded, θ is smaller than this and the wall is not so high. As the load increases, θ reaches its limiting value and the wall reaches its maximum height: the disc sinks.

Pins and needles

I wanted to find the limit of the ability of water to buoy up *steel* knitting needles. After a search, I found some (knitting needles are no longer made of steel).

No.17, No.16 and No.15 needles have diameters of 1.42 mm, 1.63 mm and 1.83 mm respectively. I cut rods 10 cm long having first removed the heads and tapering tails. To float the rods, I used a

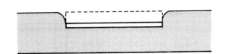

Figure 6

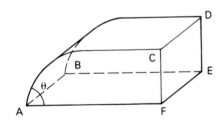

Figure 7

Figure 8

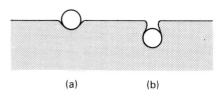

(a)   (b)

Figure 9

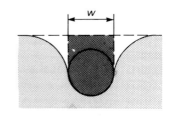

Figure 10

Lamp

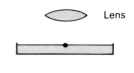

Lens

Figure 11

launcher made of copper wire (Figure 8). When the critical thickness is approached, the ends begin to sink – unless they are smeared with a fine layer of vaseline.

Unlike pins, these thicker rods will not float unless the surface of the water is first cleaned. This can be done by drawing a strip of thin paper across the surface. I had no difficulty in floating No. 17 and No. 16 rods on wiped water.

A little entertainment can be had here. When such a rod is floating, wipe your finger on your forehead and dip it into the water. The rod will move away briskly, and sink. Fish it out with the launcher, then wipe the water afresh. The rod can be floated again. A thin layer of sebum – the sweat of one's brow – reduces the surface tension of the water.

Diagrams like those in Figures 9(a) and 9(b) sometimes appear in books of popular science. They are incorrect – the idea that the water surface has a skin has been carried too far. Pins on top of homemade rice pudding (which of course has a skin) would behave like this. In neither of the two figures is the water shown as wetting the pins. But it does. Use threads to lower a pin on to a water surface so that it floats, and then lift it clear. A line of droplets will hang from the pin, showing that it has been wetted by the water.

The real cross-section of a rod floating on water is shown in Figure 10. There is a finite angle of contact between the top of the rod and the water wall. If rods are floated in a transparent vessel – for example, the lid of a sandwich box – observation confirms that for broader rods the whole rod is beneath the surface of the water.

The rod displaces not only its own volume of water but in effect the volume shown shaded in Figure 10. The weight of the total effective volume of water displaced produces an Archimedean upthrust on the rod. The vertical component of the surface tension along the two lines of contact of rod and water added to this upthrust equals the weight of the rod.

I measured the depths of immersion of the rods with a travelling microscope fixed to work vertically. The microscope was first focused on the top of the rod, and the reading taken. The rod was then pushed to the side, powder sprinkled on to the water and the new reading taken. The depth of immersion is greater for the broader rods, increasing from 1.5 mm with No. 17 rods to 2.3 mm with No. 15 rods. The uncovered part of the rod decreases as the rod sinks deeper. The width w shown in Figure 10 decreases, eventually reaching a minimum. Then the rod sinks.

Generally, rods cut from No. 15 needles cannot be floated – the critical point has been passed. I measured the density of one No. 15 rod which did float – it was only 7.0 g/cm^3, the density of cast iron, not steel.

The cross-section solved   It is a simple matter to measure the depth of immersion of a floating rod, but how can the extent of the uncovered section be measured? The answer is: by the shadow. The shadow of a rod floating in a shallow transparent vessel (the lid of the sandwich box) is much wider than the rod itself. The experimental arrangement is shown in Figure 11.

The wall of water curves down to the top of the rod. The rays are therefore bent out of line. As I have shown, the shape of the water wall is known. Each part of the wall will bend the rays differently

Figure 12

(Figure 12). From the width of the shadow and a lot of calculation, it is possible to work out the precise cross-section of the water surface. The full calculation is given in the *School Science Review*, *189*, p.775.

The No.17 needle used had a diameter of 1.44 mm and a mass-to-length ratio of 0.130 g/cm. It was immersed to a depth of 1.5 mm. The angle made with the vertical was 39°. The effective Archimedean upthrust was 35 mN/m. The upward component of surface tension was 93 mN/m, so the total upward force was 128 mN/m. This agrees better than was to be expected with the weight of 127 mN/m.

Cartesian divers

When Descartes' name is turned into an adjective, it loses a syllable at the beginning to gain one at the end. René Descartes (1596–1650) is well described as a philosopher; he was indeed a lover of learning. He made contributions to many branches of science – not only geometry, mechanics, optics and meteorology, but psychology and embryology too. His name (partly hidden) is perpetuated in 'Cartesian' coordinates and the 'Cartesian' diver.

The Cartesian diver – like pins and needles – is a 'maybe floater' but – unlike them – once sunk, it can be refloated. It is a popular toy and appears in different guises. I have seen Cartesian devils and Cartesian octopi. Pen tops and rubber teats from dropping tubes can be turned into divers.

Basically a Cartesian diver is an empty unstoppered tube floated mouth downwards in a wider tube. It only just floats. When the pressure in the wider vessel is increased, the air inside the diver is compressed and a little water enters. The diver is now denser than water and it sinks. When the pressure is relaxed, the diver rises.

If the bottle used to hold the diver is made of glass, the pressure can be increased by pushing a rubber bung further in. The pressure inside a plastic bottle can be increased by squeezing the sides.

Match-stick diver   Having read of science teachers in Cyprus who used match heads as Cartesian divers, I tried the *whole* match instead. By itself, the match was not dense enough. Thin copper wire of carefully chosen length was wrapped round the end of the stick to bring the density up to just below parity with water.

As a Cartesian diver, the match-stick has a will of its own. Increase the pressure and it sinks. Release the pressure and generally it rises – but not always immediately. Sometimes it rises after a delay of a minute – sometimes much longer. Sometimes when it is floating it will sink suddenly and without warning.

Why will a match-stick act as a diver? Is it because there is air inside it? Or because the stick is compressible, being made of soft wood? A liaison with the biology department is suggested here.

A little magic can be practised if the match-stick is floated in a plastic bottle. Tell the class to will the match-stick to sink. It sinks. Tell them to will it to rise again. It rises. The children are watching the match, not your hand which is holding (and at the right moment squeezing) the bottle.

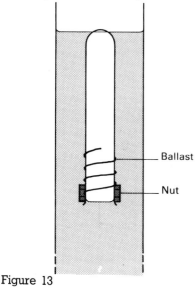

Figure 13

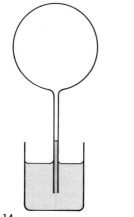

Figure 14

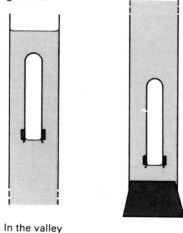

In the valley

On the hill top

Figure 15

Critical depth   The diver can be elevated in status from a toy to a scientific instrument if a suitably designed diver is floated in a transparent tube of length about a metre. An iron or steel nut is glued to the end of a test-tube (for example, of length 7 cm and diameter 1.3 cm) (Figure 13). The nut keeps the tube upright and enables it to be controlled by a magnet from outside. A length of copper wire is coiled round the end of the diver to bring its effective density to the desired value.

Float the diver. With the magnet, bring it down a short distance. Notice how the water enters a little way into the diver. Remove the magnet: the diver floats. Bring the diver down a greater distance. On being released, it floats up but is beginning to show reluctance. Eventually, at the critical depth, it will hesitate – not knowing whether to float up or to sink down of its own accord. The magnet is now used not to bring the diver down but to bring it up.

I took this magnetically controllable Cartesian diver to the Hull meeting of the ASE in 1980 and left it set up. The sixth-former who demonstrated the experiment pointed out that the critical depth was not constant but changed during the day. (Of course, if I had thought a little I should have been able not only to predict a change but also to calculate its extent.)

If the pressure on the surface of the water in the open tube (the atmospheric pressure) increases, the density of the diver will *increase*. The critical depth will therefore *decrease*. In contrast, if the temperature of the room (and therefore eventually the temperature of the air inside the diver) increases, the density of the diver will *decrease* and the critical depth will *increase*. Generally both atmospheric pressure and room temperature change, and it is not possible to apportion the change in critical depth between the two effects without measuring one of them.

Galileo made an air thermometer similar to that shown in Figure 14. If the atmospheric pressure remained constant, this would indeed be a simple and sensitive *thermometer*. Alternatively, if the surrounding temperature remained constant, the Cartesian diver would make a simple and sensitive *barometer*.

The critical depth can be measured to an accuracy of about 0.5 cm. The atmospheric pressure is roughly equal to that of a head of water of 1000 cm. Thus a change in pressure of about 1 part in 2000 will make the difference between sinking and floating.

The diver as altimeter   With a change in altitude, atmospheric pressure changes. With a rise in altitude, pressure falls. If the loading of the diver is so arranged that the critical depth is small when the diver is in a valley, then it will be large when the diver is high up a hill (Figure 15).

One of the highest points round Bradford is Soil Hill in Queensbury. With the help of Marcus Topham, I started from a height of 207 m and read the critical depth there. We then drove quickly to the triangulation station on Soil Hill, and found the new critical depth to be 22.5 cm below the first one.

The change in altitude had brought about a change in pressure equal to a head of water of 22.5 cm:

$$\frac{\text{change in altitude}}{\text{change in critical depth}} = \frac{\text{density of water}}{\text{density of air}}$$

At an atmospheric pressure of 840 mm Hg and a temperature of 15 °C, the density of water is 840 times greater than that of air.

The altitude of the triangulation point measured in this way is therefore (207 + 840 × 0.225) – that is, 392 m which is 1290 ft. The Ordnance Survey map gives the height as 1321 ft. Our Cartesian altimeter had given a satisfactory result. There was some good luck as well as good management in this: we had lagged the tube and driven quickly to avoid a change in the temperature of the water in the tube, but a change in temperature of only 0.10 °C would have altered the critical depth by 0.5 cm.

(If in wartime the altitude of an aircraft was measured by an aneroid barometer which depended on the ratio of the density of water to the density of air, how was allowance made for changes in this ratio as the aircraft changed its position?)

Chapter 4
Surface Tension

SOAP FILMS AND bubbles are delightful things but they are not 'in the syllabus'. The excellent demonstrations that can be done with them are useful to keep for open days or for the end of term when exams are over.

Nowadays, soap bubbles are generally made with detergents, not soap. They are thought of as fragile delicate things, but this is rather misleading. When they are properly treated they are quite tough.

Soap bubbles

Not as fragile as they seem   Make a film about 15 cm square by dipping a wire frame into a shallow container filled with water to which a little detergent has been added. Then carefully lift the frame out.

It is possible to poke a finger into such a film, pass a needle through it, bang it with a hammer or stab it with a knife provided that the finger, needle, hammer or knife has been wetted beforehand with soapy water. If the film is held horizontally, drops of water will pass through it.

In contrast, if you touch a film or a bubble with the tip of a feather (even very lightly), it will burst – wet doesn't like dry.

Why doesn't the bubble burst?   Blow a bubble so that it rests on top of a transparent cup. Then pour a stream of soapy water into the cup (Figure 1). The bubble grows bigger but does not burst. Why doesn't the bubble burst? One answer to this rather awkward question is that both the falling stream and the film are wet. Water doesn't dislike water.

Big bubble wanted   For a popular television programme, Cyril Isenberg and I were asked to blow a bubble big enough to hold a child. Cyril said that if we were provided with a dustbin full of water into which a detergent bottle had been emptied, a very big funnel and a child suitably dressed we would have a try! We expected a short-haired boy in bathing trunks. Instead we got two long-haired girls in their party frocks.

So as not to disappoint the girls, who wanted to 'appear on telly', we blew a big hemispherical bubble on top of a plastic container. Each girl plunged a hand through the bubble. They shook hands in the middle. Before doing this, the girls had dipped their hands into a basin of soapy water.

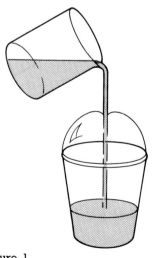

Figure 1

Expectation of life   Bubbles are not really fragile; they are, however, generally short lived. The life expectation of a bubble depends on the humidity and the temperature. Hot, dry conditions are bad for bubbles but they are good for electrostatics. So bubble and electrostatics experiments should not be attempted on the same day. In hot, dry conditions the soap films evaporate quickly and therefore thin rapidly. If bubbles are made in a closed space, they last much longer.

Fill an old-fashioned flat-sided medicine bottle with soap solution. Close the top of the bottle with your fingers, and turn the bottle upside down. By moving your fingers, let the solution out and air in, thereby filling the bottle with bubbles. They will last for days. At first they are brilliantly coloured; later they become thin, lose their colour and can only be seen from the side.

Soap films

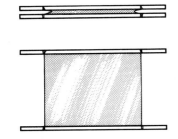

Figure 2

The ability of a film to increase or decrease in area can be shown with the help of two rods and two threads tethered to the rods (Figure 2). With the rods together, the film seems to disappear; when the rods are pulled apart, the film stretches out to a full square.

A man-in-the-moon shape (Figure 3) can be obtained with a semi-circular wire and two threads. When the central thread is released, the man in the moon disappears.

The shapes obtained when films are formed in wire frames in the shape of tetrahedra, prisms and so on are well known. Interesting effects happen with a cubic frame:

- A single dip into a bucket containing solution will produce the shape shown in Figure 4. If the 'window' in the middle is in a vertical plane, a shake will move it into a horizontal plane.
- A second dip will produce a fascinating cubic bubble. All its six faces are convex (Figure 5).

Push a drinking straw into this bubble and blow air into it: the bubble will expand. Then suck air out: the bubble will contract. There is, however, a limit to how small the bubble can become. This minimum size can be measured – no doubt it will provide a good problem for mathematicians.

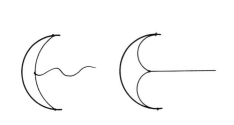

Figure 3

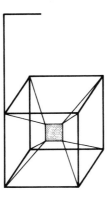

Figure 4

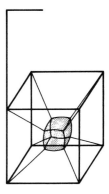

Figure 5

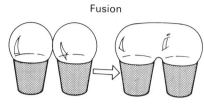

Fusion

Figure 6

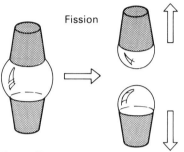

Fission

Figure 7

Bubbles again

A spherical bubble blown through a rubber tube on the end of a small funnel can be transferred to a beaker whose rim has been wetted. Figure 6 shows two such bubbles alongside each other and apparently touching. At first, they remain apart. Suddenly, for no apparent reason, they unite. This is *fusion*. If a second beaker is used as shown in Figure 7, the single bubble splits into two. This is *fission*.

We decided not to try to get a small girl into a bubble. It is, however, easy to get a small toy such as a plastic frog inside a bubble. Place the plastic frog in the middle of a saucer and pour soap solution round it. Cover the frog with a large funnel fitted with a rubber tube. Then blow down the tube and gradually lift the funnel. At the appropriate moment, turn the funnel on its side and shake it free. The frog will be left – not in a glass case, but in a bubble case.

A 'sublime' experiment

While holidaying in Paris, we were walking along the Champs Elysées when we heard a street vendor extolling her wares with as great fervour as if they had been masterpieces from the Louvre. They were in fact 'camphor ducks' on the surface of water in a tray. She had some justification for her fervour: the ducks were not circling slowly but were whizzing round.

She told her audience that before she launched the ducks she wiped the surface of the water with a strip of newspaper. This removed any mono-molecular layers, leaving the water with a high surface tension. I made use of this tip when I carried out the experiments on floating pins and needles (see Chapter 3).

The explanation generally given for the behaviour of the camphor duck is only half an explanation. Yes, the camphor flake at the rear of the duck does sharply reduce the surface tension so that the greater surface tension of the uncamphorated water at the front pulls the duck forward. But a soap flake too will reduce the surface tension of the water, and yet there are no soap-flake ducks. Why not?

The reason is that camphor sublimes. The layer of camphor produced by the action of the water quickly evaporates, leaving an uncontaminated water surface. The fact that camphor sublimes is shown by its smell; if you leave a flake or two of camphor on a table, it will have disappeared when you come back the next day.

The duck can be dispensed with. File a lump of camphor above a wiped water surface in a dish. The minute fragments of camphor dash about madly, more like eels than ducks. A particular eel may stop and then start again in the opposite direction. Pupils have compared them to spiral nebulae. Presumably the camphor fragments dissolve more quickly at the sharper points.

A camphor rotor

It is easy to make camphor floaters other than ducks. Cut out various shapes of aluminium foil. Glue a short length of light tubing (a drinking straw or balsa wood stick) to the surface of the foil. Push

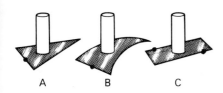

Figure 8

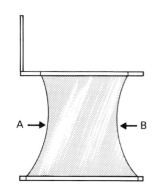

Figure 9

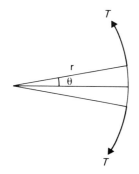

Figure 10

camphor into a cleft at one end (Figure 8). Shape A travels in straight lines; shape B moves in circles. If it is small enough (2 cm by 6 mm), shape C will whizz round very quickly in cold water and more quickly still in warm water – so quickly indeed that it is difficult to time it. Such boats will sometimes (but not always) rotate for hours on end. This leads to questions about perpetual motion.

To stop a camphor vessel, remember the experiment with the floating pins and needles (Chapter 3), wipe your finger on your forehead and dip it in the water. The vessel stops. Sheer magic!

Two calculations

1 The surface tension of a soap film

Figure 9 shows a film stretched between threads which are holding up a light rod. This is a pleasant demonstration of the tendency of a film to decrease in area. It can be turned into a quantitative experiment to measure the surface tension of the detergent solution.

Consider the equilibrium of the bottom half of the film. At A and B there are upward pulls due to the tension T in the threads. Along AB there is an upward pull due to the surface tension in the film. Since the film has two sides, if the width of the waist is w, then this pull will be $2sw$, s being the surface tension.

The tension in the thread depends on both the surface tension and the curvature of the thread. Let r be the radius of curvature. Consider the forces on that small arc of the thread which subtends an angle 2θ:

The pull to the left due to the components of T (Figure 10) will equal $T \times 2\theta$. The pull to the right will be $2s \times 2r\theta$.

These pulls are equal and opposite, so T equals $2sr$. The sum of $2T$ and $2sw$ must equal the weight mg of the rod, so

$$mg = 4rs + 2ws$$

The curvature r can be found by cutting cards with different radii and finding the best fit. The waist w can be found with dividers, and so s can be calculated:

$$s = \frac{mg}{4r + 2w}$$

2 A soap-film catenoid

I removed the bases of two coffee tins and mounted the tins on blocks of wood as shown in Figure 11. In the space between the tins, I made an open-ended soap film. Such a film is possible because the curvature at any point on its surface has two principal radii. These radii are in opposing directions and are therefore able to cancel each other out. I began with the tins near each other and slowly separated them. There was a maximum separation beyond which the film burst. For tins of diameter 99 mm, the maximum

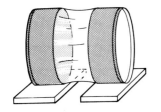

Figure 11

separation was 63 mm. Thus,

$$\frac{\text{critical separation}}{\text{diameter}} = \frac{63}{99} = 0.64$$

Consider Figure 11. Let r be the radius of the central section. The surface tension force F_0 pulling to the left equals $2\pi rT$.

Let y be the radius at a distance x from the centre (Figure 12). The horizontal component of the surface tension force to the right equals $2\pi yT \cos\theta$.

Since the two forces are equal,

$$y \cos\theta = r$$

and

$$y = \frac{r}{\cos\theta}$$

Since the tangent of the slope is $\dfrac{dy}{dx}$

$$\frac{1}{\cos\theta} = \sqrt{\left\{ 1 + \left(\frac{dy}{dx}\right)^2 \right\}}$$

and so

$$y = r \sqrt{\left\{ 1 + \left(\frac{dy}{dx}\right)^2 \right\}}$$

This is the catenary equation. The shape of the film is a catenoid. The general solution is

$$y = r \cosh\left(\frac{x}{r}\right) + k$$

When x is 0, $\cosh(x/r)$ is 1 and k is also 0. Thus

$$y = r \cosh\left(\frac{x}{r}\right)$$

By means of cosh tables, the greatest possible value of separation/diameter can be estimated. It came to 0.66. Thus the biggest separation that I had been able to get came within 3% of the theoretical maximum.

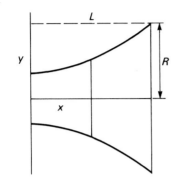

Figure 12

Chapter 5

Mechanics, Tricks and Toys

Balancing

A simple lever balance

WHEN I RETIRED, I made a simple but useful lever balance (Figure 1). The lever – bought in a model shop – was a wooden stick 500 mm × 3 mm × 6 mm. Strips of graph paper glued to the stick gave the length of the two arms.

A piece of stick was glued along the top of the lever, and a pin 1.4 mm in diameter was pushed through it. The pin is 3 mm above the top of the lever. (3 mm is a compromise – a smaller distance is required for maximum sensitivity, and a greater distance for maximum stability.)

The pin is supported on metal plates. Strips of cardboard prevent the pin from slipping sideways. The arrangement is mounted on a wooden block as shown. The gap is small to prevent undue tilting of the arms.

The masses to be compared are suspended by cotton threads: in most cases the threads have negligible mass. Coins can be used as standard masses (Table 1). The values given are not whole numbers but in these days of calculators who is afraid of multiplying?

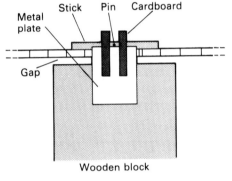

Figure 1

Table 1

Coin (in p)	½	1	2	5	10	20	50
Mass (in g)	1.782	3.564	7.128	5.65	11.31	5.00	13.50

This home-made balance has several advantages (besides cost) over electrical top-pan balances: it is not temperamental; it can be moved from place to place; suspended things can be weighed; it does not require electricity.

Balancing: two fingers

Balance a long stick (a metre rule) on two fingers (Figure 2). Use one of your fingers (A) and one finger belonging to a member of the class (B). Before trying, ask which finger will get to the centre of the rule first when the two fingers are moved slowly inwards. Generally the answer is B – it is the nearest and so has less distance to travel. In fact, neither finger gets there first – they arrive at the same moment.

This pleasant little demonstration is not in the books: physics

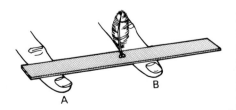

Figure 2

textbooks deal with one theme at a time. This has three themes: centre of mass, law of moments and friction. From the first two, we can deduce that the downward force on finger A will be less than that on finger B. Finger A will therefore not have as much grip on the stick and will slide to the centre.

When the two fingers are equidistant from the centre of mass of the stick, the two downward forces will be equal and the fingers will have equal grip: both fingers will slide inwards.

Once when I did this experiment with a young girl, she became so alarmed when her finger did not move that she cried out 'My finger's stuck!'

The experiment can be performed with other objects such as brooms and window poles. The point where the two fingers meet gives the centre of mass.

Swinging

There are several versions of this balancing effect. If the centre of gravity of a body free to swing about an axis is below that axis then, given a slight displacement, the body will swing to and fro. If the axis is only slightly below the centre of gravity, the time of swinging will be longer.

Figure 3 shows a swinging duck. Its head is made of cardboard, its body is a cork, its legs are pins. The duck is balanced by a stiff wire at the end of which is a heavy steel bolt.

Without a feather in its tail, the duck looks rather pathetic; with it, the swaying dies down more quickly.

Balancing: one finger

It is possible to stand a pencil, 15 cm long, upright on a table (provided that the end of the pencil is flat). It is not possible (for a normal person, anyhow) to keep the pencil upright on a finger for any length of time.

In apparent contradiction to this, a metre stick will not stand upright on a table. It can, however, be made to balance on your finger for as long as your patience permits. As soon as it begins to topple, you make a correcting movement with your finger.

A pencil or a metre rule on a table is static. It is possible to stand the pencil up because of its short length and circular base. It is not possible to stand the metre rule up because of its greater length and, in one direction, its very narrow base. Time does not come into it.

But balancing a pencil or a metre rule on your finger is very much a matter of time. The time taken for a long thin rod to topple through a given angle depends on the square-root of its length. Thus, the metre stick will take $\sqrt{(100/15)}$, i.e. 2.6 times, longer to topple than the 15 cm pencil. Any movement of the pencil is too quick to be countered.

It is always a pleasure to find a use for an empty wine bottle. Insert a long thin rod into the neck of a wine bottle. Having taken due precautions, balance the arrangement on your finger – bottle on top. You should have no difficulty provided that you watch the top of the bottle (Figure 4). Attempts to balance the bottle on a finger when the rod is on top usually fail: the wild movements of the rod are uncontrollable.

Figure 3

Figure 4

Falling

Galileo was able to make great progress in his study of falling by 'isolating the variables' – studying only those cases where the effect of air resistance could be neglected. It is a good idea to show examples of non-Galilean falling during a lesson on the acceleration due to gravity.

Nature, or biology, will provide a rich variety of examples: dandelion fruit, rose-bay willowherb fruit, sycamore keys and (best of all) feathers. Man-made examples include cotton threads, tissue paper, trays of expanded polystyrene and flour.

The phrase 'line of least resistance' can lead one astray. Hold a cotton thread or a short fluffy feather vertically. Let it fall. Very soon, it takes a position of *maximum* resistance.

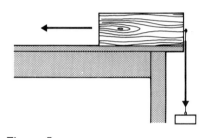

Figure 5

Gravity toys

Lessons on mechanics can become tedious. To bring a moment or two of light relief, keep a stock of gravity toys. It is safe to say that any toy that moves has some physics in it. Among those that appear in the shops from time to time are the duck that waddles downhill when placed on a slope and the dog that is pulled by a thread. The thread hangs over the edge of the table and is weighted. The dog walks to the edge of the table and stops. At the edge of the table, the tension in the string becomes a *vertical* force and therefore cannot any longer overcome the *horizontal* frictional resistance to motion (Figure 5).

Street salesmen sometimes have on their trays the toy shown in Figure 6. When placed on a slope, the ball bearing rolls down inside the tube, acquiring rotational energy. On hitting the bottom of the tube, the rolling ball brings the tube round with it. The ball is now at the top; the process is repeated.

'Pecking birds' such as that shown in Figure 7(a) seem to have disappeared from the shops, but they are easy to make. The bird is connected via a short spring to a wooden ring which fits loosely on the dowel. Given a slight tap to set it off, the bird pecks its way steadily to the bottom.

Such birds are good time-keepers: one that I had took 22 seconds to fall from top to bottom. This device is in some ways similar to an old-fashioned grandfather clock. Once a fortnight, grandfather lifted up two great lead cylinders. These fell in a series of steps (the number of seconds in a fortnight), each fall providing the kinetic energy required to keep the pendulum clock going.

In place of a wooden dowel, a steel rod can be used and in place of the wooden ring a short wire spiral (Figure 7(b)). A fourth-form girl suggested the substitution of the bell. Other gravity toys which can be kept in a toy-box are the yoyo, the slinkie and the whirling wheel.

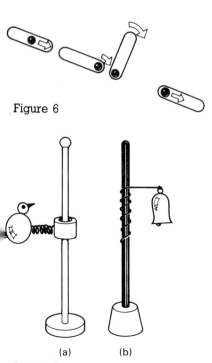

Figure 6

(a)   (b)

Figure 7

Terminal velocity

Feathers, those non-Galilean fallers, provide one good example of terminal velocity. If the works of a discarded musical box are removed, they provide another. Once it has been wound up, a spiral spring keeps the drum of the musical box (with its many tongues) rotating. The torque of the spring decreases as the spring unwinds and yet the drum must rotate at an approximately constant speed for the music to be acceptable. Besides turning the drum slowly, the spring turns very quickly two vanes mounted on a spindle. The resistance of the air through which the vanes move makes the drum rotate at a more or less constant speed. Thus a musical box and the fall of a feather have this in common – terminal velocity.

Another example of terminal velocity is provided by a cyclist: the cyclist can be pedalling hard without the speed of the bike increasing. When the sum of the resistive forces (chiefly wind resistance) reaches the size of the propulsive force, no acceleration takes place.

Free fall

If a box with a loose stone inside it is allowed to fall, the stone will become 'weightless' – it will cease to press down on the base of the box.

Toy shops sell cardboard cylinders which give out a bleating sound when turned upside down. This is meant to represent the mooing of a calf but sounds more like the bleating of a lamb. The cylinders are about 6 cm high and are of Chinese origin.

In one part of the cylinder there is a flat iron cylinder; in the other part are bellows, fitted with a squawker. When the cylinder is turned upside down, the iron presses on the bellows and forces air out through the squawker (Figure 8). (If the toy is shaken up and down, it 'quacks' like a duck, instead of bleating.)

To illustrate weightlessness, turn the toy upside down and, before it has had time to bleat, throw it up into the air. As it falls, it will remain silent. There is no surprise here: although the iron is on top of the bellows, it is not pressing down on them. But what does seem surprising is that the cylinder is silent on the upward journey also. On this half of the journey the iron, though moving upwards, is accelerating downwards, but so too (and just as quickly) are the bellows. Thus the bellows and the iron are weightless both when they are going up and when they are coming down.

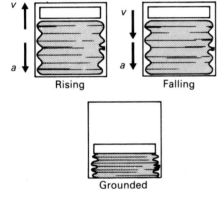

Rising   Falling

Grounded

Figure 8

Projectiles

A middle-school science teacher asked me if I could help him with a projectile problem. He had wanted his class to find by experiment the angle at which a projectile should be fired to give it maximum range. He had decided to use a stream of water as the projectile. Each pair of pupils had a detergent bottle full of water. Setting the bottle at a definite angle, they squeezed it and noted where the stream of water landed. To the teacher's surprise the class found – quite definitely – that the angle for maximum range was 25°, not the 45° the textbooks predict for more conventional projectiles. The teacher wanted to know why.

In a toy shop, I found suitable projectiles under the name of 'jumping frogs'. A plastic frog is mounted on to a suction cup, a

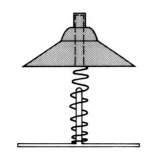

Figure 9

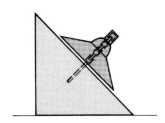

Figure 10

spring and a base (the last three of these are shown in Figure 9). The frog is pushed down so that, by atmospheric pressure, the suction cup adheres to the base – but only for a few seconds. Air leaks in and, suddenly, the spring is released. Up shoot the frog, cup, spring and base into the air. I removed the frog since it is an unnecessary burden for the projectile. When I measured the height to which the cup (with its spring and base) would jump when fired upwards, I found it to be sufficiently consistent for useful measurements to be made.

Wooden triangles were cut with angles of 30°, 45° and 60°. A metal rod was set into each piece of wood; the toy was fitted over each rod in turn (Figure 10), and then launched.

As theory predicted, the maximum range was obtained with a slope of 45°. Theory also predicted that this maximum range should be twice the height reached when the projectile is fired vertically. This turned out to be not quite the case; the maximum range was a little less than twice the height.

The reason is not difficult to find. The path of a projectile fired at 45° is 15 per cent longer than that of a projectile fired vertically, so there will be 15 per cent more air resistance. The calculation for this, involving hyperbolic integration, is an interesting one for the mathematically minded. It requires the integration

$$\int \sqrt{(a^2 + x^2)}\,\mathrm{d}x = \tfrac{1}{2}x\sqrt{(a^2 + x^2)} + \frac{a^2}{2}\,\sinh^{-1}\left(\frac{x}{a}\right)$$

But why did the middle-school children get 25° rather than 45°? Perhaps for the smaller angles they pressed down with their arms but only pressed with their hands for bigger angles.

Nijinski

Rebecca West wrote this about the famous dancer Nijinski: 'The climax of his art was his jump. He leaped high into the air, and stayed for what seemed several seconds. Face and body suggested he was to mount still further, do the Indian rope trick with himself as rope, hurl himself through an invisible ceiling and disappear. But then he came down – and here was the second miracle – more slowly than he had gone up, landing as softly as a deer clearing a hedge of snow.'

It is possible that Nijinski's downward fall *did* take a little longer than his ascent. In fact, a cricket ball thrown vertically upwards takes longer to come down than it does to go up. Suppose that one of the toy projectiles was fitted with strips of tissue paper which trailed behind the projectile when it was going up but which opened up rather like a parachute when it came down. This would slow the projectile's descent. Was Nijinski's costume designed to slow down his descent?

A projectile myth

Along with other raw recruits, I was instructed by a drill sergeant how to throw a hand grenade. He described dramatically the path of the grenade: it went upwards and away from us until it reached the top of its flight; and then it swooped straight down. 'Shades of

Galileo', I thought to myself. 'What am I to do? Should I let gross error pass uncorrected or should I risk rebuke by the drill sergeant?' I waited until I was alone with him. Then I pointed out that the grenade having reached the top of its path continued to move forwards as well as dropping down.

His face was a study: annoyance at the presumption of a recruit but a nagging fear that the recruit might be right. Always a lover of demonstrations, I offered to show him the path. I asked him to stand to the side and then I threw the grenade. Its parabola persuaded him. 'Blimey', he said. 'I never knew that.'

I recounted this story to Swedish friends. They too had heard this myth from their sergeant instructors. It is not quite as absurd as it seems. The thrower of the grenade being in the plane of the parabola cannot judge its shape. Only an observer standing to the side can do this, and when grenades are being thrown in combat one cannot observe the symmetry of the parabola.

Stranger than friction: a skidding car

Jam the *back* wheels of a toy car. Place it on a sloping board and gradually increase the slope. Eventually the car moves but before it has gone far it turns round so that the jammed wheels are at the front. The car then proceeds in a straight line down the slope. To some people this is surprising: they expect the jammed wheels to be dragged along by the front wheels.

Now place two toy cars on a slope: one with jammed back wheels, the other with jammed front wheels. (Do not let the class know that you have jammed the wheels.) Increase the slope: one car turns round, the other does not and gets ahead. Ask the class to suggest why only one car has turned round, and then show them why.

If the car with the jammed back wheels is lined up exactly down the plane, it may travel some distance before making up its mind (so to speak) to turn round. Even if the angle with the line of the plane is as small as 1°, it will determine which way the car turns.

To understand the behaviour of cars with jammed wheels, let us first consider the behaviour of a normal car on a slope. The car will accelerate in the direction shown in Figure 11(a). This acceleration has a component across the slope, so there must be a force acting across the slope. This can only come from the sideways friction F of the wheels acting in the direction shown. (On an icy slope, a car left at an angle across the road with its brakes on might slide down sideways if the friction is insufficient to stop it.)

Figure 11(b) shows the force on a car with jammed back wheels as it begins to move forwards. The frictional force F_1 on the back wheels will be in the opposite direction to the initial motion. The sideways frictional force F_2 on the front wheels will produce an anti-clockwise movement, and so cause the car to turn further out of line.

The corresponding diagram for a car with jammed front wheels (Figure 11(c)) shows that the movement will now be clockwise, and so the car will be brought into the line of the slope.

The phenomenon shown here with toy cars happens with real ones too. If the back brakes are suddenly applied, the car may swing right round.

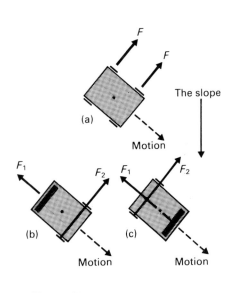

Figure 11

For the toy car the slope is not necessary. The car can be pulled forwards by a thread attached somewhere near the centre of mass. An alternative is to place the car on a long strip of paper which is pulled forwards while a thread attached to the car prevents forward movement. This produces a puzzle: which end of the car is now the front end?

If a car is let go at a definite angle (say 10°) on a plane of definite slope, the path it follows is reasonably consistent. I have not as yet been able to work out an equation for this path.

Newton's cradle

No list of mechanical toys and curiosities would be complete without Newton's cradle (Figure 12). Known by other names, it is stocked by firms which sell items to adorn the desks of business executives. Newton studied the collisions of suspended spheres and put forward an experimental law:

> 'the relative velocity along the line of centres immediately after impact is −e times the relative velocity before impact'

The value of e for hard substances like steel or ivory is nearly 1. It is called, rather vaguely, the coeffecient of restitution.

When sphere 1 is pulled back and let drop, it comes to rest on colliding with sphere 2. Sphere 5 swings out – the momentum of sphere 1 has been transferred to sphere 5. Sphere 5 falls back and transfers its momentum back to sphere 1. And so on. Some of the fascination of the toy comes from the apparent immobility of the three inner spheres. They do not seem to take part in the proceedings.

If spheres 1 and 2 are used instead of sphere 1 alone, spheres 4 and 5 collect their momentum. If spheres 1, 2 and 3 are used, spheres 3, 4 and 5 swing out. Sphere 3 is then privileged: it is swinging all the time. If spheres 1, 2, 3 and 4 are used, spheres 2, 3, 4 and 5 swing out. Now spheres 2, 3 and 4 are always swinging.

If sphere 1 is released from the left at the same time as sphere 5 is released from the right, both spheres swing out. If sphere 1 is given a small swing and sphere 5 a large one, sphere 1 will pick up the larger swing of sphere 5.

If two spheres only are used, the momentum is transferred from one to the other. Is it possible to deduce the behaviour of five spheres from the behaviour of two? In the Newton's cradle with which I am familiar, there is a slight gap between the spheres. When sphere 1 collides with sphere 2, sphere 2 can acquire momentum which it then transfers to sphere 3, and so on. But what would happen if the spheres were touching?

If any one of the three inner spheres is held between thumb and forefinger, sphere 1 will still be able to transfer its momentum to sphere 5.

It is sometimes claimed that Newton's cradle illustrates, or even 'proves', the conservation of momentum. But suppose that the spheres were made of lead or putty – their behaviour would be quite different, and not at all interesting to watch. I don't think that the cradle proves anything. But it does illustrate in a spectacular way the transfer of momentum made possible by the excellent resilience of steel.

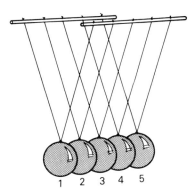

Figure 12

Figure 13

Inertia?

Party tricks

There are several party tricks which claim to illustrate 'inertia'. In one simple trick the bottom draught in a pile is given a sharp sideways blow with a thin ruler. The draught flies out and the remaining draughts fall down, leaving the pile one short.

Figure 13 shows a card standing on a wine glass. A coin rests on the card. If the card is given a quick flick, the coin falls into the glass. More skill is required for the next trick in which a wine glass is placed on a handkerchief. The idea is then to pull the hankie away, leaving the glass unscathed – this requires both speed and nerve.

A still more ambitious demonstration is to snatch a tablecloth away from a loaded table. It is not a trick for the slow or the faint hearted.

Ganot claimed that a clay tobacco-pipe suspended by two hairs could be cut in two by a powerful stroke with a sharp sword without breaking the hairs. Possessing neither a clay pipe nor a sword, I have not been able to confirm this.

A school demo

A school demonstration which does not require courage but which does require speed can be done with a cardboard cylinder on a strip of paper (Figure 14). When the strip is pulled, one of three things can happen:

1 If the strip is pulled slowly, the cylinder moves with it.
2 If the strip is gently snatched away, the cylinder topples over backwards.
3 If the strip is snatched away quickly, it leaves the cylinder standing. The cylinder doesn't move – or so it seems. Careful observation of the position of the cylinder before and after the strip is snatched away shows that it has moved forwards slightly.

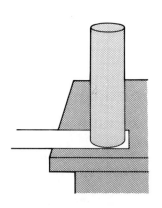

Figure 14

The greater the ratio of the height of the cylinder to the diameter, the more exciting this demonstration becomes. For success, the paper and the bottom of the cylinder should be smooth, and the strip should not overlap on the far side. You can play this trick on a volunteer. When you do the snatching, leave no strip on the far side. Make a quick snatch. Success: the cylinder remains upright. But when you stand the cylinder up for the volunteer let some strip overlap, distracting the volunteer's attention while you do so. The cylinder is more likely to topple this time.

Snatches

Consider a snatch as a big but short-lived acceleration. A block of wood rests on a strip of paper (Figure 15). Let the coefficient of limiting friction be μ, a typical value being 0.20. If the acceleration of the strip is less than $\mu \times g$ (where g is the acceleration due to gravity), the block will move forwards with the strip.

If the acceleration of the strip is greater than μg, the block will accelerate forwards but only with an acceleration of μg. This

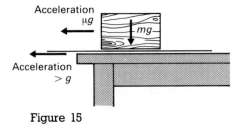

Figure 15

acceleration will be maintained as long as there is some strip left underneath. If the snatch is a big acceleration and the protruding strip is short, this will not be for long. In this case the block will not move far but, like Galileo's earth, it will move.

A little consideration shows that the distance that the block moves is independent of the mass of the block and so also of the size of its inertia. Provided that the snatch is greater than μg, a block of wood will move, and it will move no less than a cardboard box.

So what do the tricks show? Inertia? Or that frictional forces have limits?

Horsedrawn trams and Newton's first law

Some seaside resorts have – or had – horsedrawn trams along the promenade. To get the tram moving from a standing position, the horses have to use all the strength of their huge legs. Once the tram is moving, they use much less force.

Why is this mighty and painful effort necessary? A small force – Newton's first law tells us – should produce an acceleration, though only a small one. Why is starting so difficult? Is it due to the difference between the limiting friction μ_1 at the start and the smaller limiting friction μ_2 once movement has begun? The frictional force of resistance depends on the *weight* of the tram. On an imaginary *lunar* tramway, horses would have a much easier time.

_____ *Chapter 6* _____

Acceleration

Linear acceleration

The toppling block

STAND A RECTANGULAR wooden block on a trolley. The width of its base should be a small fraction ($\frac{1}{2}$ or $\frac{1}{4}$) of its height. To prevent it from sliding backwards, the block is taped to the trolley – the tape acts as a hinge. Move the trolley forwards gently; the block does not topple. Move the trolley forwards more rapidly; the block will topple.

Ask the class why the block toppled the second time and not the first. Someone will say that the trolley was moved too quickly, that the *speed* was too great. But speed is not the cause. To demonstrate this, use a hanging weight to make the trolley accelerate (Figure 1). If the weight is small enough, the trolley and block will gain speed but the block will not topple.

Next, use a bigger weight to increase the acceleration. The block will topple straight away before the trolley has had time to gain any speed. *Acceleration*, not speed, causes the block to topple.

In this experiment the block topples *backwards*. Toppling *forwards* is an everyday occurrence. If a bus driver applies the brakes too quickly, passengers standing up will topple forwards. The block on the trolley topples backwards because of a positive acceleration. The bus passengers topple forwards because of a negative acceleration.

The lurch forwards is predictable. But on many buses there is a second lurch, this one being backwards. Presumably the suspension system of the bus is responsible for it.

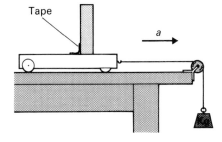

Tape

a

Figure 1

Acceleration game

An acceleration game can be played with a trolley and a block. The object is to move the trolley by hand from one end of the bench to the other in the minimum time without the block toppling backwards. Let several volunteers try, and find who has clocked the least time. Next, use a hanging weight to accelerate the trolley – one that will just not cause the block to topple. The time now will probably be considerably shorter than the previous shortest time.

The theoretical minimum can be calculated. If the block is n times taller than it is wide, then the acceleration must not be greater than g/n. To travel a distance L, it must take a time not less than

$$\sqrt{\frac{2Ln}{g}}$$

A pendulum bob

Now stand a pendulum on the trolley (Figure 2). Use a bifilar suspension to prevent the bob from swinging sideways. Then by means of a hanging weight make the trolley accelerate. The bob will move backwards relative to the trolley. For the bob to accelerate, there must be a horizontal force on it. This is provided by the horizontal component of the tension in the suspending threads.

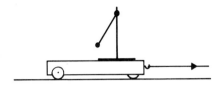

Figure 2

The bob acquires kinetic energy as it moves backwards. This makes it overshoot the mark and so it swings to and fro as the trolley moves along the bench. It does not have time to settle down to its final position. Eventually, the bob would reach a position in which the pendulum threads made an angle of $\tan^{-1}(a/g)$ with the vertical, where a is the acceleration of the trolley and g is the acceleration due to gravity. Because of the swinging, it is not possible to measure this final angle.

As an alternative experiment, replace the pendulum with a tube such as that shown in Figure 3. When the trolley is accelerated, the liquid is forced into the back limb of the tube. If the liquid had time to settle down, then the angle θ would be $\tan^{-1}(a/g)$, but once again oscillation prevents measurement. I looked next for a *damped* acceleration detector; I found one in a spirit-level.

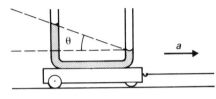

Figure 3

The spirit-level

The tube of a spirit-level is curved. In an ordinary spirit-level this curvature is very slight, making the instrument a sensitive detector of tilt. Place a spirit-level lengthways on a trolley and accelerate the trolley by hand. The bubble, having less inertia than the spirit, will move forwards; an acceleration of $g/50$ will take the bubble out of sight. If three spirit-levels are mounted as shown in Figure 4 and the acceleration is increased, bubble A will move into the central position first, then bubble B and finally bubble C.

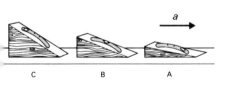

Figure 4

I took an arrangement of two such spirit-levels on the train to Leeds. It fitted snugly on to the window sill. (To allay any fears in the minds of other passengers, I took my son with me.) The slope of the railway line had to be added to or subtracted from the tilt registered. I found that the trains started off with a bigger *acceleration* than they maintained. (This was not predictable.)

Next, I replaced the three separate spirit-levels with a single spirit-level made out of a curved glass tube (Figure 5). I accelerated the trolley for a short distance using a falling weight; the bubble moved forwards. When the weight hit the floor, the trolley continued to move but ceased to accelerate. The bubble, knowing (so to speak) the difference between constant velocity and acceleration, resumed its place in the middle.

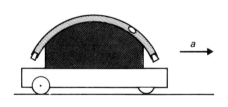

Figure 5

Circular motion

A model flying swing

To introduce middle-school children to some aspects of circular motion, I made a model flying swing as shown in Figure 6. The central axis is a No.8 knitting needle (this just fits Meccano parts).

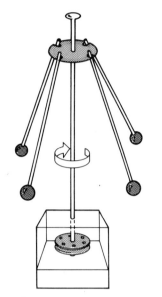

Figure 6

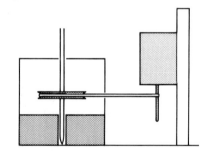

Figure 7

Four baubles, each at the end of a light wooden rod, hang from a Meccano faceplate. Slots are cut in the faceplate, and the rods are supported so that they are free to swing outwards. The roundabout is mounted vertically as shown in Figure 7. A rubber band transmits the drive from the axle of a 1.5 V model motor to a Meccano pulley, and in so doing reduces the rpm to a required lower level.

The revs can be controlled by a 10 Ω resistor in series with the cell. If the revs fall below a critical value, the baubles hang down vertically and press against the central axis. As the revs increase, the baubles move out and fly in ever-increasing circles. Why do they do this? In answering this question, we must choose our words very carefully. Some pupils will already have the answer, but unfortunately the wrong one – centrifugal force.

I suggest an explanation using the words 'centrifugal effect'. Bodies go in straight lines unless a force makes them do otherwise. If a body is moving in a circle, it is because a force acting towards the centre is making it do so. If the force is not big enough, the body will fly off at a tangent; this is the centrifugal effect.

The flying swing can be adapted to show this. Remove one of the baubles from its rod and re-attach it using only a thin sliver of blu-tack. Increase the revs gradually; the bauble will fly off at a tangent – not because 'centrifugal force' makes it do so but because the restraining force can no longer stop it from doing so.

The direction of rotation of the roundabout can be reversed by reversing the terminals of the cell. It is useful to do this with younger pupils since it demonstrates that a current is something which can be reversed. (They have to look down from above to see the reversal; viewed from the side, it is not obvious).

The science sixth, on being shown this toy, might look down on it in another sense as being too childish for their consideration. If they do, set them this problem: find the critical rate of rotation at which the baubles no longer press against the central axis.

The flying swing and g   We can adapt the merry-go-round to measure g. Figure 8 shows how. Suspend two spheres (pendulum bobs) from a cross-tree by a bifilar suspension. Place this on a gramophone turntable (preferably a discarded one) and set the turntable in motion. The bobs will fly out, swinging up and down before eventually settling into their orbit.

Measure the vertical separation h of this orbit from the plane of suspension. Then let out more thread and measure h again. Surprisingly, h is found to be constant. If the suspending threads are long enough to allow the bobs to move away from the axle, the bobs will orbit in a plane whose height depends only on the rate of revolution of the turntable, n Hz.

To verify this, suspend the bobs by threads of different lengths. Set the turntable going and let the bobs settle down in their orbits. Then look at the roundabout from the side, and you will see that the bobs are in the same plane. Analysis shows that

$$g = 4\pi^2 n^2 h$$

Thus by measuring n and h we can calculate g.

In effect, two accelerations have been compared: the acceleration of the bobs in their circular orbit, and the linear acceleration g that the bobs would have on being allowed to fall.

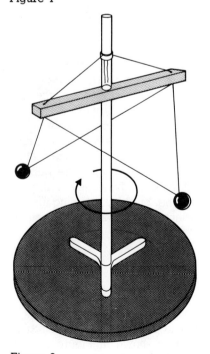

Figure 8

A seaside trick

It is a common sight at the seaside to see fathers (rarely mothers) entertaining their children by swinging a bucket of water round so quickly that not a drop falls out. No doubt some fathers would give the incorrect explanation that, because of the great speed, the water has not time to fall out. However, once the speed of rotation has passed a critical value, the water in the bucket does not even begin to fall.

On returning from the seaside many summers ago, I wondered what I could do in the lab to find this critical speed. I found an old-fashioned gramophone turntable worked by a spring. This had the advantage that the speed of rotation of the turntable was adjustable over a limited range – from 66 through 78 to 84 rpm. I determined to use this veteran turntable to repeat the seaside trick.

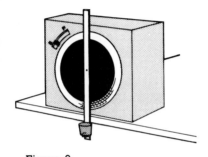

Figure 9

The turntable method   Figure 9 shows how the experiment was set up. The turntable was turned on to its side and a 0.5 metre rod was attached at the centre. A wooden block holding a shallow cardboard cup was fitted on to one end of the rod, and a brass washer was placed in the cup. The idea was that the rod would be whirled round with the speed control set at F (84 rpm). At this speed, the washer was expected to stay in the cup. The speed would then be reduced until the washer flew off at a tangent.

The chief problem was that the turntable did not attain its full speed in half a rotation. This was solved by starting the rotation with the turntable tilted and only slowly bringing it into a fully vertical position.

A stroboscope was used to determine the critical speed at which the washer was ejected. For this, four concentric stroboscopic rings were used. Intermittent light was provided by a beehive-type neon bulb. The result was fascinating to watch; two rings rotate slowly clockwise while the other two rotate anti-clockwise.

I took this experiment to the Manchester meeting of the Science Masters Association in 1963 where a visitor from Holland told me of a similar experiment with a bicycle wheel. A copper ring is wound round one of the spokes of the wheel so that it is free to move up and down the spoke. When the wheel is spun round quickly, no clicking is heard; the ring is pressed against the rim of the wheel, regardless of the position of the spoke. As the rate of rotation drops below the critical rate, a clicking sound is heard. This is caused by the ring sliding down the spoke as it goes over the top and being brought back to the rim with a click a little further on.

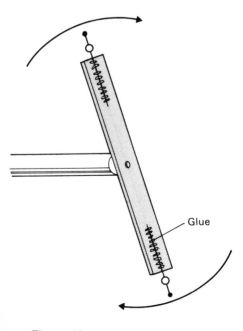

Figure 10

A use for hat pins

The story of the bicycle wheel led to the experiment shown in Figure 10. A stick about 50 cm long is free to spin on a nail. Hat pins carrying metal bobs are fastened to each end of the stick. The stick is rotated using a finger. When it is rotated slowly, clicks are heard as the stick approaches the upright position. As the speed of rotation increases, the clicks suddenly cease: the critical speed has been passed. Each bob is now firmly pressed against the end of the hat pin for the whole rotation.

With practice, the stick can be rotated so that clicks are sometimes heard and sometimes not, as the speed drops below and rises above the critical value. The average speed will now be the critical speed. Three people are required to do the experiment: one to be the twirler, one to take the time and one to count the rotations.

The calculation   The difficult part of this experiment is the calculation. Consider what is happening when the stick is rotating at a speed greater than the critical speed, and the bob is approaching the top of its path. The bob will press against the hat-pin head. The hat-pin head will therefore press down on the bob. There will be two downward forces on the bob – the reaction R of the hat pin and the force of gravity. These two forces give the bob its downward acceleration $r\omega^2$ where r is the distance between the hat-pin head and the nail, and ω is the angular velocity.

$$R + mg = mr\omega^2$$

In the critical case when the bob is just about to fall, R becomes zero and g equals $r\omega^2$.

If the number of rotations per second in the critical case is n, then ω equals $2\pi n$ and g equals $4\pi^2 n^2 r$. Rather than regarding the experiment as yet another method of finding g, it is perhaps more helpful to think of it as a method of verifying that the acceleration of a body moving in a circle is $r\omega^2$ and is directed towards the centre.

Cartwheels

With the advent of spring, young girls delight in doing cartwheels in any suitable place. They spring up and do a complete rotation in one movement: girls rather than boys because their centres of mass are lower and so it is easier for them. Young girls because, as they go over the top, their skirts fall down (like the pendulum bobs in the hat-pin experiment) and, being young, they have no embarrassment about this.

The fall of a space-lab

I happened to show the 'hat-pin' experiment at a sixth-form conference one day when a space-lab satellite was in the news. Its angular velocity having dropped below the critical value, the space-lab was due to come crashing down somewhere. The $r\omega^2$ for the space-lab being only just below the $r\omega^2$ for the hat pin's critical case, we could call them equal (for they both equal g). Hence, getting rid of constants,

$$\frac{R}{r} = \frac{T^2}{t^2}$$

where R is the radius of the earth, r is the radius of the bob on the stick, T is the orbiting time of the space-lab and t is the orbiting time of the bob. We wondered what kind of a value we could get for R from these figures.

We were told that T was about 90 minutes, i.e. 5.4×10^2 s, t was 1.0 s and r was 0.30 m:

$$R = \frac{T^2 r}{t^2} = \frac{(5.4 \times 10^2)^2 \times 0.30}{1.0^2}$$

$$= 87 \text{ km}$$

This is well above the correct value (64 km). The 'about 90 minutes' is probably the cause. It was a disappointing result but the opportunity was too good to miss.

Toppling once again

When I used to tell a class that 'a body moving in a circle with constant speed is accelerating towards the centre', I would watch their faces as I came out with this apparent contradiction. Constant speed and yet acceleration – some faces would show polite disbelief.

Toppling can be used to help with this rather knotty piece of theory. A 2 cm metal cube (the 'toppler') is placed on a turntable. Just as the block of wood in Figure 1 toppled *backwards* when the trolley passed a critical linear acceleration, so the metal cube topples *outwards* when the turntable passes a critical rate of rotation.

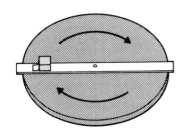

Figure 11

The cube is fastened to the turntable by a hinge made of tape (Figure 11). As the following calculation shows, at a speed of 78 rpm the cube is about to topple if its centre is 14.6 cm from the axis of the turntable. With a variable-speed turntable, the speed can be set a little below 78 rpm and then increased until toppling occurs.

With a turntable whose speed is fixed at 78 rpm, the cube is placed first at 14.6 cm from the axis and then progressively nearer to the axis until the critical distance is found. With slower turntables, two cubes can be used – one on top of the other.

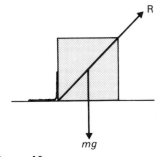

Figure 12

The theory   Consider the two forces acting on the cube when it is on the point of toppling (Figure 12). There is a force mg acting vertically downwards through the centre of mass of the cube.

There is the reaction R of the plane on the cube which acts through the taped edge. At the critical rate of rotation, the line of action of this reaction must pass through the centre of mass.

At this point, the horizontal and vertical components of R are equal. The vertical component must equal mg, so the horizontal component equals mg also. But this component gives the cube its acceleration, $r\omega^2$. Hence $g = r\omega^2$. The cube is therefore on the point of toppling when its acceleration in its circular path equals the acceleration due to gravity.

$$g = r\omega^2 = 4\pi^2 n^2 r$$

Ball bearings in grooves

A turntable suitable for doing experiments with ball bearings in grooves can be made from a small dc motor, a rubber band and Meccano pulleys.

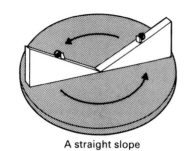

A straight slope

Figure 13

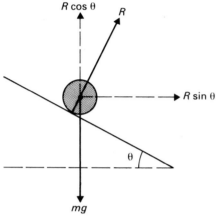

Figure 14

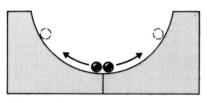

A circular slope

Figure 15

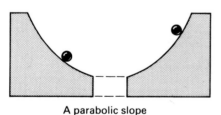

A parabolic slope

Figure 16

1 A straight slope

Set up a turntable as shown in Figure 13, with the two ball bearings free to roll up the slopes. If the ball bearings are at the bottom of the slopes when the turntable is started, they will not move up. But if they are placed at a critical height on the plane (with stops to support them), they will roll up the slopes once the turntable has started moving.

Figure 14 shows the two forces acting on each ball. The vertical component of R equals the weight of the ball. The horizontal component provides the force which gives the ball its acceleration towards the centre. If θ is the angle of the slope and r is the radius of the circle round which the ball is travelling, then $g = \tan \theta \, r\omega^2$.

At the critical height, the ball is in a state of unstable equilibrium: once it has rolled up the slope, a slight reduction in turntable speed will not bring it back.

2 A circular slope

The stability of ball bearings is different if a circular slope is used instead of two straight slopes. Place two balls at the centre and set the table rotating. The balls roll apart and after oscillating up and down settle in their orbits. These are decided by the rate of rotation of the turntable and the curvature of the slope (Figure 15). Increase the speed: the orbit widens. Decrease the speed: the orbit narrows.

3 A parabolic slope

The stability of a ball on a parabolic slope makes an interesting contrast with that on a circular slope. If the parabola is cut so that

$$y = \frac{2\pi^2 n^2}{g}x^2$$

where n is the rate of rotation, then the ball is in equilibrium in any orbit. If the turntable is speeded, up the ball rolls up the slope to the top: if the speed of the turntable is reduced, the ball rolls down. Because of the difficulty in shaping the parabola near the middle it is better to leave out the central part (Figure 16).

In place of a ball, liquid can be used. When a dish containing liquid is rotated, the surface of the liquid becomes a paraboloid whose shape is governed by the above equation. This can be done with water; the drop of the surface in the centre can be measured by lowering a pin until it touches its image. In the old days, mercury could be used. If the amount used was suitable, at first a paraboloid would appear. Then suddenly surface tension would prevail and a big circular hole was formed in the middle.

Roundabout in the park

It is fitting to end this chapter, which has dealt with sandbuckets and the seaside, with an account of an experiment using a roundabout in a park.

One summer evening, when the rightful users of the roundabouts were in bed, I set out with my family to the local park, armed with spirit-level, inclined planes, stop-watch and metre rule. One member of the family provided the power to keep the roundabout in motion; because of its considerable inertia, the roundabout rotated steadily. A second member of the family measured the rate of rotation; each rotation took 3.0 seconds.

A third member of the family sat on the roundabout. She rested the spirit-level accelerometer on one of the inclined planes. She found that the bubble was in the centre of the level when the level was 80 cm from the centre of the roundabout and when the slope of the inclined plane had a tangent of $\frac{1}{3}$.

Her acceleration towards the centre of the roundabout was thus $\frac{1}{3}g$, i.e. 3.3 m/s^2. Substitution in the formula $4\pi^2 n^2 r$ gave for her acceleration 3.5 m/s^2, in reasonable agreement with the experimental result. Thus we had verified this formula.

One member of my family asked, 'What is the point of all this?'. I didn't say 'To find g' – that would have been to invite the reply, 'I didn't know it was lost'. The real point was to show that physics is not just something that applies in physics labs.

Chapter 7
Mainly Mirrors

Pin-hole cameras

During the war, I spent some time in Egypt. I found it to be a good place for pin-hole camera effects, since the sun was nearly always shining. It rarely rained, so it didn't matter that the roof of the NAAF1 building was full of holes. Inside, bright elliptical patches of light could be seen – sometimes on the floor and sometimes on the walls. As we watched them, they would slowly creep round the room.

10 July 1945

By 1945 I had moved from Egypt to Germany. On the sunny afternoon of 10 July, I was walking with companions through a leafy wood in Wolfenbüttel. I startled them by suddenly stopping and pointing to the ground crying out in glee, 'An eclipse! An eclipse of the sun is taking place!' We watched as the bites taken out of the elliptical patches of light grew bigger, reached their maximum and then dwindled to nothing.

The newspapers came a day late, so after the event we were told that an eclipse was to take place. One of my companions reading this declared that I had been right, it was an eclipse whose effect we had noticed the day before. Obviously he had not believed me until he had 'seen it in the paper'.

The pin-hole camera effect can be used to measure the angular diameter of the sun (Figure 1). Make a small hole in a piece of card, and hold the card up to the sunlight. Catch the light which passes through the hole on a second piece of card. Tilt this card until the patch of light is circular, not elliptical. By measuring the separation of the two cards and the diameter of the circular patch, you should then be able to calculate the angle subtended by the sun.

Accurate measurement shows the angle to be 32' or $\frac{1}{108}$ rad. If the separation of the two cards is 1.08 m, the diameter of the patch of light will be only 1 cm.

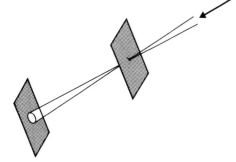

Figure 1

Shadows

Shadows are so commonplace that some interesting features of them are often ignored. Look at the shadow cast by a railing. At the bottom, near the ground, the shadow is sharp; higher up, the shadow gets progressively less sharp. This is due to the 32' subtended by the sun.

One's shadow cast by the evening sun on level road is amusingly distorted: the legs are generally enlarged, the head diminished.

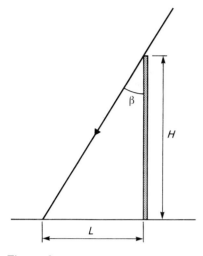

Figure 2

Latitude

In September 1982, I took advantage of being retired and stayed with relations in Zambia. I asked them if they knew the latitude and longitude of their home – they did not, so I decided to measure it. I assumed that September 23rd was the autumnal equinox, and on that day measured the length of the shadow cast by a long pole as the shadow became shorter, reached its minimum and then grew longer again. There was a difficulty: because of the finite angular size of the solar disc, the shadow starts with a penumbra before the umbra is reached. This limits the precision with which the shadows can be measured.

At the equinox the sun is overhead at noon along the equator. Therefore, when the shadow is shortest, the angle β equals the latitude θ (Figure 2). Thus the latitude is $\tan^{-1}(L/H)$. So a simple measurement of two lengths at the equinox gives the latitude.

Longitude

As well as measuring the length of the shadows, I noted the time at which each length was measured. The town of Kitwe where I was staying is east of Greenwich, so the shadows would be at their shortest in Kitwe earlier than in Greenwich. From this difference in time, I expected to be able to find the longitude of Kitwe. I realised that I should have to correct for Zambian local time and British summer time and did so. But my value for the longitude was considerably different from that given by the map.

I had forgotten the equation of time (it doesn't come into school physics). A solar day is the length of time between two successive solar crossings of the meridian. It is not constant, varying slightly between one day and the next.

We used to teach that 'day' was the real unit of time, a second being one-sixtieth of one-sixtieth of one-twenty-fourth of a day. To avoid too much explanation, we did not point out that the day was the length of the day averaged over the whole year (not Greenwich Time but Greenwich *Mean* Time).

The graph in Figure 3 shows the equation of time. From it we see that in February and November the meridian crossing can be as much as 15 minutes out. On September 23rd it is about 8 minutes out, and this accounted for my poor result.

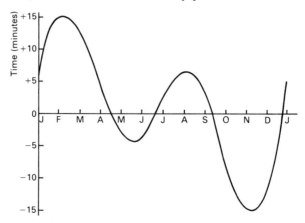

Figure 3

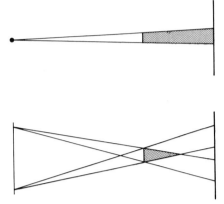

Figure 4

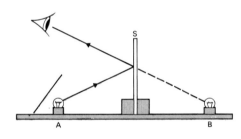

Figure 5

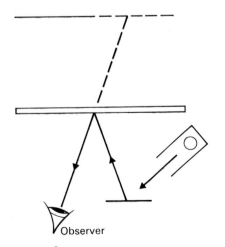

Figure 6

More shadows

1 A surprise with gauze

The coil of one type of car headlamp bulb is 8 mm long and 1 mm wide. As a shadow maker, it is practically a line source of light. If a screen is placed at a suitable point in front of the lamp, the bulb will cast a sharp shadow of a rod parallel to its length and a blurred shadow of a rod perpendicular to its length (Figure 4).

If the rods are replaced with a sheet of metal gauze, the result is surprising. The wires parallel to the coil produce shadows; at first glance, the other wires cast no shadows. Rotation of the gauze produces interesting pictures.

2 The Heiligenschein

The walk to Thornton Grammar School took me down a steep grassy slope which faced east. In spring and autumn, as the sun came up over the hill it would cast very long shadows on the dew. Sometimes I would see around the shadow of my head a faint but definite halo. It was not around the head of any boy or girl walking alongside me. But each of them could see a halo around their own head. I tried to photograph the halo, holding the camera up in front of my eyes, but the photo does not capture the fascination of the effect.

Minnaert's book *The Nature of Light and Colour in the Open Air* gives an interesting account of this halo – the Heiligenschein. The explanation of it is complex; it depends on not one but several effects.

Reflections

Pepper's ghost

Glass both reflects and transmits light. This caused difficulties for the upholders of the corpuscular theory of light. If corpuscles were attracted to glass and so speeded up when they fell on to it, why should some of them be reflected? Thus simultaneous reflection and transmission provided a *problem* for some people, but for magicians it provided *opportunities* for tricks of the Pepper's ghost type.

Figure 5 shows a simple way of setting up a Pepper's ghost. Lamp A is lit but hidden behind a black card. Lamp B is not lit. The sheet of glass S is on the perpendicular bisector of A and B. An observer looking past A thinks that B is lit until his or her head is moved to the side.

If you are in a playful mood, you can suggest a fanciful explanation: the observer's head switches off lamp B. A careful observer will notice something not quite right about B. Since the sheet of glass has two surfaces, the image of A seen in the position of B is in fact double.

For another arrangement (shown in Figure 6), a more powerful lamp, e.g. 24 W, is used. The observer looks through the glass sheet in the direction shown. Screens suitably placed shield his or her eyes. The card behind the glass sheet carries the letter A. The card in front carries the letter B which must be inverted.

Ask the observer to look through the glass sheet and say what he or she can see: two letters A and B. Ask the observer to pick up A. No problem – he or she does this. Ask the observer to pick up B – bewilderment ensues.

Next draw a nose – frontal view – on a piece of card. Find your nearest point of distinct vision (NPDV) by bringing the card up to your eyes as near as you can focus. Measure the NPDV. Now replace the card with a mirror. Look at your nose in the mirror, and find the new NPDV – it will be about half the first one. Draw a second nose, this time on a smaller piece of card. Hold the drawn (object) nose alongside the real (image) nose and bring the mirror close up. The drawn nose will then look 'more real' than the reflected nose.

Mirrors

The size of the mirror

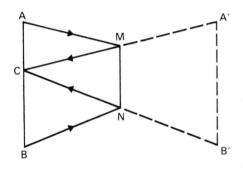

Figure 7

Ask a class how big a mirror must be to show the whole length of your face. Probably somebody will say that it depends on your distance from the mirror. It does not, however. A mirror half the length of your face will show the whole of your face, at whatever distance it is held.

Figure 7 shows why. AB represents the face: A'B' its image. The eye is at C. The mirror is halfway between the face and its image. It need extend only from M to N for rays from the extreme points A' and B' to enter the eye. MN is only half A'B', and so only half AB.

This diagram explains another observation. If your mirror is lightly 'steamed up' and you trace the outline of your head on it with a finger, the outline will not be lifesize, but only half lifesize.

The shape of the mirror

When we were very young, we loved playing with small mirrors on sunny days. By reflection, we made patches of light dance up and down neighbouring walls. This, of course, is the principle of the optical lever. Some daring spirits actually took mirrors into the classroom, risking the wrath of the teacher but gaining the admiration of the rest of us.

The shape of the reflections is of interest. If the wall is near and the mirror square, the shape will be square too. If the wall is far away and the mirror small then, whatever the shape of the mirror, the patch of light will be either circular or elliptical.

Which shape is observed depends on two angles: α, the angle subtended by the sun's disc on any point on the mirror and β the angle subtended by the mirror at any point on the wall.

Suppose that, instead of a large mirror at MN, there are two very small mirrors at A and B (Figure 8) and that they are at right-angles to the sun. The cone of light from the sun falling on A will be returned as a cone of the same angle. The same thing applies for the cone of light falling on B.

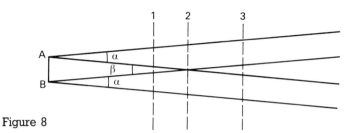

Figure 8

If the wall is in position 1, the two reflected cones will not overlap: two separate spots of light will be seen. The patch of light will have the shape of the mirror.

If the wall is in position 3, the two cones will overlap: only one patch of light will be seen and it will be approximately circular. The further away position 3 is, the more nearly circular will the patch become.

Position 2 is the critical position. As the figure shows, in this position β equals α. Thus when β is considerably bigger than α the shape of the mirror counts. When β is considerably smaller than α, the shape of the sun prevails.

The angle α is, as we have seen, about $\frac{1}{2}°$. To get a circular patch of light from a square mirror, the mirror must be small and the screen far away. If the screen is at the bottom of a box with blackened sides, the circular patch shows up better.

Curved mirrors

Convex mirrors

Many objects act as convex mirrors, forming small bright images of the world that is in front of them. Apples, grapes, raindrops – these are convex mirrors beloved of artists.

Turning our attention to people, we can start with the toe caps of brightly polished shoes. Finger nails, being cylindrical, just about qualify. Our foreheads and noses have mirror properties, though shiny noses are regarded as undesirable. Our cheeks are specially interesting as they have controllable curvature. We say that our cheeks mirror or relect our mood. In a serious or sombre mood, our cheeks are flat; in a laughing mood, they are strongly curved. The image formed by a convex mirror is small but a lot of light has been collected. The image is therefore bright, and so we have the bright shining faces of young children.

The light in your eyes

Last, and most important, are our eyes. Their function is to be convex lenses. But they cannot be convex lenses without being convex mirrors at the same time.

The dictionary points out that 'pupil' is a diminutive form of the Latin *pupus* (boy) and *pupa* (girl). If we look at ourselves in other people's eyes, we are indeed diminutive. If we take the radius of curvature of an adult eyeball as 5 cm, this makes the focal length about $2\frac{1}{2}$ cm. At the standard 25 cm away, an observer looking 'into' your eyes will see an image of his or her head about one-tenth of its linear size but only one-hundredth of its actual area.

The Elizabethan poet John Donne in one of his sonnets has this to say about courtship:

Pictures in our eye to get
Was all our propagation.

Looking towards windows indoors during the daytime, the image is that of the windows. To see yourself in someone's eyes, the light must fall on your face. The other person must be in the shade.

Concave mirrors

Some years ago, I took my family to see the camera obscura in Edinburgh. A large mirror in the ceiling throws an image of people moving about in the street outside, looked at from above, on to a horizontal white screen . The guide explained how the camera worked: it was a plane mirror. 'Plane?' I quietly questioned. 'Perfectly plane,' came the confident reply. I was squashed. My children were embarrassed. 'Dad, you put your foot in it again,' they said, when we got outside. I defended myself of course and said that there was no simple connection between the truth of what is said and the confidence with which it is uttered. I could have pointed out that, if plane mirrors did form real images, Isaac Newton had wasted a lot of his valuable time grinding concave mirrors. But then they would have complained of another of my sins – being heavy.

Concave mirrors are fascinating because they form real images – images that can be thrown on to a screen. Before they took any measurements of focal lengths, I let my pupils use concave mirrors and 12 V lamps to project images of fingers, hands, faces and finally the lamp itself. The lamp is used to illuminate the object (Figure 9). Two screens are needed: one to shield light from the lamp, the other to catch the image.

The beating of one's pulse can be demonstrated by using a galvanometer mirror as an optical lever. Wet the mirror and stick it on your pulse. Shine a beam of light on to the mirror and catch the reflected beam on a screen. With a 1 metre focal length mirror, I made the spot of light on the screen move through 5 cm.

The up-and-down movements of the spot are different: the outward movement of the pulse is faster than the return movement. The return took place in two stages, the second being slower than the first.

Soap bubbles

A soap bubble is at one and the same time a concave and a convex mirror. It produces not one but two images, as the famous painting *Bubbles* by J.E. Millais clearly shows (Figure 10). The image formed by the front surface is upright and between the front surface and the centre of curvature: that formed by the back surface is inverted and between the centre and the back surface. The two images are thus not far apart. The inverted image will be slightly smaller. This should make a good subject for a photograph.

Cusps

When rays of light from a parallel beam are reflected from a wide-angle strip of cylindrical mirror, they form the 'caustic curve'. How

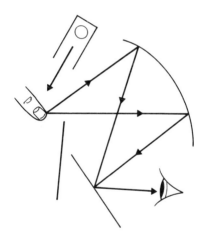

Figure 9

Figure 10

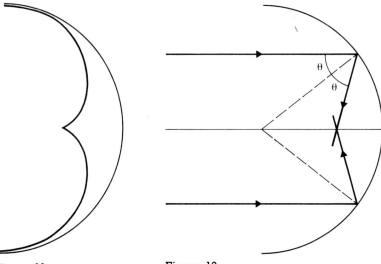

Figure 11   Figure 12

such a pleasant sight acquired such an unpleasant name is hard to understand. The shape is that of a cusp, a word almost onomatopoeic, and with pleasant associations (Figure 11).

Reflection cusps can often be seen on the surface of tea or coffee in a partly filled cup. A very good reflection cusp is formed by a lamp hanging above a cylindrical bucket. It becomes even better if the bucket is partly filled with water. Young children sometimes have a quiet giggle when they see these curves – they look like babies' botties.

Not being able to work out an equation for the cusp, I drew ten parallel lines in the top quadrant and, using the law of reflection, followed their paths (Figure 12). The cusp is the common tangent of the reflected rays. Drawing it is a pleasant task for a retired science teacher, especially in these days of calculators.

As others see us

O wad some Pow'r the giftie gie us
To see oursels as others see us!

So wrote Burns. If anybody protests that the Pow'r had given us the giftie because he had given us mirrors, Burns could have justly replied that mirrors do not show us ourselves as others see us.

The difference between an object and its mirror image is hard to put into words. 'Inversion' is often used, but to some people inversion means 'turning upside down'. There was once a suggestion that 'perversion' should be used but this did not find many supporters.

Shakespeare described the effect of the immersion of a human body to a depth of 'full fathom five' as producing a 'sea change rich and strange' in the appearances of the body. Why should we not follow Shakespeare's example and coin a new word 'mirror-change'? The difference between an object and its image seen in a looking-glass is that the image has suffered a mirror-change.

Before dealing with three-dimensional objects, a few words first about two-dimensional ones.

Figure 13

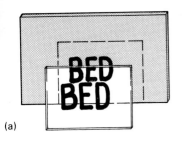

(a)

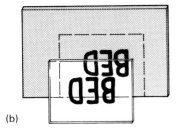

(b)

Figure 14

Two-dimensional objects

A mirror does not make any change in a two-dimensional object. Loud protests from the class: what about written or printed words? They are only turned round. All the mirror does is to allow us to look at the words from behind. Bend a wire into the shape of the letter G and hold it up in front of a mirror. Look past the object G to the image G. There is no inversion here! (Figure 13).

If 'BED' is written on the glass, we can turn it back to front by turning the glass round. If we look *from behind*, BED remains BED (Figures 14(a) and 14(b)).

Mirror games   Write your name on thin paper. Copy the name as seen *through* the paper on to your forehead using a suitable pen. Look at yourself in the mirror. Your name will be the right way round.

Light entertainment can be provided for open days by Magic Mirrors. A trickster says that he has a mirror which can distinguish between red and yellow. Paint one half of a strip of card yellow, and the other half red. Write 'OTTO' on one half and 'GLEN' on the other. Hold it up in front of a mirror. One name changes, the other doesn't.

If it is considered unwise to play tricks in rooms meant for serious instruction, then simply ask the observer to explain why one is changed, the other not.

Three-dimensional objects

Reflection in a mirror does bring about a change in such three-dimensional objects as hands, golf clubs, hockey sticks and motor cars. Hold a toy car (British version) in front of a mirror. It becomes its Continental counterpart. Also, a right hand becomes a left hand (Figure 15).

When we look at our own face in a mirror, we see the mirror-changed version of it – not the real thing. If we look at a familiar face in the mirror, we may experience a feeling of unease: there is something different about it, something wrong. What is wrong is that left has become right, and right has become left.

A wartime circus act depended on this mirror-change. The batman-servant of a captain broke the mirror in which his master admired himself on returning from drinking at HQ. Fearing his master's wrath, the batman decided to substitute for the captain's mirror-image his real batman self.

The captain came home drunk and began to undress. The batman followed his movements doing with his left hand what his master was doing with his right. The captain took his tie off but, becoming suspicious, decided to put it back on. This was too difficult for the batman: he got a sound thrashing.

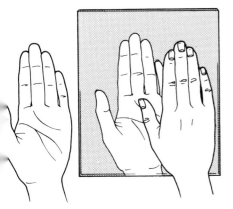

Figure 15

A double mirror

Burns was wrong: we can see ourselves as others see us if we use a double mirror – two mirrors at right-angles. The first reflection turns left into right and right into left, so the second reflection restores right to right and left to left. It is a case of two wrongs making a right. Your left hand remains your left hand.

To make a double mirror, I bought two mirrors 12 cm by 20 cm.

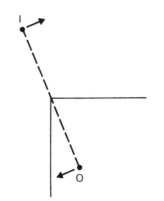

Figure 16

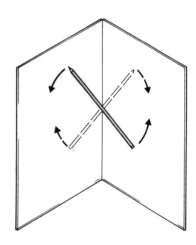

Figure 17

The glazier bored holes in them so that they could be firmly screwed to a wooden base. Having the holes made cost more than the mirrors. Owing to the thickness of the glass, a slight gap is left down the centre of the image. If I could have afforded front-surface mirrors, this would not have happened.

Stand or sit upright. Hold the double mirror upright, that is, with its axis vertical. Look at yourself and wink. If you wink with your left eye, a left eye will wink back at you. You see yourself as others see you, not mirror-changed.

The double mirror has another surprise for you. Pick it up and rotate its axis. Your image rotates too. Your face will still be 'the right way round' but it will not be the right way up. For a fraction of a second, you may even think that the double mirror can distinguish between horizontal and vertical.

It cannot do so, of course. It can only tell when your facial plane of symmetry is parallel to its own axis. Hold a pencil upright in front of the double mirror. The image will be upright too. Tilt the pencil – the image will tilt but in the opposite direction.

The image of O (Figure 16) formed by a double reflection is at I. If O moves to the left, I moves to the right. If the object pencil (Figure 17) turns anti-clockwise, the image pencil turns clockwise.

Benham reflected

When the black-and-white Benham disc shown in Figure 18 is rotated (especially in bright sunlight), coloured rings appear. If it is rotated in a clockwise direction, the order of colours from inner to outer ring is bluish, pinkish, dark. If the disc is rotated in the opposite direction, this order of colours is reversed too.

When the disc shown in Figure 19 is used instead of the first disc, the colours are again reversed. So the order of colours for the first disc rotated clockwise is the same as that for the second disc rotated anti-clockwise.

If either disc is rotated in front of an upright mirror, the order of colours seen is the *same* in the reflected image as in the object. The reason for this is that there are two mirror-changes, not one.

1 The stationary image of disc 1 is disc 2.
2 The object disc and image disc rotate in opposite directions.

If the first disc rotates clockwise, we see the second disc rotating anti-clockwise. Two mirror-changes have restored the original, as two negatives make a positive.

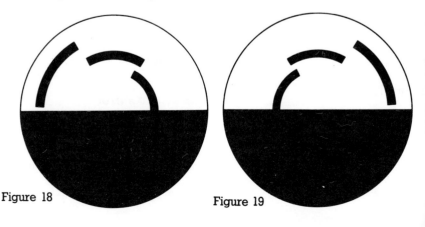

Figure 18   Figure 19

Chapter 8

Refraction: the Slowing Down of Light

Ptolemy

The Greek philosopher Ptolemy studied the refraction of light. He measured the angle of incidence i and the angle of refraction r when light was refracted at a water surface. The first two lines of Table 1 show his results; the third line, r_2, shows the results that comply with Snell's law of refraction and a refractive index of 1.333.

Table 1

i	10°	20°	30°	40°	50°	60°	70°	80°
r_1	8°	$15\frac{1}{2}$°	$22\frac{1}{2}$°	29°	35°	$40\frac{1}{2}$°	$45\frac{1}{2}$°	50°
r_2	$7\frac{1}{2}$°	15°	22°	29°	35°	$40\frac{1}{2}$°	45°	$47\frac{1}{2}$°

Only for 80° is the difference between r_1 and r_2 greater than $\frac{1}{2}$°. For large angles of incidence, accurate measurement becomes difficult as the dispersive effect becomes greater and so more troublesome.

Professor Lipson has pointed out an interesting feature of the r_1 values: they make an arithmetical progression. The successive values of r_1 increase, but each increase is $\frac{1}{2}$° less than the previous one.

Irreverent students could declare this to be an example of Cook's Law: 'If your results don't fit, make 'em fit'. Perhaps it was the delight in discovering a regularity that lured Ptolemy into choosing 50° in the 80° case.

Refractive powers

Isaac Newton in *Opticks* reported that astronomers had not only observed the refraction of air but had also measured it. The sine of the angle of incidence was to the sine of the angle of refraction as 3201 was to 3200. This gives $n = 1.00031$. (n is not constant but varies with temperature and pressure.) Newton stated that the difference between the refractive index and unity ($n - 1$) was a measure of the 'refractive power' of the body. Thus air had a refractive power of only 0.00031 and rainwater a refractive power of 0.335.

Newton regarded light as made up of corpuscles which possessed mass. He was interested in the densities of the media through which the corpuscles passed, and he tried to find connections between refractive power and density. In Table 2 he gives the 'refractive power of the body in respect of its density' for 22 substances. The table includes some exotic-sounding substances, for example, 'Sal Gemmæ', 'Crystal of the Rock' and 'Spirit of Wine well rectified'. For air the ratio is 5208; for Glass Vulgar it is 5436. For a number of substances the ratio is in the region of 6000. 'By the foregoing Table all Bodies seem to have their refractive Powers proportional to their Densities.' Except when they don't, he ought to have added.

Table 2

The refracting Bodies.	The Proportion of the Sines of Incidence and Refraction of yellow Light.		The Square of BR, to which the refracting force of the Body is proportionate.	The density and specifick gravity of the Body.	The refractive Power of the Body in respect of its density.
A Pseudo-Topazius, being a natural, pellucid, brittle, hairy Stone, of a yellow Colour.	23 to	14	1'699	4'27	3979
Air.	3201 to	3200	0'000625	0'0012	5208
Glass of Antimony.	17 to	9	2'568	5'28	4864
A Selenitis.	61 to	41	1'213	2'252	5386
Glass vulgar.	31 to	20	1'4025	2'58	5436
Crystal of the Rock.	25 to	16	1'445	2'65	5450
Island Crystal.	5 to	3	1'778	2'72	6536
Sal Gemmæ.	17 to	11	1'388	2'143	6477
Alume.	35 to	24	1'1267	1'714	6570
Borax.	22 to	15	1'1511	1'714	6716
Niter.	32 to	21	1'345	1'9	7079
Dantzick Vitriol.	303 to	200	1'295	1'715	7551
Oil of Vitriol.	10 to	7	1'041	1'7	6124
Rain Water.	529 to	396	0'7845	1'	7845
Gum Arabick.	31 to	21	1'179	1'375	8574
Spirit of Wine well rectified.	100 to	73	0'8765	0'866	10121
Camphire.	3 to	2	1'25	0'996	12551
Oil Olive.	22 to	15	1'1511	0'913	12607
Linseed Oil.	40 to	27	1'1948	0'932	12819
Spirit of Turpentine.	25 to	17	1'1626	0'874	13222
Amber.	14 to	9	1'42	1'04	13654
A Diamond.	100 to	41	4'949	3'4	14556

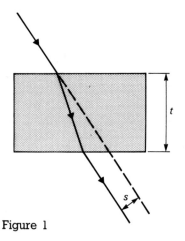

Figure 1

Prefabricated results

Glass

It is possible for junior forms who have done no trigonometry to measure the refractive index of a glass block provided that the calculations have been done beforehand.

A ray of light falls at an angle of incidence of 30° on to the block. Its passage through the block is traced (Figure 1). The distances *s* and *t* are measured and the ratio *s/t* found. The measurements are repeated at 45°, 60° and 75°. A little trigonometry shows that

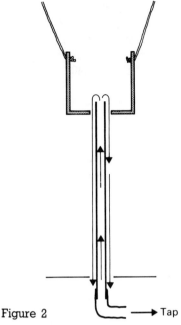

Figure 2

Figure 3

Figure 4

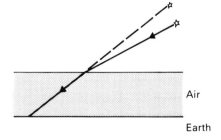

Figure 5

$$\frac{s}{t} = \frac{\sin(i - r)}{\cos r}$$

From given values of i and n, first r can be found and then s/t. In this way a table of s/t values can be calculated (Table 3). Pupils can read off their four values for refractive index from the table. They will want to know if they have got the 'correct answer'. There is in this case no single correct answer: different kinds of glass have different refractive indices. However, they are generally in the range 1.49–1.52.

Table 3

n	1.45	1.48	1.50	1.52	1.55
30°	0.18	0.19	0.195	0.20	0.21
45°	0.31	0.32	0.33	0.34	0.35
60°	0.49	0.50	0.51	0.52	0.53
75°	0.73	0.74	0.75	0.75	0.76

Water

Next fill a hollow transparent box with water. Proceed as before, and so find the refractive power for water. For an angle of incidence of 60°, s/t values of 0.43, 0.44 and 0.45 will correspond to values of n equal to 1.31, 1.33 and 1.35 respectively. The fact that the refracting power of water is different from that of glass can be shown by dipping a glass rod into water. It will still be visible, though it will not stand out as clearly as it does in air.

The relatively slight bending of rays going from water into glass makes possible a trick for open days. Water appears to be endlessly streaming from a can suspended by string from the ceiling. In fact, the water is flowing from a concealed source up the inside of a glass tube and down the outside. The unsteadiness of the water stream helps to hide the glass tube (Figure 2).

Refraction: stars

Figure 3 shows the sun low down in the sky above Lake Kariba in Zimbabwe. Figure 4 shows the sun sinking below the horizon over the same lake. The flattening, squashing effect obvious in the first picture is more pronounced in the second one. (By an optical illusion, the flattening effect is also perceptibly increased if the picture is turned through 90°.)

Because of atmospheric refraction, the actual height of a star in the sky is less than it seems. A star at a height of 45°0′ appears to be at a height of 45°1′ (a calculation easily done with an eight-digit calculator). Figure 5 exaggerates and simplifies this effect. Since the density of air decreases with altitude, there is no abrupt change in direction.

The deviation increases as the star approaches the horizon. For angles of incidence of 89°, 89.5° and (say) 89.99°, the angles of refraction become 88.28°, 88.57° and 88.60° respectively with angles of deviation of 0.72°, 0.99° and 1.40°. The diameter of the sun subtends an angle, as we have seen, of 0.50°. As the sun approaches the horizon, its bottom edge is bent up more than its top edge: hence the flattening of the sun.

A full treatment of the effect has to take into account the curvature of the earth. If the earth were flat, we should never see the sun set. Its lower edge would never get below 1.40°. (I doubt if flat-earthers would be impressed by this calculation.)

Two other phenomena resulting from atmospheric refraction are well known: twinkling stars, and mirages. From where I live – up on a hill in Bradford – I do not have to wait for the stars to come out. If I look across the valley on a clear evening, I see the street lights merrily twinkling. As for mirages, motorways with their long stretches of straight level road provide many examples. In the early days, drivers were known to slow down, thinking that they were approaching a wet patch of road only to find that it was dry when they got there. Total internal reflection had produced a mirror image. For obvious reasons it is not possible to stop and photograph this phenomenon.

Rings around the moon

When rays fall on a parallel-sided glass slab, the deviation caused by refraction at the first surface is cancelled out by an equal and opposite deviation at the second surface. When rays fall on a prism, the deviation at the second surface is in the same sense as that at the first surface: the ray emerges with a deviation (Figure 6).

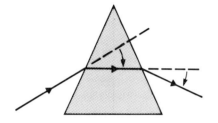

Figure 6

The deviation depends on the angle of incidence; it is a minimum when the ray passes symmetrically through the prism, as in Figure 6. The angle A of the prism, the angle D of minimum deviation and the refractive index n are connected by the equation

$$n = \frac{\sin(\frac{1}{2}\overline{A + D})}{\sin(\frac{1}{2}A)}$$

If a ray of light falls on one face of an ice crystal and emerges at the next face but one (Figure 7) it will, in effect, have passed through a 60° prism.

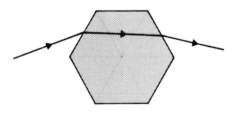

Figure 7

The moon is sometimes seen surrounded by a halo which subtends an angle of 44° to the eye. This angle can be measured by finding the distance from the eye at which a circular card has to be held for it to fit the halo. There is sometimes also a halo of this size around the sun. To see it, a card has to be held up to prevent dazzling.

These haloes are formed by the minimum deviation of light by hexagonal ice crystals. For the haloes to be complete, the crystals must be randomly orientated: this does not often happen.

The refractive power of ice

For the ice crystals, the angle of minimum deviation D, being half the subtended angle, is 22°. Substituting this in the equation gives a value of 1.31 for the refractive index of ice. As Newton expected, since ice is a little less dense than water, it is also a little less refractive.

This difference can be confirmed in very cold weather. Remove

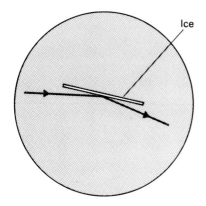

Figure 8

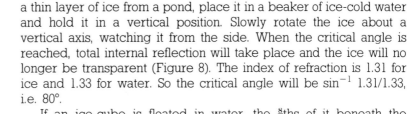

a thin layer of ice from a pond, place it in a beaker of ice-cold water and hold it in a vertical position. Slowly rotate the ice about a vertical axis, watching it from the side. When the critical angle is reached, total internal reflection will take place and the ice will no longer be transparent (Figure 8). The index of refraction is 1.31 for ice and 1.33 for water. So the critical angle will be $\sin^{-1}$ 1.31/1.33, i.e. 80°.

If an ice-cube is floated in water, the $\frac{8}{9}$ths of it beneath the surface is hardly visible since the two refractive indices are nearly equal. If the ice-cube is floated in warm water, streaks of what looks like an oily liquid can be seen sinking down. Cold water is denser than warm water: it has a different refractive power. This explains the oily streaks. However, it is not possible to deduce from them that the cold water is *more* refractive than the warm water.

Total internal reflection

Bathing baby

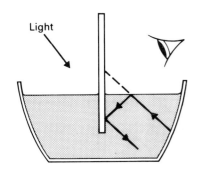

Figure 9

I noticed an amusing example of total internal reflection while giving baby a bath. Before I had used any soap, the part of baby's leg that was in the water looked cleaner than the part above the water. Water, by itself, had washed it whiter. Once you know where to look for it, the effect is common – I have seen it looking down at my feet in sea-water. To demonstrate the effect, dip a stick into water in a white basin and illuminate the stick from the left. An observer on the right will then notice that the part of the stick under water looks brighter (and therefore cleaner) than the rest of the stick. Figure 9 shows why. The critical angle for total internal reflection in water is 48°. The rays that get into the bowl are scattered in all directions: if the critical angle is exceeded, the rays cannot get out. Some of the rays never emerge to light up the top half of the rod, but are redirected to give the bottom half more than its fair share of light.

The glass cube trick

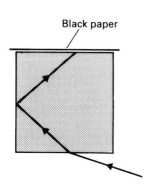

Figure 10

Glass cubes are almost indestructible and seem to last for ever, so they are still to be found in some schools. If you can find one in your school, try this simple demonstration. Stick a square of dark paper on the top of the glass cube, and place a coin with its date uppermost underneath the cube. Everyone knows that glass is transparent, and it seems reasonable to expect that by looking through the side of the cube you should be able to see the coin. 'If you can tell me the date you can keep the coin.' Guessing should be penalised. In fact, since the critical angle for glass ($n = 1.52$) is 41.1°, no rays entering the bottom of the cube can get out of the side (Figure 10). You don't lose your money.

Next, fill a hollow cube with water. This time, the coin (though distorted) can be seen and its date correctly named. The critical angle for water ($n = 1.333$) is 48.6°. Glass, a denser substance than water, is a better bender of light.

Convex lenses

Like concave mirrors, convex lenses have the pleasing ability to form 'real' images – images that can be projected on to a screen. It is easier to do this with lenses than it is with mirrors as only one screen is needed (Figure 11).

With a 24 W lamp and condenser (use a round-bottomed flask filled with water), images of colour slides can be projected, and rules about upside-down and left-to-right can be worked out (Figure 12).

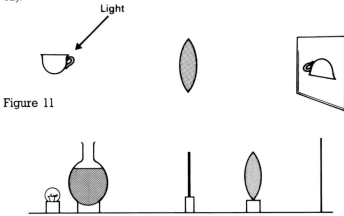

Figure 11

Figure 12

Raindrops

A raindrop on a window pane is a plano-convex lens shaped just well enough to form a real image. Normally, the top half of a raindrop looks darker than the bottom half. The world outside consists of such things as buildings below and a sky above. The image in the raindrop is inverted, so the bright sky ends up below. Sometimes, however, the raindrop is brighter at the top. This happens when the ground is covered with snow. Since raindrops on windows and snow on the ground don't often happen at the same time, it is a fairly rare sight.

Sunspots

As we have seen, the angle subtended by the sun at any point on the earth is 0.0093 rad. If an image of the sun is produced by a convex lens of focal length f, the diameter of its image will be $0.0093f$. If a 2 m convex lens is used, the diameter will be 1.9 cm; if a 4 m lens is used, the diameter will be 3.7 cm.

I used to have a 4 m lens. Since it was not at first sight obviously different from a plane glass circle, it was nearly lost more than once.

On one occasion I was using it to demonstrate the solar image it cast on to a screen to a form of 12 year olds. One girl said that she could see spots on the image. She was right. It was 1958 – a year of sunspot activity. It had never occurred to me that sunspots could be demonstrated so easily.

A 4 m lens can also be used to demonstrate a solar eclipse. Outlines of the solar image formed on the screen can be quickly drawn and the progress of the eclipse timed.

If a pinhole card is mounted alongside the lens, it too will form an

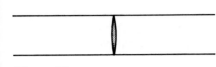

Figure 13

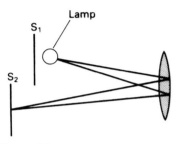

Figure 14

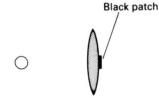

Black patch

Figure 15

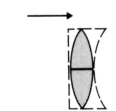

Figure 16

image of the sun. It will be much fainter than the lens image, but the same size. There is a practical problem in dealing with a lens of long focal length: one's arms are not long enough to arrange the lens so that it is at right-angles to the axis. If the lens is mounted in the centre of a cardboard tube (as shown in Figure 13), the tube can be lined up by observation of its shadow. When the tube is lined up, so is the lens. The lens, even though it is a weak one, should not be used for direct observation of the sun.

Four focal lengths

In addition to the main image, a convex lens produces three other images which are easily found if the focal length of the lens is long enough. The lens has four focal lengths corresponding to these four images.

Suppose that the lens is made of glass, is equiconvex and has a main focal length f_1 of 1.00 m. Then there will be a real image on the same side as the source of light, corresponding to a focal length f_2 of approximately 0.25 m. To observe this image, a screen S_1 is positioned as shown in Figure 14, so that light from the lamp does not fall on the screen S_2. It helps if the object distance u is made slightly less than the image distance v. From u and v, f_2 can be found.

The third real image is on the same side of the lens as the main image and corresponds to a focal length f_3 of about 0.14 m. To observe this image, the centre of the lens should be covered with a black patch to keep the light from the main image out of the way (Figure 15).

The fourth real image is on the same side as the source, and corresponds to a focal length f_4 of about 0.10 m. If u is made about 0.15 m, v can be measured and f_4 can be calculated.

The focal lengths f_2, f_3 and f_4 are very nearly $\frac{1}{4}$, $\frac{1}{7}$ and $\frac{1}{10}$ of f_1. These figures can be neatly explained by the wave theory and can be used to give a value for n.

Light is slowed down as it passes from air into glass. If the refractive index of glass with respect to air is n, then it takes a ray of light n times longer to travel through the central part of the lens (Figure 16) than it does for it to travel the same distance in air. If the thickness of the central part of the lens is t, then light travelling through the air will be ahead by a distance $nt - t$, i.e. $(n - 1)t$.

The second of the four images is formed by light which has been 'there and back' through the lens. The light travelling through air will therefore be ahead by $2nt - t$, i.e. $(2n - 1)t$.

The third of the four images is formed by light which has been 'there' twice and 'back' once. The distance by which the light is ahead is now $3nt - t$, i.e. $(3n - 1)t$. For the fourth image, this distance is $(4n - 1)t$.

For the first focal length for an equiconvex lens, it is a simple matter to show (from the slowing down of the light travelling through the glass) that

$$\frac{1}{f_1} = (n - 1)\frac{2}{r}$$

where r is the radius of curvature of either surface.

For glass, n is about $1\frac{1}{2}$, and so $n - 1$, $2n - 1$, $3n - 1$ and $4n - 1$

have the simple relationship $\frac{1}{2} : 2 : 3\frac{1}{2} : 5$ (or $1 : 4 : 7 : 10$) found by the measurements. The regularity has been explained by the 'slowing down' idea.

For a transparent material other than glass, a straight-line graph can be obtained by plotting the reciprocal of the mth focal lens against m. Both r and n can be found from the intercepts of the line. Alternatively, since

$$\frac{f_1}{f_3} = \frac{3n - 1}{n - 1}$$

by measuring only f_1 and f_3, n can be found.

Concave lenses

Anyone who wears spectacles will know that in addition to the desired image there are other images. Some light gets in from the back. If I hold my biconcave lenses in front of me, I can see two sets of images of lamps above. One set is formed by a single reflection at the first surface; the second set is formed by light which has passed through the lens, has been reflected from the second surface and has then travelled back through the lens.

With my spectacles back in their normal position, if I look carefully at the lamps in the room and slightly tilt my spectacles, I can see a faint and diminished (but upright) second set of lamps. The light to form this second set has passed through the lenses three times.

It is *tilting* the spectacles that separates the main first set of images from the second set. The second set is there all the time but is only noticeable with bright lamps. I have known people be distracted by them and, thinking that they are caused by greasy lenses, try to get rid of them with a polishing cloth. This has not improved matters, and the cloth has been blamed. The secondary images are out of focus and are not easily recognisable.

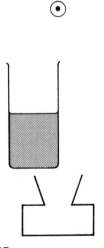

Figure 17

Microwaves

The bending of microwaves in paraffin can be shown using a prism filled with paraffin. Just as light waves are bent towards the base of a glass prism, microwaves will be bent towards the base of a paraffin-filled prism. Hertz in his original experiment with electromagnetic waves needed a huge prism of pitch. It weighed half a ton.

The refractive index of paraffin for microwaves can be measured by an interference method. Since microwaves travel more slowly in paraffin than in air, their wavelengths must be shorter. In a given length, there will be more microwaves in paraffin than in air.

Figure 17 shows the arrangement. A perspex container of depth at least 8 cm is held above the horn of the transmitter so that it covers half of it. The probe detector receives waves from two sources: some waves have travelled through the paraffin, some through the air. The two lots of waves will get out of step and in step as the depth of paraffin is increased. The probe detector is connected to an amplifier and then to a CRO.

When the waves are out of step, there will be a minimum; when they are in step, there will be a maximum. In an actual experiment it was found that the minimum became a maximum with a change in depth of paraffin of 4.0 cm. If in this distance there are x waves in air, there will be $x + \frac{1}{2}$ waves in paraffin.

The wavelength of the microwaves in air was 3.2 cm. If the refractive index of paraffin is n, then the wavelength in paraffin will be 3.2/n. Thus

$$x = \frac{4.0}{3.2} \quad \text{and} \quad x + \frac{1}{2} = \frac{4.0n}{3.2}$$

from which we find that $n = 1.4$.

A verse for weak spellers

If you want to spell *LENS*
You've no need to guess
There's only one 'e'
And it ends in an 'ess'

Chapter 9

Rainbows – Real and Artificial

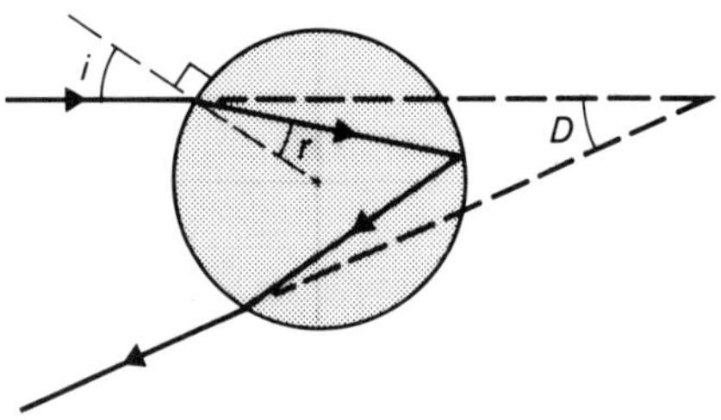

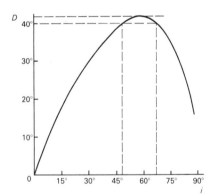

Figure 1

Newton

'This Bow never appears, but where it rains in the Sun-shine, and may be made artificially by spouting up Water which may break aloft, and scatter into Drops, and fall down like Rain. For the Sun shining upon these Drops certainly causes the Bow to appear to a Spectator standing in a due Position to the Rain and Sun. And hence it is now agreed upon, that this Bow is made by Refraction of the Sun's Light in drops of falling Rain . . . .

The interior Bow is made in round Drops of Rain by two Refractions of the Sun's Light, and one Reflexion between them, and the exterior by two Refractions, and two sorts of Reflexions between them in each Drop of Water.'

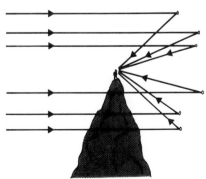

Figure 2

The inner bow

Figure 1 shows a ray passing through a drop. It suffers a refraction, a reflection and then a second refraction. If i is the angle of incidence and r is the angle of refraction, then the angle D shown in the diagram equals $4r - 2i$.

Figure 2 shows the graph of D against i when the index n of refraction equals 1.333. D has a maximum value of 42°. A glance at the graph shows that a large number of the incident rays have values of D near the maximum value. The light returning from the drops after a simple reflection is contained within a cone but it is not evenly distributed, it is concentrated near the edge. Newton quoted the analogous case of the solstices: 'When the Sun comes to his Tropicks, Days increase and decrease but a very little for great while together'.

Imagine an observer standing on a peak with a shower of rain falling in front of her and the sun shining at her back (Figure 3). Rays will be returned to her at all angles up to 42°. There will be a complete circular area of brightness but the brightness will be greater towards the perimeter, and only at the perimeter will the colours appear. From a peak, a complete coloured ring can be seen but it does not often happen that we are on a peak in suitable weather. Normally we see only part of the circle: it is in the shape of an archer's bow so we call it the rainbow, not the rain-circle.

The lower the sun is in the sky, the greater the arc of the circle will be. A rising or a setting sun will give a semi-circular bow. To see the bow, we must have our back to the sun. The centre of the

Figure 3

circle of which the arc is a part, our head (more accurately one of our eyes) and the sun are in a straight line. Our shadow points to the apex of the arc. We cannot see a rainbow from the side though Rubens in a famous painting *The Rainbow Landscape*, thought that we could.

That rainbow mnemonic

As a primary schoolboy, I was taught a mnemonic for the colours of the rainbow. 'Richard of York gained battles in vain'. Red, orange, yellow, green, blue, indigo, violet.

With classes of 12 year olds I used to set up a spectrometer, a prism and a lamp to get a pure spectrum. I asked each child to say nothing as he or she looked at the spectrum but to *write* down the order of the colours. In this way they would not influence those who had not yet looked.

I stressed that each one had to write down what he or she saw, not what they thought they ought to see. Nobody ever wrote down indigo. Some said that the spectrum ended in purple, not violet. For them the mnemonic should become: 'Richard of York gained battles profitlessly'.

Being only 12 years old, the children (seeking approval) would ask if their order of colours was correct. I would reply that it was bound to be correct. 'Nobody except you knows what you have seen.' (I realise that my reply is not completely sound: for example, some child, in a desire to show off, might have imagined colours.)

Rainbow colours

It is not obvious that the rainbow marks only the outer edge of a circle of brightness. It is the colours that catch our eyes and make our hearts leap up when we behold them. Some photographs show the inner brightness clearly.

I once showed a classical friend an article of mine about rainbows which included calculations. He tutted, saying that to measure a rainbow would be to destroy its beauty. I denied this, and asked him for how long he ever looked at a rainbow. I claimed that the pleasure was enhanced by study – our hearts leap up just as much and for a longer time.

The colours are due, of course, to the dispersion of the rays as they pass through the raindrops. Figure 4 shows two rays, the red one and the violet one. Their dispersion is exaggerated. As the maximum value for D is greater for red, the rainbow is red on the outside.

Like the spectrum formed by sunlight falling on a prism, the colours formed by raindrops are impure, but they are impure in a different way. In the spectrum, each colour is mixed with its neighbours on either side. In the rainbow, the extreme red is relatively pure but, even for the red, the finite size of the sun prevents total purity. Elsewhere, orange is mixed with a little red, yellow is mixed with a little orange and still less red, and so on.

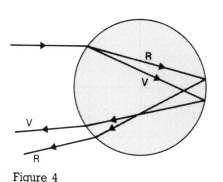

Figure 4

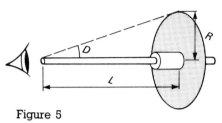

Figure 5

Measuring a rainbow: an irisometer

The semi-angle of the rainbow cone is about 42°. Because of its dispersion, it cannot be measured very accurately. To make a measurement, you must have in readiness a rainbow stick. This consists of a rod with a cardboard disc which slides along it (Figure 5). The disc has a short cylinder fastened to it to prevent it from tilting.

Hold the rod with the disc up to your master eye, and move the disc until it covers the rainbow arc. Measure L. If time permits (i.e. if the bow persists) measure L first when all the bow is just covered by the disc and then when it is just exposed. From L and R, the angle D can be found.

From D, the refractive index of water can be obtained:

$$D = 4r - 2i$$

and since it is a maximum

$$\frac{di}{dr} = 2$$

Simple calculus and trigonometrical steps give an equation for i:

$$\sin i = \sqrt{\left(\frac{4 - n^2}{3}\right)}$$

Starting with a value for n in a suitable range, we can find in turn i, r and $4r - 2i$, i.e. D. Table 1 has been derived in this way. Thus, from the measured value of D, n can be read off.

Table 1

D	40°	$40\frac{1}{2}°$	41	$41\frac{1}{2}°$	42°	$42\frac{1}{2}°$	43°
n	1.347	1.344	1.340	1.337	1.334	1.330	1.327

Mosi-oa-Tunya

When David Livingstone explored the Zambesi River in 1855 he came across a series of superb waterfalls as the river dropped 100 m along a 1600 m ledge. Being a loyal subject of the Queen, he called them the Victoria Falls, and it is by this name that they are still known today. We say that he 'discovered' the Victoria Falls but this is rather absurd: the falls needed neither discovering nor naming. Long before Livingstone, the Zambesi people had their own name for the Falls: *Mosi-oa-Tunya* or 'the smoke which thunders'.

As the water pours noisily over the ledge into the gorge below, it throws up a permanent spray. The sun shines more often than not, so Mosi-oa-Tunya is the place for rainbow lovers and photographers. From a colour photo of such a rainbow (spraybow?), it is possible to calculate the dispersive power of water. The extent of the dispersion will depend on the characteristics of the colour film used.

On one such photo, the central yellow line of the bow had a radius of curvature of 16 cm. The breadth of the bow cannot be measured with precision but it can be given a minimum width – it

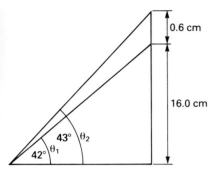

Figure 6

was at least 1.2 cm broad. Assume that for yellow n is 1.333 and that D, the minimum deviation, is 42.0°. This will make the radius for the red 16.6 cm and the angle 43.0° (Figure 6). The radius for blue–violet will be 15.4 cm and the angle 40.9°. Thus the angular dispersion of the beam is 43.0° − 40.9°, i.e. 2.1°.

Newton and the rainbow

Before Newton, Des-Cartes (as Newton called him) and others had explained the 42° angle of the bow as a result of the 1.333 refractive index of water. They were unable to give a satisfactory explanation for the colours, since they did not understand the relationship between white light and colour.

As we have seen, Newton had found this relationship by means of *glass* prisms and sunlight. The most wonderful example of colour in nature being provided by the rainbow, Newton needed to show qualitatively and quantitatively that its colours were due to the dispersion of sunlight by *water*.

By means of a 'Prismatic vessel of water', Newton measured the dispersion produced by water. For the most-refracted rays the ratio of the sine of refraction to the sine of incidence was 109 : 81 (1.346); for the least-refracted rays it was 108 : 81 (1.333). The difference in refractive indices was thus 0.013.

Newton had to show that the breadth of the rainbow could be deduced from these two indices. He 'computed' that for the most-refrangible rays the angle would be 42°2′ and that for the least-refrangible rays it would be 40°17′ – a difference of 1°45′. Since the sun is a disc of light rather than a point source, 30′ have to be added to this angle. This gives a total breadth of $2\frac{1}{4}$°.

So the predicted width was $2\frac{1}{4}$°. It is not easy to measure rainbows – in England, anyhow. On one occasion when Newton tried, he was able to measure the breadth of the red, yellow and green but the blue and violet were obscured by the brightness of the clouds. He *supposed* that the blue and the violet between them would be as broad as the rest of the bow. This gives (not really surprisingly) the total breadth of the bow as $2\frac{1}{4}$°.

At another time (without any supposing) he was able to measure 'the breadth of the interior Iris 2Gr10″. (A 'grad' (Gr) is one-hundredth part of a right-angle.) Theory and practice agreed. From a Zambian rainbow photograph, I had deduced a breadth of 2°6′. Since neither the red edge nor the blue edge is sharp, the margin of error is at least 10 per cent – the good agreement has an element of luck about it.

The 'Theory of Colours' now being universally accepted, it is not as important as it was in Newton's day that theory and practice should agree so exactly.

Polystyrene bows

In the lab

Some years ago I received a letter from Zsúdel Laszló, a physics teacher in Hungary. He had read my article 'Rainbows when and where you want them' in which I described how I had obtained

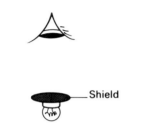

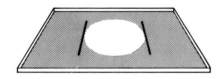

Shield

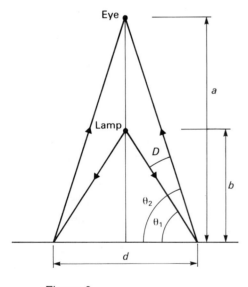

Figure 7

rainbow effects by using polystyrene beads. Stimulated by the article, he had sent to England for the beads, but when he obtained them he was unable to get any 'rainbows'. He sent me some of his beads and the reason for his failure was soon discovered – the beads were opaque instead of being transparent. Fortunately I had a good stock of transparent beads. I soon heard from Laszló again: the rainbows were shining in Hungary.

It was a former pupil of mine, Jamie Brown, who told me that if polystyrene beads were scattered on to a table, rainbow effects could be seen. My heart leapt at the mere mention of rainbows, so I got a supply of beads. I was able to obtain not just rainbow effects but *complete rainbow circles*. No longer had I to wait for the sun to shine and the rain to fall at the same time.

Figure 7 shows the arrangement needed. The beads are scattered on to a black tray which has a raised edge to prevent the beads from rolling away. A small lamp illuminates the beads from above. A black card shields the lamp from the eye. Three things are immediately obvious.

1 The whole circular area is bright as theory requires.
2 At the edge, the circle is brightly coloured with red on the outside. The blue is not always strong – it can be made more prominent by increasing the voltage of the lamp up to fusing point.
3 Each eye sees a different bow. Switch from one eye to the other: the bow moves. With both eyes open, the master eye wins.

A fourth feature of the bow is that it is polarised. Testing with polaroid shows this.

Measuring the refractive index of polystyrene

If the diameter of the circle is measured, it is possible to deduce the refractive index of polystyrene. The diameter d depends on the distance a of the eye from the board and the distance b of the lamp from the board (Figure 8). The diameter is measured with the help of two thin rods. They are placed as in Figure 7 so that they are tangents to the circle. Suitable values for a and b are 30 cm and 15 cm; d will then be about 20 cm.

The edge of the bow is set by the critical value of the semi-angle D, which is the difference between θ_2 and θ_1.

$$D = \theta_2 - \theta_1$$

$$= \tan^{-1}\left(\frac{2b}{d}\right) - \tan^{-1}\left(\frac{2a}{d}\right)$$

In this way I found D to be $15\frac{1}{2}°$.

A preliminary calculation, similar to that with real rainbows, showed that if n was 1.600, D would be 15.0°. From this, I compiled Table 2. The semi-angle of 15.5° gives a refractive index of 1.590. This is a lot bigger than the refractive index of water: the big refractive index leads to a small bow.

Figure 8

Table 2

n	1.580	1.590	1.600	1.610
D	16.2	15.5	15.0	14.2

A direct calculation Having become a lecturer, Jamie Brown set his students the problem of finding by trial and error the value of n from the semi-angle $15\frac{1}{2}°$. One of his students, disdaining trial and error, went directly from D to i to r and so to n. The equation connecting D and i is

$$\tan\left(\frac{D}{4}\right) = \tan^3\left(\frac{i}{2}\right)$$

I have many times learned from my own pupils. On this occasion I learned from the pupil of a pupil.

It is possible to measure the diameter of the polystyrene ring with only two beads. Start with them close together under the lamp. They will shine. Separate them slowly, keeping them equidistant from the central point. Suddenly they will disappear. This happens when their separation is greater than the diameter of the ring.

Each eye has its cwn bow. This is true for rainbows, but it is much more obviously true for polystyrene bows.

People are often puzzled by the exact whereabouts of a rainbow – it is wherever your eyes are focusing. If you are looking at a cloud, then (as Genesis says) the bow is set on that cloud. If you are looking at a fountain in the city square, then the rainbow is on that fountain. When photographs are taken of polystyrene bows, they are in the focal plane of the camera.

Polystyrene beads have another property: when they are scattered on to a smooth hard surface they reduce friction almost to zero. Objects placed on the surface slide about as if by magic. Practical jokers soon realise this and, in consequence, the stock of beads drops sharply.

Figure 9

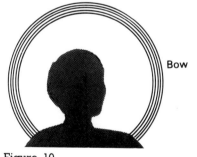

Bow

Figure 10

Out of doors

When the sun is shining, the beads scattered on to a horizontal board will show bows with the colours greatly enhanced. As with a rainbow, the sun, the observer's head and the centre of the circle of which the bow is an arc will be in line.

If the observer is standing, only a small arc will be seen (Figure 9); if he or she is kneeling down, the arc will be greater and more impressive.

The beads can be fixed to the board by painting the board with black poster paint and sprinkling on the beads just before the paint dries. The board can then be held up vertically, and the bow will extend much further (Figure 10). In the words of the song, there will be a 'rainbow round your shoulder'.

The secondary bow

Occasionally a faint secondary bow can be seen outside a bright inner bow. It is formed by rays which have undergone two internal reflections as well as two refractions (Figure 11). It is red on the inside: thus the red of the secondary bow faces the red of the primary bow. The space between them is darker. It has a name – Alexander's dark band. Figure 12 is taken from *Opticks*.

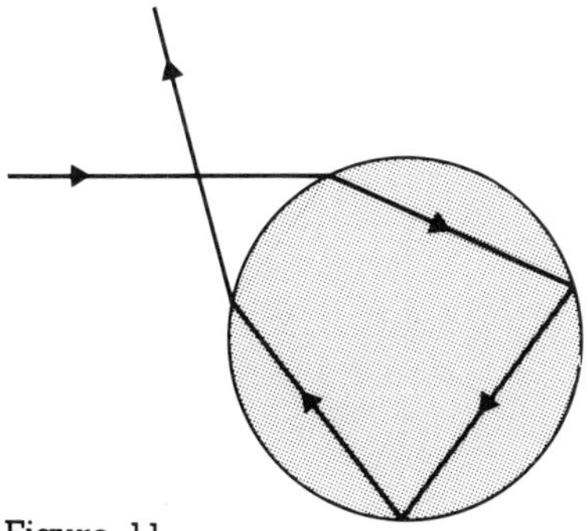

Figure 11

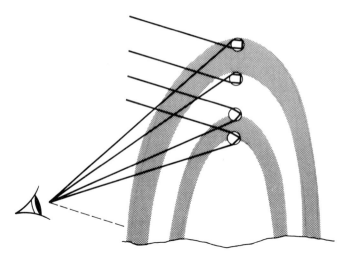

Figure 12

The deviation $4r - 2i$ of the primary bow becomes $6r - 2i$ for the secondary bow, and

$$\sin i = \sqrt{\left(\frac{9 - n^2}{8}\right)}$$

On a visit to Australia, Professor David Layton was giving a lecture when he chanced to see through the window not *two* but *three* rainbows – a very rare sight indeed!

If a ray undergoes three internal reflections, it emerges on the same side as the sun and is therefore invisible. This is also the case for four internal reflections. After five internal reflections, the ray will emerge on the usual rainbow side. It is no wonder therefore that a third rainbow is a very rare sight.

Myths

Rainbows are, of course, of interest to people other than physicists. Poets have enthused about them, artists have painted them, photographers have snapped them and D.H. Lawrence called a novel after them.

The rainbow story appears in the ninth chapter of Genesis after the story of the flood. God showed the bow on a cloud as a covenant that 'the waters shall no more become a flood to destroy all flesh'. Fundamentalists will have some problems with this story. It suggests that before God made his covenant there were no rainbows: afterwards there were rainbows. God therefore had changed the properties, in particular, the dispersive powers of water.

Chapter 10

The Shadow of a Hair

Grimaldo, a Jesuit Priest in Bologna, studied the diffraction of light in detail. His great work was *Physico-Mathesis de Lumine, Coloribus et Iride*. He died in 1663 at the early age of 45. In his *Opticks*, Newton wrote, 'Grimaldo has inform'd us, that if a beam of the Sun's Light be let into a dark Room through a very small hole, the Shadows of things in this Light will be larger than they ought to be if the Rays went on by the Bodies in Straight Lines, and that these Shadows have three parallel Fringes, Bands or Ranks of Colour'd Light adjacent to them'.

Newton repeated and extended Grimaldo's observations. He measured the pattern produced by the passage of a narrow beam of sunlight past a hair. The hole through which the sunlight shone was $\frac{1}{42}$ in in diameter. It was made by a pin in a lead sheet. (The breadth of 21 such pins laid together was half an inch.) The hair, $\frac{1}{280}$ in thick, was 12 ft away from the hole. Newton measured the pattern on a screen first 6 in away from the hair and then 9 ft away from the hair.

Newton thought that the shadow had definite edges and that it was several times broader than the geometrical shadow. On both sides of the shadow he noted three bright-coloured fringes. He made many measurements of their positions.

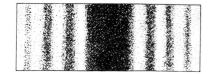

Figure 1

Intensity

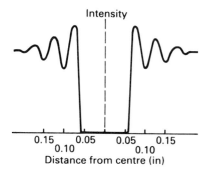

0.15   0.05   0.05   0.15
    0.10   0.10
Distance from centre (in)

Figure 2

The pattern

I have drawn in Figure 1 a black-and-white version of the pattern which Newton recorded. Figure 2 represents the positions of the maxima and minima accurately; their heights are merely guesses.

Table 1 is taken from Book III, Part I, of *Opticks*. I have had the audacity to add the right-hand column. This is the ratio of the size of a particular part of the pattern on the distant screen to its size on the near screen. Some of the measurements are intriguing: how did Newton measure $\frac{4}{17}$ in?

The first ratio (6.0) is the odd one out. The other nine range between 5.3 and 5.7 with an average of 5.5. To our eyes, the shadow does not have a definite measurable edge. Was his determination to measure the unmeasurable (the breadth of the shadow) the cause of Newton's undoing? If it had not been for the discordant 6.0, might not Newton have tried harder to discover why an 18-fold increase in distance brought about a 5.5 ± 0.2 increase in pattern size?

Table 1

At the Distance of	half a Foot	Nine Feet	Ratio
The breadth of the Shadow	$\frac{1}{54}$	$\frac{1}{9}$	6.0
The breadth between the Middles of the brightest Light of the innermost Fringes on either side the Shadow	$\frac{1}{38}$ or $\frac{1}{39}$	$\frac{7}{50}$	5.4
The breadth between the Middles of the brightest Light of the middle-most Fringes on either side the Shadow	$\frac{1}{23\frac{1}{2}}$	$\frac{4}{17}$	5.5
The breadth between the Middles of the brightest Light of the out-most Fringes on either side the Shadow	$\frac{1}{18}$ or $\frac{1}{18\frac{1}{2}}$	$\frac{3}{10}$	5.5
The distance between the Middles of the brightest Light of the first and second Fringes	$\frac{1}{120}$	$\frac{1}{21}$	5.7
The distance between the Middles of the brightest Light of the second and third Fringes	$\frac{1}{170}$	$\frac{1}{31}$	5.5
The breadth of the luminous Part (green, white, yellow, and red) of the first Fringe	$\frac{1}{170}$	$\frac{1}{32}$	5.3
The breadth of the darker Space between the first and second Fringes	$\frac{1}{240}$	$\frac{1}{45}$	5.3
The breadth of the luminous Part of the second Fringe	$\frac{1}{290}$	$\frac{1}{35}$	5.3
The breadth of the darker Space between the second and third Fringes	$\frac{1}{340}$	$\frac{1}{63}$	5.4

Where Newton went wrong

Newton thought that the pattern arose because the hair 'acted upon' (i.e. repelled) the rays of light. This immediately explains why the shadow was so broad. The nearer the ray got to the hair, the more it was repelled. Figure 3, adapted from *Opticks*, shows this clearly. At some places AA', because of the re-directing of the rays, there will be an increase in brightness with a consequent decrease in other places such as BB'.

Newton, being Newton, must have tried to turn this from a qualitative explanation into a quantitative theory. We can imagine him trying an inverse square law of repulsion. If he did, he did not succeed – he was looking at the wrong distances.

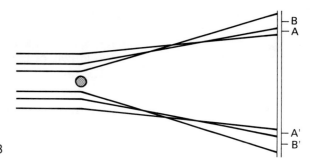

Figure 3

Path difference

The distance that Newton should have been interested in was the 'path difference': the difference in path between a ray of light travelling directly from P to M (Figure 4) and a ray travelling first to Q and then to M.

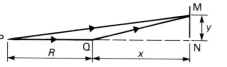

Figure 4

Let R be the hole-to-hair distance

x the hair-to-screen distance

y the distance of a particular maximum from the central line and

p the path difference, i.e. PQ + QM − PM.

Since y is small in comparison with R and x, it is a simple matter of Pythagoras and the binomial theorem to show that

$$y = \sqrt{\left\{2px\left(1 + \frac{x}{R}\right)\right\}}$$

Screen distance

Let us suppose that the path difference p is all important: that it decides the pattern size and that for a particular part of the pattern (the middle of the first bright band, for example) p will be the same in the 9 ft case as in the 6 in one.

Since p is common, the ratio of the two pattern sizes will be the ratio of the two values of

$$\sqrt{\left\{x\left(1 + \frac{x}{R}\right)\right\}}$$

Thus

$$\frac{\text{size at 9 ft}}{\text{size at } \frac{1}{2} \text{ ft}} = \frac{\sqrt{\{9(1 + \frac{9}{12})\}}}{\sqrt{\{\frac{1}{2}(1 + \frac{1}{24})\}}} = 5.5$$

5.5! This is the average value of the ratio of the pattern sizes. The supposition is justified – path difference has shown a connection where ray repulsion could not.

Relationships discovered

The table of breadths was for Newton a happy hunting ground. He found several numerical relationships between the breadths; moreover, these relationships were independent of the screen distances. To take an example: 'The distance between the middle of the first, and middle of the second Fringe, was to the distance between the middle of the second and middle of the third Fringe, as three to two, or ten to seven'.

The ratio of ten to seven equals 1.43.

Path differences calculated

If y_n is the distance from the central line of the nth maximum, then the path difference p_n is given by the equation

$$p_n = \frac{y_n{}^2}{2x\left(1 + \dfrac{x}{R}\right)}$$

As Figure 5 shows, before substituting for y, the thickness of the geometrical shadow must be calculated and allowed for. Fortunately Newton had measured the thickness of the hair ($\frac{1}{280}$ in). The geometrical shadow in the 6 in case will have a thickness

$$\frac{12 + \frac{1}{2}}{12} \times \frac{1}{280}$$

i.e. 0.0037 in.

The distance y_1 (Figure 5) will be half the separation of the first maxima, i.e.

$$\left(\frac{1}{38.5} - 0.0037\right) \text{ in}$$

$$y_1 = \frac{1}{2}\left(\frac{1}{38.5} - 0.0037\right) = 0.0112 \text{ in}$$

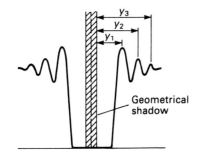

Geometrical shadow

Figure 5

Hence for a screen at a distance of 6 in,

$$p_1 = \frac{y_1{}^2}{2x\left(1 + \dfrac{x}{R}\right)} = \frac{0.00112}{2 \times \dfrac{1}{2}\left(1 + \dfrac{1}{24}\right)}$$

$$= 1.2 \times 10^{-5} \text{ in}$$

Table 2 gives the path differences for the three maxima for the two distances multiplied by 10^5.

Table 2

	6 in	9 ft	Average
First maximum	1.20	1.18	1.19 inches
Second maximum	3.62	3.49	3.56 inches
Third maximum	6.25	5.72	5.99 inches

Small whole numbers are beginning to emerge. Well within the experimental error,

p_2 is three times p_1 and p_3 is five times p_1

Newton had discovered that

$$\frac{y_3 - y_1}{y_2 - y_1} \simeq 1.43$$

Let us suppose that the three path differences are exactly in the ratio 5 to 3 to 1. Since y is proportional to $\sqrt{p}$

$$\frac{y_3 - y_1}{y_2 - y_1} = \frac{\sqrt{5} - \sqrt{1}}{\sqrt{3} - \sqrt{1}} = 1.43$$

This is further confirmation of the idea that path difference decides the pattern – our first supposition. It also confirms the idea that there are units ('atoms') of path difference – our second supposition.

The first maximum occurs when the path difference is one unit, the second when it is three units and the third when it is five units. Taking all six values from the table into consideration, we obtain for the average value of the path difference a length of 1.19×10^{-5} in.

Small whole numbers

A century after Newton, Dalton put forward his atomic theory because he found small whole numbers cropping up in the relations between masses of combining chemical elements.

Oh, Sir Isaac Newton Knt! If only you had looked *along* the rays instead of *at right-angles* to them! You might have seen that path difference decided the pattern and that path differences had small whole-number relationships. Moreover, you might have seen that path difference was the link between your diffraction experiments and your interference experiments.

Sunbeams in the cellar

Experiments that require sunlight are best done during the holidays – sunbeams do not often fit into school timetables. During the summer of 1964, I was able to repeat Newton's measurements in the cellar at home. First, the cellar was blacked out. A pinhole made in an aluminium sheet let the sunbeam in. For obstacles, besides hairs (insulators) I used pins and wires (conductors). When looking for a stand for the pin, I could not resist the temptation of sticking it into an apple (Figure 6).

There are problems in taking measurements of the pattern. Only for a short period during the day is the sunbeam – if there is one – in the right direction. The sunbeam does not stand still, so readings have to be recorded quickly. I started by marking the centre of the three maxima on both sides with a pen point, but later found pin points to be more satisfactory. The separation of the points I measured with a travelling microscope.

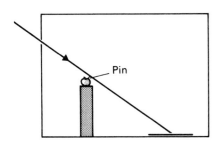

Figure 6

In one set of measurements, R was 43 in and x was 71 in. The hair had a diameter of 0.005 cm so its geometrical shadow was 0.013 cm broad. The average of 12 readings of the separation of the first maxima was 0.349 cm, that for the second maxima being 0.581 cm. Subtracting the geometrical shadow and dividing by 2 gave y_1 and y_2 as 0.168 cm and 0.284 cm respectively.

$$\frac{y_2}{y_1} = \frac{0.284}{0.168} = 1.69$$

This is in fair if not good agreement with $\sqrt{3}/\sqrt{1}$, i.e. 1.73.

From measurements of the second maxima, I calculated the unit of path difference. Four sets of readings with the same hair, but with a range of values for R and x, gave 2.8 cm, 2.9 cm, 2.8 cm and 3.0 cm with an average of 2.9 cm (1.14 in). From Newton's measurements, I had deduced 1.19 in. I have a deficiency in colour vision: the 'Middle of the brightest Light' for Newton need not have been the middle for me, so the agreement is as good as can be expected. (The mixture of inches with centimetres is awkward, but to quote Newton's measurements as centimetres is absurd.)

Internal fringes

Since Newton thought that the diffraction was due to the repulsion of the light rays by the hair, there could not be (for him) any light within the shadow. There was therefore no need to look for internal fringes so Newton did not look – at least, he did not record seeing anything.

I found a faint but definite maximum along the central line of the shadow of the hair (diameter, 0.1 mm) (Figure 7(a)). With the pin (diameter, $\frac{2}{3}$ mm) or the needle (diameter, 1 mm) I found both maxima and minima (Figure 7(b)).

To check that I was not 'seeing things', I asked other people – including young children and teenagers – to report what they saw. Being careful not to put any ideas into their heads and with only one observer at a time, I moved a pointer slowly across the pattern. They all saw a maximum with the hair, maxima and minima with the pin.

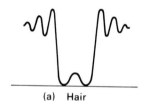
(a)   Hair

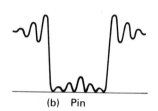
(b)   Pin

Figure 7

Fits and starts

As well as studying the diffraction patterns produced when light passed a hair, Newton studied the patterns produced by interference when light passed through narrow spaces. In particular, he measured the diameters of the coloured rings (Newton's rings) produced when light passed between a weakly curved convex glass surface and a plane glass one.

From the radii of the rings, he calculated 'the Thicknesses of the Air at the most luminous Parts of all the Brightest Rings' and found that they increased in the ratio 1 : 3 : 5 etc. (As we have seen, this ratio 1 : 3 : 5 occurs in the path differences of the shadow pattern.) Newton explained the rings by supposing that as the light passed through the gap between the two glass surfaces it had 'Fits': 'Fits of easy Reflexion and easy Transmission' – a fit and a start, we might say. He calculated the length of a fit. 'If the Rays which paint the

Colour in the Confine of yellow and orange pass perpendicularly out of any Medium into Air, the Intervals of their Fits of easy Reflexion are the 1/89000 part of an Inch'. (1/89000 is 1.12×10^{-5}.)

As we have seen, in the diffraction pattern of a hair there is a unit of path difference. From Newton's measurements, it was 1.19×10^{-5} in; from my measurements it was 1.14×10^{-5} in. Shadow measurements are difficult, and great accuracy cannot be expected. Within the error of experiment, the two measurements of the atom of path difference equal the length of the fit for yellow–orange: 1.12×10^{-5} in.

If we add the length of a fit to that of a start, we get 2.24×10^{-5} in. This is 5.69×10^{-5} cm, the wavelength of yellow light. *The unit of path difference from the shadow measurements is half the wavelength of light!*

How near and yet how far! Newton's corpuscles have a lot to answer for. They led him to see things that he ought not to have seen, such as measurable edges to a shadow. He did not see things that he ought to have seen – the fringes inside the shadow. He did not see that the shadow measurements led to a unit of path difference equal to 11.9 micro-inches and that this was practically the same length as the 'Fit of easy Reflexion' (11.2 micro-inches).

The poet Alexander Pope wrote a famous couplet about Newton:

Nature and Nature's Laws lay hid in Night
God said: Let Newton be and there was light.

This is not, as we have seen, the whole truth and to get a fuller picture I add another couplet:

To which the Devil said, 'Not quite
I'll see that Isaac does not get it right'.

Work interrupted

The third book of *Opticks* is entitled: 'Observations concerning the Inflexions of the Rays and the Colours made thereby'. 'Inflexions' are diffractions.

Newton wanted to improve the measurements. 'When I made the foregoing Observations I design'd to repeat most of them with more care and exactness, and to make some new ones for determining the manner how the Rays of Light are bent in their passage by Bodies, for making the Fringes of Colours with the dark lines between them. But I was then interrupted, and cannot now think of taking these things into farther Consideration.'

I too would like to repeat my measurements of 20 years ago but, alas, my neighbour has in the meantime erected a garage in his garden. The sunbeams no longer travel in fits and starts, waves or corpuscles, down into my cellar.

Chapter 11
Poisson's Bright Spot

Obstacles

Fresnel's triumph

In 1818 a French engineer, Augustin Fresnel, submitted an entry to a competition organised by the Académie des Sciences on the subject of diffraction. One of the judges, Poisson, who was an opponent of the wave theory deduced from Fresnel's entry that there should be a *bright spot* at the centre of the shadow cast by a circular obstacle.

This was obviously absurd. Had not Newton himself more than a century before studied the shadow of a hair? He had not reported a central bright line. Moreover, it was contrary to common sense – the centre of the obstacle should be the centre of darkness.

Arago was the Chairman of the judging committee. Prompted by Poisson's scorn, he looked at the centre with Fresnel. Lo and behold, there was a bright spot! Common sense – not for the only time – had misled. The scoffer had to eat his words. Ironically the spot, one of the most dramatic ·sights in the history of physics, was named after neither Arago nor Fresnel, but Poisson. In these days of electric lamps, we do not have to wait for the sun to shine to see it.

A footnote deterrent

A famous textbook *The Theory of Light* by Thomas Preston, first published in 1890, had its fourth edition in 1912. It was in that edition that I read a footnote on p.231 which referred to Poisson's bright spot: 'This experiment is difficult to perform satisfactorily since even when the disc is cut with utmost care each of the minute inequalities in its edge is magnified and accompanied by fringes which mix and cross so as to totally confuse the whole appearance'.

Deterred by this warning, I didn't try the experiment until I had retired from teaching. Thus I never had the pleasure of showing my pupils this and some other delightful surprises that diffraction has to offer.

How to show Fresnel diffraction

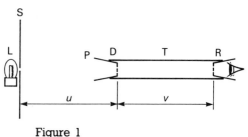

Figure 1

Figure 1 shows the arrangement. A 12 V headlamp bulb sends light through a pinhole in a screen. To get a bright picture, the lamp should be as near the pinhole as possible. P is a plastic tub with its end removed. It has been chosen to fit into the cardboard tube T. The obstacle to be studied, the diffractor D, is mounted across the end of P. Quick changes from one diffractor to another are possible. The tube T keeps out stray light and facilitates lining up.

There are two methods of viewing the diffraction picture:

1 It can be viewed on a translucent screen mounted on a second plastic tub. Suitable plastic sheets for the screen are not hard to find, but the picture is not bright. It is small but can be magnified by an eye-lens, and for measurements of distance there is no doubt where the picture is – it is on the screen.

2 It can be viewed directly by an eye-lens. The picture is now bigger, brighter and coloured. Younger students, however, experience difficulty in knowing where to look.

The obstacles

The Poisson bright spot can be seen at the centre of the shadow of an 11 mm drawing pin when u and v in Figure 1 are each about 1 m.

I mounted such a drawing pin on a microscope slide. Viewing through the translucent screen, I could just detect a faint spot. With the eye-lens it was most definitely there but in addition there were 'intruders'. Preston had warned about 'faint spokes irregularly distributed'. In addition, where the shadow ended, there were the usual two or three edge-effect fringes.

Small ball bearings can be suspended from the end of a magnetised needle. Two diffraction pictures will now be seen – that of the linear obstacle and that of the circular one. With 6 mm ball bearings the bright spot became more pronounced and the spokes were fainter. With 3 mm balls the eye-lens showed a bright spot surrounded by two or three faint narrow rings. With 1.5 mm balls there was a marked change in appearance: the rings around the central spot were now broader and brighter.

Small balls are difficult to handle, so eventually I cast Preston's warning aside and, with a fine brush, painted black dots on a microscope slide in the range 1.0 mm down to 0.5 mm. Even dots that were far from circular gave good diffraction pictures. I painted dots of different sizes on the same slide so that the effect of different sizes could be seen at a glance. As the dots got smaller, the bright centre expanded until it occupied most of the picture.

Small round holes

Small round obstacles produce pleasing diffraction effects, but small round holes are even better. (Victorian textbooks talk about 'apertures'.) Figure 2 is an attempt to capture what is seen when the size of the hole is increased in six stages. F1 is the pattern formed by the smallest hole. F2 and F4 show central *dark* spots.

'If what you say is true,' Poisson said (though not in these words), 'at the centre of a shadow there will be a bright spot and this is absurd.' He need not have stopped there: 'and at the centre of a circular patch of light there can be a dark spot, which is even more absurd'.

The centre of the diffraction pattern of a round obstacle is always a bright spot. The centre of the diffraction pattern of a round hole alternates between bright and dark as size increases.

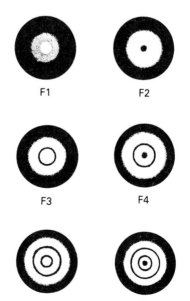

F1   F2

F3   F4

F5   F6

Figure 2

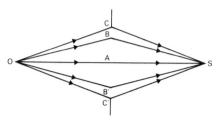

Figure 3

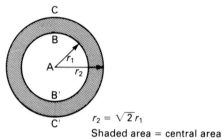

$r_2 = \sqrt{2}\, r_1$

Shaded area = central area

Figure 4

Theory

Two waves, unlike two corpuscles, can cancel each other out.

Consider the waves of light starting from the point O which pass through the hole CC' (shown – greatly exaggerated – in Figure 3) to arrive at point S. If the path difference between the wave which has travelled from O to C and then to S is one wavelength greater than that of the wave which has travelled directly from O to S, then by the usual argument the effect of the waves passing through the outer ring CB in Figure 4 will cancel out the effect of the waves which have travelled through the circle BA.

At S (Figure 3) there will be no light. This is how the dark spot of F2 comes about.

Let OA be u and AS be v and let f be the distance such that

$$\frac{1}{u} + \frac{1}{v} = \frac{1}{f}$$

Let the diameter of the hole be w. It is a simple matter to show that the dark spot of F2 will appear when

$$\frac{\omega^2}{4f} = \lambda \text{ (one wavelength)}$$

Similarly it can be shown that n, the number of the Fresnel picture in Figure 2, is given by

$$n = \frac{\omega^2}{4\lambda f} = \frac{\omega^2}{4\lambda}\left(\frac{1}{u} + \frac{1}{v}\right)$$

Practice

The equation shows how with a given hole the picture can be changed by changing u and v and so f. As f is decreased, the picture passes from F1 with its dark centre to F3 with a bright centre to F4 which has not only a dark centre but a dark ring as well. For a given hole, as f decreases n increases. For a given value of f, the bigger the hole is, the bigger the F number is.

Four at once

It is fascinating to see the first four Fresnel pictures at the same time. The diameters of the holes have to be in the ratio of $\sqrt{1}: \sqrt{2}: \sqrt{3}: \sqrt{4}$, i.e. $1 : 1.41 : 1.73 : 2$. Inch drills go (or went) up in sixty-fourths: $\frac{3}{64}, \frac{4}{64}, \frac{5}{64}, \frac{6}{64}$. Their ratios are therefore $1 : 1.33 : 1.67 : 2$. By means of a reamer, the $\frac{4}{64}$ and $\frac{5}{64}$ holes can be enlarged to the right size.

Four such holes were bored 5 mm apart in a brass square of side 30 mm. The square was mounted on the end of the plastic tub. The No.1 picture was at its best when f was 0.59 m. The length v of the sighting tube was 0.9 m, so u had to be about 1.6 m.

Emboldened by the sight of F1, F2, F3 and F4, I wondered if I could get F5. Calculation showed that a No.36 drill (2.72 mm) would be the right size. There was room for it (just) in the middle of the other four holes. I drilled the hole, and I got the required F5 picture with its bright centre and two dark rings. But I got something more. In the spaces between the central hole and its four satellites, there were strong and beautiful interference fringes.

The measurement of wavelength

It may seem straightforward to measure the wavelength of light by circular hole diffraction using the equation

$$\lambda = \frac{\omega^2}{4nf}$$

All that has to be done is to decide on a pattern (say F4), to obtain the pattern and then to adjust f until F4 appears at its best. The distance f can be adjusted by adjusting the distance u. However, it takes time to adjust u and in that time the impression of the first picture is fading.

Simultaneous viewing is needed. This can be done by using three nearly equal holes side by side. Having decided on F4, I bored three holes side by side with a $\frac{5}{64}$ inch drill. One hole I left as it was, 2.0 mm; I enlarged the second hole with a reamer to 2.1 mm and the third to 2.2 mm. A preliminary calculation shows that for light with a wavelength of about 6×10^{-7} m the 2.1 mm hole will give F4 when f is about 0.50 m. I used this information to get the three F4 pictures side by side and then adjusted f until the middle picture was better than its neighbours.

If white light is used, λ is the wavelength of yellow light. By using red and green filters in turn, the wavelength for red and green can be found. With red light, I was able to get brighter pictures, F6 and even F7. I drilled a bigger hole with a $\frac{1}{8}$ inch drill, calculated from λ_R the required value of f to get F6 and set up u and v so that f equalled this value: in the same way, I obtained F7.

From bigger holes to smaller ones: when

$$\frac{\omega^2}{f\lambda} < 1$$

the bright centre of F1 spreads out (Figure 5). It is surrounded by rings which get ever fainter and nearer to each other.

Linear obstacles

In Chapter 10, Newton's measurements of the diffraction pattern produced by a hair and my repetition of some of them have been described. Having passed the hair, the sunlight fell on to a white card, and the shadow on the card was examined. It would have been possible for Newton to dispense with the card and to look at the sunbeam with a magnifying glass after it had been passed through the hair. It would have been possible, but not easy – even for Newton.

There are two disadvantages of using sunbeams to study diffraction. One is obvious – the sun is not at our beck and call. The other is that the angle at which the sunbeams come down is awkward: horizontal sunbeams would be much more convenient.

Today we can use electric lamps to study diffraction at any time of the day or night, and the direction of the beam from the lamps is for us to decide. We can use the arrangement of Figure 1 to study the diffraction of light past linear obstacles and through slits. It is not necessary to use a slit source at S to line up with the obstacle, in fact a pinhole at S will serve as well as a slit and is easier to use.

The diffraction pattern that appears has two distinct parts, external fringes and internal fringes. If we use progressively thinner obstacles – from needles down to pins, from thick wires down to fine wires – we find that the external fringes do not change in appearance, being just as they were when Newton described them. In contrast, the internal fringes (which Newton never saw) change as the thickness of the obstacle changes. More precisely, their appearance depends on the same quantities ω, f and λ as with holes. The formula $\omega^2/f\lambda$ again applies, but not quite exactly.

If we start with f at 0.5 m, u and v each being 1 m, we find that a 1.6 mm needle gives a strong outer pattern but only a faint inner one. An eye-lens will show that the inner pattern has five maxima and six minima, as shown in Chapter 10, Figure 7(b). For a 0.8 mm pin, there is a central bright line with a dark fringe on either side. Whatever the thickness of the obstacle, if there is a pattern of maxima and minima, the centre will be bright.

It takes time to change from one diffractor to another – from a pin to a needle – so some of the contrast is lost in making the change. Instead of using a cylindrical object such as a pin, I used a flat strip mounted on a simple homemade turntable controlled (literally) by pulling strings. A strip of thin steel 5 cm long × 3 mm broad was a satisfactory object but even a postcard can be used. As the turntable is rotated, the various patterns are shown quickly, one after the other.

Several linear obstacle patterns can be shown at once if the strip is cut in the shape of a wedge. The central line being always bright, we could call it Poisson's bright line.

Transparent obstacles

The diffracting obstacle need not be opaque. Figure 6 shows the pattern formed by diffraction along the edge of a microscope slide. It is the usual straight-edge effect shown with an opaque obstacle but shown twice, not once. For waves going through the air, the *glass* behaves as if it were opaque; for waves going through the glass, the *air* behaves as if it were opaque.

The light streaming from the lamp is not a continuous coherent wave but comes in bursts of waves, occupying finite lengths. Because of the thickness of the glass, the waves travelling through it lose all coherence with the waves travelling through the air. Each part of the beam of light makes its own diffraction pattern quite unaffected by the other part.

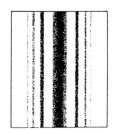

Figure 6

Linear holes: slits

We have seen that as far as patterns are concerned

> linear obstacles ≡ round obstacles

similarly,

> linear holes ≡ round holes

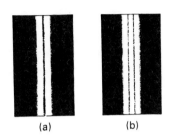

(a)   (b)

Figure 7

With obstacles, there is no alternation between bright and dark as size increases; with holes there is.

> In Figure 2 the dark spot of F2 becomes the bright spot of F3.
> In Figure 7 the dark line of Figure 7(a) becomes the bright line of Figure 7(b).

Newton made a tapering slit from two tilted knives. Figure 8 is taken from *Opticks*. Careful examination will show that the central line is alternately bright and dark.

The qualitative agreement between the patterns for slits and holes is not exactly matched by a quantitative one. I mounted a slit on the turntable and measured the angles at which the slit had to be set to change from first dark to bright and then to second dark.

Using the value of λ that I had obtained from the hole experiments, I found that for the holes

$$n = \frac{\omega^2}{4f\lambda}$$

whereas for the slits

$$n - \frac{1}{4} \simeq \frac{\omega^2}{4f\lambda}$$

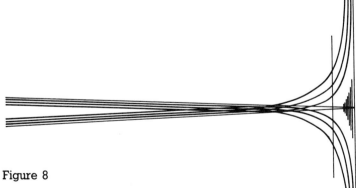

Figure 8

'Transparent holes'

In addition to transparent obstacles, we can make 'transparent holes' – holes bored in a sheet of acetate. To get a smooth edge round a hole in an acetate sheet, I clamped the sheet tightly between wooden sheets and then drilled it. The diffraction pattern produced by such a hole was surrounded by broad dark rings like the moat round a castle wall.

In an acetate sheet I drilled four holes with the same diameters as the first four holes made for Figure 2. The diffraction patterns were those of Figure 2 but this time enhanced by dark rings.

Five effects

It is not necessary for a long thin obstacle to be straight. It must however be narrow. If a steel washer (external diameter, 7 mm; internal diameter, 3 mm) is suitably suspended, a fascinating picture is seen through the eye-lens. There are three different diffraction effects with the washer: the edge effect outside the shadow, the obstacle effect within the shadow, and the round hole effect in the middle.

The washer has to be suspended: it can be held up by a magnetised needle. There will then be two more effects from the needle itself, making five effects in all.

Chapter 12

Odds and Ends: Optics

The colours of soap films

Figure 1 shows an arrangement with which the colours of soap films can be shown – not to one or two people but to the whole class. The films are not only full of beauty, but full of physics too.

A flat source of light (a 150 W floodlight) is mounted behind a translucent screen. An opaque screen shields the observers from direct light; a black screen prevents light getting into the film from behind.

The film is formed in a frame of copper rods. The solution – a weak solution of detergent liquid – is poured into a shallow tin. The frame, which is held by its base, is dipped into the tin and then removed.

For a second or two, nothing much happens. The film behaves like a mirror and forms a colourless image of the translucent screen as far behind the film as the screen is in front of it. Then, slowly and steadily, horizontal bands of brilliant colour appear across the film.

As the number of bands increases, they descend gracefully. Eventually a silvery band appears at the top: it heralds the appearance of a dark space. Although the film is by now very thin, the dark space may descend more than halfway down the frame before the film bursts.

To explain the colours seen by white light it is a good idea to describe first what happens when the films are seen by a single colour, e.g. red light.

Red and black

The film looks very different when viewed through a colour filter, particularly a red filter. In place of the brilliant colours, horizontal red and black bands are seen. These become closer together as they move down the film (Figure 2). The contrast between black and red decreases down the film but it is possible to count up to ten bands.

The black bands occur when the red waves reflected from the back surface of the film are out of phase with the waves reflected from the front surface of the film. As the film increases in thickness, the path difference increases. For every increase of half a wavelength, 'out of phase' is replaced by 'in phase': black is replaced by red.

'But why,' some bright student might ask, 'when the film is at its thinnest and the path difference is at its least, is the film black? Where has the half wavelength come from?'

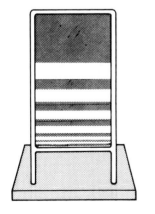

Figure 1

Figure 2

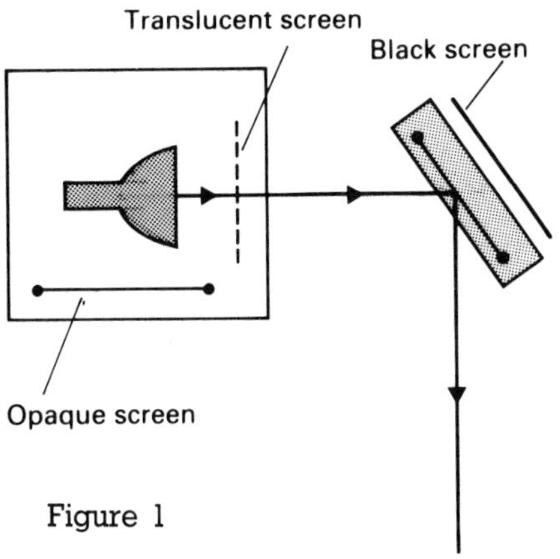

Translucent screen

Black screen

Opaque screen

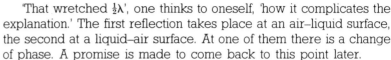

'That wretched $\frac{1}{2}\lambda$', one thinks to oneself, 'how it complicates the explanation.' The first reflection takes place at an air–liquid surface, the second at a liquid–air surface. At one of them there is a change of phase. A promise is made to come back to this point later.

The red waves which pass through the filter have a spread in wavelength of perhaps a tenth. When the film is about 20 or so wavelengths thick, some part of the red light will be reflected; the contrast will weaken. With strictly monochromatic light, bright and dark bands would appear whatever the thickness.

The range of wavelengths in white light is about 2 (red) to 1 (violet). In consequence, only with films a few wavelengths thick will particular colours be suppressed to allow the other colours to shine brightly. With white light, the bright colours at the top of the film become subdued further down.

Figure 3

If the soap film were a plane wedge, the bands seen through the red filter would be equidistant. From the appearance of the bands, we can deduce that at the top there is a discontinuity where a very thin film is formed (Figure 3). Below the discontinuity, the film is bi-concave.

Expectation of life

Though the life of a particular film is unpredictable, there are some regulating factors to bear in mind. Films are constantly evaporating – becoming thinner and therefore weaker. A hot dry atmosphere means a short life; a cold damp atmosphere means a much longer life.

At a temperature of $7\frac{1}{2}$ °C and a humidity of 75%, I found the average life of a film to be 145 seconds: but at a higher temperature (18 °C) and a lower humidity (45%) this had dropped to only 16 seconds, not leaving much time to make observations.

Hot and dry – these are the best conditions for electrostatics, the worst for soap films. No day will be good for both.

The life expectation of a film can be extended by adding glycerine to the soap solution. The glycerine, being viscous, slows down the movements within the film; local inequalities build up, and lurid colours are seen swirling about. If psychedelic effects are required, add glycerine: if a more serious study of the colour is needed, don't.

Turbulent tadpoles

If a film is held in a vertical frame, it thins at the top for two reasons: not only is it draining to the bottom, but it is also evaporating. Both these changes are slow ones; the coloured bands slowly, steadily and gracefully descend. Everything is serene.

Now switch your attention from the centre of the frame to the edge and look closely at it, using a magnifying glass. Here there is a very different picture. Small brilliant circles with long waving tails (resembling tadpoles) come from nowhere, stream hurriedly up the edge of the frame and then disappear. The swift turbulent ascent of the 'tadpoles' is in striking contrast to the slow descent of the coloured bands.

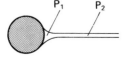

Figure 4

Figure 4 is a horizontal cross-section of the film near the edge.

The film wets the edge of the frame, producing a concave curvature there. The pressure at P_1 is less than the pressure at P_2, so liquid moves inwards and upwards.

A topless bubble

With the help of a funnel, blow a hemispherical bubble on the top of a beaker. Illuminate it from the side with the floodlamp. The room should be free from draughts and preferably damp. Look at the bubble from the side. The colours are of course similar to those formed by a flat frame but, unless you have successfully suppressed all the draughts, the colours tend to swirl around and the pattern will go through a series of quick changes before it settles down again.

Eventually, there will be a surprise: the bubble will become topless, or so it seems. It will acquire the shape of an egg that has been beheaded. Three stages are shown in Figure 5. Careful examination of the missing top may show up very small speckles.

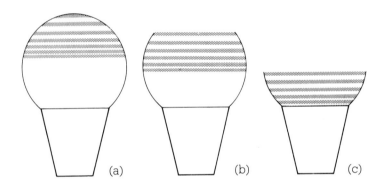

(a)   (b)   (c)

Figure 5

The rainbow cup

The rainbow cup was invented by Professor Boys of 'soap bubbles' fame. A soap film is formed across the top of a shallow cup. The cup is rotated rapidly by hand and the film thins out in the centre producing brilliantly coloured rings.

At the Warwick Meeting of the ASE in 1981, Mr D Dyson showed a rainbow cup which he had kept for many years. This stimulated me to make a modern, more brightly lit, version. The cup is now an empty bean tin of diameter 7 cm by depth 5 cm. The inside is painted dull black.

Figure 6 shows the arrangement, drawn from above. The light comes from a lamp such as that used to illuminate soap films (Figure 1). The can is mounted on a horizontal axis. The film, which is formed across the mouth of the can by dipping it into a soap solution, is in a vertical plane. This means that more people can see it at once. A small motor, pulley wheels and rubber bands make the can rotate. The rate of rotation is not critical.

Before long, a black dot appears in the centre surrounded by brilliantly coloured rings (Figure 7). The dot becomes a circle which may eventually fill the entire space before the film bursts.

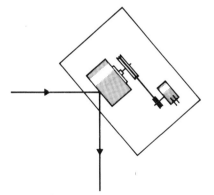

Figure 6

Figure 7

The soap film thins out at the centre to thicken further away. (There will be the usual desire to attribute this to 'centrifugal force'.) Its cross-section will bear some resemblance to the cross-section of the space between the two surfaces which produce 'Newton's rings'. Textbooks say that the central spot of Newton's ring is dark but, in my experience, this is not always so. The two surfaces must be spotlessly clean for the centre to be dark. There is no difficulty at all in getting a dark centre to the rings of the rainbow cup.

Beware of editors

I was asked by the editor of a US journal to write an account of the rainbow rings. This I did, and it was duly edited. When I saw the printed version, the rate of rotation which I had put at 5 Hz had speeded up a thousandfold to become 5 kHz. Some can! Some speed!! Gee whizz!!!

Peacock's feathers

The wings of some insects and butterflies are iridescent; the colours glitter and change when the angle of viewing changes. Peacock's feathers also are iridescent and are more suitable for the physics lab than insects' wings since they are more durable.

The centre of the 'eye' is a dark velvety patch. The most vivid change in colour takes place in the surrounding ring. As the direction of light changes, the colour goes from a brilliant blue through green to gold. With the help of a torch, the changes can be studied: when the deviation of the rays is large (approaching 180°), the ring appears to be blue; when the deviation is reduced to 90°, the ring appears to be golden.

If the feather is held up to a mirror and positioned so that the feather and its mirror image can be seen at the same time, it may happen that the object and image have different colours.

Some people say that the colours are produced by interference but thin-film interference requires smooth surfaces which do not occur in the filaments of the feathers.

Other people say that the colours are due to diffraction. If this were the case, the colours would change when the feather was rotated about an axis perpendicular to its plane – they do not.

So what causes the colours?

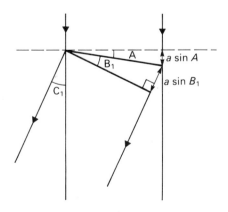

Figure 8

A diffraction grating short cut

In setting up a grating on a spectrometer, time is taken up in setting it exactly at right-angles to the collimator. If time is short, this can be avoided.

With a set-square, put the grating perpendicular to the collimator (by eye). It should not be far out, perhaps 2°. Take the reading of the angle of a spectral line, first to the right C_1 and then to the left C_2. Their average will be very nearly the correct value θ. An example will show this (Figure 8).

Let the grating constant be a, θ be 20°, the angle of mis-setting 2°, one of the angles which the telescope makes with a perpendicular

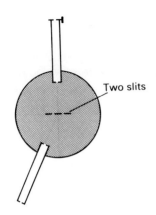

Two slits

Figure 9

to the grating B_1 and the other B_2, and let C_1 be the setting of the telescope. From the diagram it is clear that

$$a \sin \theta = a \sin A + a \sin B_1$$

From this we find that B_1 is 17.89°, and so C_1 is 19.89°. Similarly

$$a \sin \theta = a \sin B_2 - a \sin A$$

B_2 is 22.14° and C_2 is 20.14°. The average of C_1 and C_2 is 20.015° or 20° 1'.

Young's third slit

There are advantages in doing Young's classical experiment with a spectrometer (see Figure 9): the fringes are easy to find; the arrangement is practically knock-proof; angles, not widths are measured; Pythagoras is not needed. The separation of the fringes in radians equals the ratio of the wavelength λ to the slit separation s:

$$\theta = \frac{\lambda}{s}$$

The experiment is usually known as a double-slit experiment, but three slits are involved. Because the collimator slit of the spectometer is adjustable, the part played by this third slit can be studied. When the slit is very narrow (almost closed), the fringes show good contrast but are faint. As the slit is opened the fringes become brighter and, as we would expect, the contrast weakens. What perhaps is not expected is that further widening improves the contrast; still further widening reduces it once again. The explanation of this is a good exercise for senior pupils.

A drinking-straw wave machine

Figure 10

A barber's pole driven round by the wind seems one moment to be endlessly screwing its way downwards: the wind changes, and the pole now soars endlessly heavenwards (Figure 10).

Some drinking straws are decorated with spiral stripes. Slip four such straws along a steel rod of length 1 m. Glue the straws to the rod, making sure that the stripe does not show the joins. Mount the ends of the rod horizontally in suitable supports, and fix one end to a hand drill. Turn the drill. The illusion that the stripe is moving forwards (or backwards) is strong: you feel that you could mark a spot on the straw and follow it from one end to the other.

It is possible with this wave machine to verify the fundamental wave equation $v = n\lambda$. Three assistants are required: one turns the drill steadily; a second times the rate f of rotation of the drill; a third measures the time of a particular wave as it progresses from one end to the other. From this time and the total length of the straws, the velocity v of the wave motion can be found. The gear ratio N of the drill is measured; the frequency of the wave motion will be Nf. The wavelength λ equals the separation of the stripes. Typical values for N, f and λ are 4, 1 Hz and 1.5 cm respectively, giving a wave velocity of 6 cm/s.

A wooden dowel

Next, I converted a wooden dowel into a barber's pole. It was 1 cm in diameter and 90 cm long. To illustrate change of velocity with change in wavelength, the stripe had a pitch of 2 cm for one half of the rod and 3 cm for the other half. The ratio 3 : 2 corresponds to the passage of light from air into glass. A ratio of $2\frac{1}{2}$: 1 would give a more vivid demonstration; it would represent the passage from air into diamond.

The wooden rod was supported on short steel rods inserted into its ends. A circular hole in a piece of hardboard placed at the middle of the rod was a third support. It corresponded to the surface of refraction.

To make the 2 cm spiral, mark a series of dots at 2 cm intervals along the first half of the rod. The angle that the spiral will make with the surface of the rod will be

$$\tan^{-1}\left(\frac{2}{\pi d}\right)$$

where d is the diameter of the rod. At each of the dots, cut a short groove at this angle with a hacksaw. Wind a black thread around the rod, fitting it into the grooves. Then follow the course of the thread with a marker pen.

The machine brings out the importance of frequency for a wave motion. Because it is easier to measure wavelength than frequency, the latter is sometimes overlooked. Red waves are thought of as longer than blue waves but in diamond a blue wave is longer than a red one.

Calculus and the convex lens

1 Find the minimum distance of separation of an object and its real image formed by a convex lens. (While invigilating practical examinations, I have seen candidates vainly trying to focus an image when the separation was too small.)

Let f be the focal length and D the separation of object and image, i.e. $u + v$.

$$D = \frac{u^2}{u - f}$$

Differentiate with regard to u

$$\frac{\mathrm{d}D}{\mathrm{d}u} = \frac{2u}{u - f} - \frac{u^2}{(u - f)^2}$$

When D has a minimum value,

$$\frac{\mathrm{d}D}{\mathrm{d}u} = 0$$

Therefore

$$\frac{2u}{u - f} = \frac{u^2}{(u - f)^2}$$

and

$$u = 2f$$

v also equals $2f$ and thus the minimum separation is $4f$.

2 For a convex lens, show that when the real image distance is approximately equal to the object distance, a small change in the one will result in an equal but opposite change in the other.

If we differentiate the equation

$$\frac{1}{u} + \frac{1}{v} = \frac{1}{f}$$

with regard to u we find that

$$\frac{\mathrm{d}v}{\mathrm{d}u} = -\frac{v^2}{u^2}$$

Thus when u and v are equal or nearly equal a small change in u will produce an almost equal but opposite change in v. The sum of u and v is constant for a small change in either v or u. With a convex lens, an illuminated object and a screen, focus the image with u and v nearly equal. Move the lens slightly; the image will remain focused.

A problem with two solutions

Question   A simple microscope is made from two convex lenses. When they are separated by 20.5 cm, the magnifying power is 50. When the separation is increased to 35.5 cm, the magnifying power becomes 100. In both cases the final image is at infinity. The nearest point of distinct vision is to be taken as 25 cm.
Find the focal lengths of the objective lens and the eye-piece lens.

Answer   If care is taken to keep the signs correct, the data lead to a quadratic equation. The two roots are real and positive, giving focal lengths of 3 cm and 2.5 cm, or 2.5 cm and 3 cm. The reversibility of a simple two-lens microscope is thus neatly demonstrated.
Look the 'wrong way' down a microscope; it will still remain a microscope. Look the wrong way down a telescope; objects, instead of appearing to be brought nearer, appear to be banished to greater distances.

A stroboscopic surprise

To show the stroboscope effect, I painted a black Maltese cross on a white card (Figure 11) and with a small dc motor made the card

Figure 11

spin. The card was illuminated by a 'fluorescent' lamp.

By varying the rate of rotation of the motor, I obtained the usual stroboscopic effects. The cross could be brought to a standstill, or made to rotate slowly forwards or backwards. Cinema viewers have learned not to expect agreement between the motion of the stage coach and the rotation of the wheels.

What I did not expect, however, was the appearance of colours in the stroboscopically stationary cross. In place of white sectors we saw blue--grey ones; in place of black sectors, browny-orange ones.

A fluorescent lamp is also a phosphorescent lamp. In it, by electronic bombardment of the mercury vapour, ultraviolet radiation is produced and this is absorbed by the phosphor lining the tube. The phosphor molecules are raised from the ground state to an excited state. Some of them very quickly fall back to the ground state with the emission of electrons. This is fluorescence (Figure 12). Others fall into an electron trap, an intermediate state from which there is no further falling. Eventually, by thermal agitation, they escape upwards. This takes time. Once again, a proportion will fall from the excited state to the ground state. The delayed radiation is phosphorescence. Different level changes take different times – these times are of the same order of magnitude as the periodic time of an alternating current and so different colours appear on the stroboscopic card.

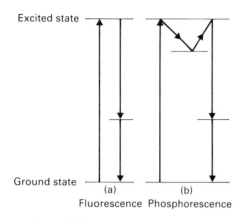

Figure 12

Polaroids and polythene

Polaroids can be used to study the elastic properties of polythene. Cut a strip from a thin sheet of polythene a few centimetres wide and hold it between two crossed polaroids: no light will pass. Pull gently: brightly coloured patterns appear. Let go: the patterns disappear. Now pull the polythene with increasing force. Eventually, the pattern will remain after the tension has been removed; the polythene strip has been stretched beyond its elastic limit.

Light and magnetism

The electromagnetic theory of light is now taken as a fact rather than a theory. Before Maxwell, Faraday sought and found connections between light and magnetism. Figure 13 is taken from Ganot's monumental 19th century work *Physics*. It shows one such connection. The drawing itself is a superb piece of craftsmanship. Light passes through the central holes in the soft iron core of the electromagnet. At *a* and *b* there are Nicol prisms. At *C* there is a block of glass. When the current is switched on, a strong magnetic field is produced parallel to the direction of the light from the lamp. The plane of polarisation is rotated by the magnetic field. Magnetism has affected light.

Figure 13

The blue sky

'Please sir, why is the sky blue?' Philosophically speaking this is an interesting question. Its asker is wanting a simple answer. Any explanation should move from the more-difficult to the less-difficult concept, from the less-familiar to the more-familiar phenomenon. Inverse fourth-power laws are not simple concepts and nothing could be more familiar than the blue sky.

So how do we answer the question? We can begin with explaining what and where the sky is. The sky is light that comes to us from the atmosphere – the air around and above us. It is not the result of water droplets; those are seen separately as clouds. The blue sky is not caused by dust particles floating in the air; the sky is at its bluest when a shower has cleared all the dust.

The air is made up of molecules. The light of the sky is light from the sun that has been scattered from the molecules of air. The moon has no atmosphere. It therefore has no sky.

So far so good. But by now the questioner will be getting impatient. 'But why is it blue?' Here a change of tactics is indicated. The questioner must be questioned. 'You are asking the wrong question. The question that you should ask is: what can we deduce from the blueness of the sky? This question is answerable.

The blueness of the sky shows that the blue waves (the short ones) are more strongly scattered than the long waves (the red ones). Only if the questioner is mature enough to appreciate it need Rayleigh's law of scattering be invoked. Rayleigh showed that the intensity of the light scattered is proportional to $1/\lambda^4$, where λ is the wavelength. If we take red waves to be about 1.5 times longer than blue waves, then blue light should be scattered 1.5^4, i.e. 5 times, more than red light.

The blueness of the sky is not an isolated phenomenon. It is connected with the redness of the setting sun. If blue light is scattered more than red light, the light that gets through greater distances of the atmosphere will appear red.

The setting sun

Professor John Tyndall (1820–1893) succeeded Faraday as the Superintendent of the Royal Institution in 1867. It was still possible in those days to achieve fame in more than one field of science. Besides his discoveries in physics, Tyndall made discoveries in bacteriology and glaciology. Not only glaciers were named after him, but also mountain peaks, for he was an intrepid mountaineer. He was a gifted lecturer and a populariser of scientific ideas. To him is due a well-known experiment which helps to explain the blueness of the sky and the redness of the setting sun.

A weak solution of hydrochloric acid is added to a weak solution of sodium thiosulphate. This results in the liberation of minute particles of sulphur which slowly grow.

The mixture is contained in a gas jar (Figure 14). A lamp sends light upwards through the jar to be reflected from the tilted mirror. At first, the liquid is clear. Slowly it begins to scatter blue light from the side, and as the blue light becomes more intense the redness seen in the mirror increases.

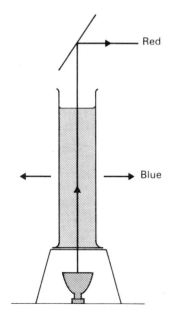

Red

Blue

Figure 14

Chapter 13

Our Eyes, our Glasses

Seventy years ago, school medical examinations were sterner affairs than they are today. The nurses treated both children and mothers as potential wrong-doers from whom no nonsense was to be taken. At the age of six or seven, my sight was tested. 'Mother,' barked out the nurse, 'this child cannot see.' It was a triumph for authority. A very juvenile delinquent – an optical Oliver Twist – had been caught, if not red-handed, then short-sighted.

If the nurse had said that I was verminous, my poor mother could not have been more upset. I had never before heard my mother rebuked, and rebuked severely. As for myself, I could not understand what wrong I had done. I was not conscious of any guilt; I knew that I could see – what was all the fuss about?

If the nurse had known more physics, if she had been better trained, she could have pointed out to my mother that I could not focus on distant objects but that this could be put right by wearing spectacles. It was put right and I have worn spectacles ever since.

The safety of my spectacles has always been of great concern to me – something that only a fellow myope can appreciate. In crowded army barracks, I tucked them away in one of my boots before settling down for the night.

A few years ago I saw the Italian farce about black-marketeers *Can't pay, won't pay*. Sacks of black-market goods had to be got rid of. They were thrown into the audience: one of the sacks on being thrown back to the stage knocked my glasses off. My heart sank. The leading actor shouted down to me, 'Are you all right, guv?' 'No, I'm not. I've lost my glasses and until I find my glasses I can't start looking for them.' This got a laugh, my first and last in a West End theatre.

'Please sir, why do you take your glasses off?' Thermometer scales are hard to read: a short-sighted teacher, who by removing his concave lenses can bring his nearest point of vision down from 20 cm to 4 cm, can gain a fivefold improvement in seeing.

Children's eyes

Children's eyes, being smaller than those of adults, have smaller radii of curvature and so shorter focal lengths. It is not surprising therefore that their nearest point of distinct vision (NPDV) is much nearer than that of the middle-aged people who write textbooks. For example, it can be about 7 cm rather than 25 cm.

A biology colleague asked me why young children seemed reluctant to use the magnifying lenses that they were provided with.

The focal length of these lenses was 5 cm. Suppose that the diameter of a child's eye was 2 cm and that the NPDV was 7 cm. The focal length of the unaided eye would be $\frac{14}{9}$, i.e. 1.6 cm. A 5 cm lens in contact with the eye would bring the resultant focal length down to about 1.2 cm; the NPDV would be 3 cm. If the lens was held at a distance of 1 cm, then the effective NPDV would be about 4 cm. The advantage gained ($\frac{7}{4}$) does not really compensate for the awkwardness of holding the lens. If magnifying glasses are to be of much use to young children, then their focal lengths should be less than 5 cm.

Co-op stamps are useful tests for the ability to read small print, i.e. the ability to focus at near distances. At normal reading distance the background seems to be a wavy line. Close to, this becomes 'Co-operative Wholesale Society'.

Some coins have the engravers initials on one of their faces but they are very small. The reverse side of a two-shilling coin contained the initials EF and CT.

A one-lens telescope

My NDPV being 5 cm, not 25 cm, I made a one-lens telescope with a 50 cm convex lens mounted at the end of an extensible cardboard tube (Figure 1). I used it to look at the moon, adjusting the length of the tube so that the image of the moon was at the NPDV. The magnifying power was about 10. If I had persevered and mounted the tube on a stand, I should have been able to get young children to use this one-lens (and very cheap) telescope. As it was, they were unable to hold an unmounted tube steadily.

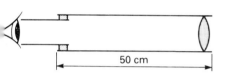

Figure 1

What big eyes you've got!

Short-sighted people wear concave lenses to give themselves a normal range of vision. If these lenses were worn pressed against the eye, then the eye would appear to other observers as of normal size. There is, however, a gap of between 1 and 2 cm between lens and eye. In consequence, an observer will see a slightly smaller eye. Long-sighted people wear convex lenses. There will be a gap between their lenses and their eyes. In consequence, their eyes appear bigger than they really are. A normally sighted person wishing to have lovely big eyes could wear convex lenses. The lenses would, of course, have the effect of making their wearer short-sighted.

Shaggy dogs

Some shaggy dogs look at the world through a curtain of hair. Little children don't push their hair back when it falls across their eyes. Eventually they are taught to do so – 'your hair must be getting in your way' – but it isn't really. The hairs are so near the eyes that they are out of focus and do not distract. They cut down the amount of light falling on the eye, but generally there is plenty of light anyhow.

Spectacle wearers know that it is not dust on the lenses that bothers them but greasy streaks. These do not block the light but re-direct it and so distract. The greatest nuisance of all for spectacle wearers is rain. Each drop on the spectacle lens is a competing lens. 'Singing in the rain' may be all right for some people, but it is not on for myopes. A fortune awaits the inventor who can devise an instant rain dispeller.

Accommodation

With advancing years, the ability to focus at different distances weakens. To overcome this, some people have two pairs of spectacles; with myopes the lenses must be stronger for distance, weaker for near vision. Other people have bifocals; the lower part of the lens is used for near vision and so is weaker. A third, unofficial and not to be encouraged method is to wear the spectacles halfway down the nose. (This weakens the side pieces.)

People who are very myopic have strongly curved lenses. Such lenses generally have small transverse diameters: from the great big diameters commonly seen today, it can be deduced that their wearers are not very myopic.

On very bright days I can read without changing my spectacles. The iris has so contracted that only a narrow beam of rays enter the eye. As photographers know, a smaller aperture allows a bigger depth of focus (Figure 2). On such days I can see without my spectacles if I look at distant objects though a pinhole held up to one eye.

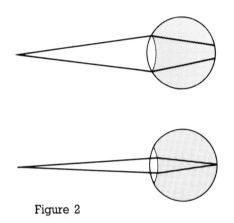

Figure 2

Sherlock Holmes

The usual picture of Sherlock Holmes shows him wearing a deer-stalker hat and a waist-length coat and armed with a great convex lens. A much smaller convex lens would of course be more effective but would not make so impressive a drawing. A big convex lens held at arm's length is useful for reading small print and can be used as a reading glass; it is a misnomer to call it a magnifying glass.

A cock and hen story

I came across some strange ideas during my days in the army. A lance-corporal who had been a farmer told me in all seriousness that a hen sees a cock three times its real size. I did not argue with him: I did not know where to start. I suppose that it is just possible that Pertelote, either from fear or hope, could *imagine* Chanticlere to be three times *nearer* than he actually was and therefore three times bigger. I could have asked the lance-corporal how he knew it was three times and not four times or twice. I did not ask him; he appeared to be at least three times bigger than I was.

Binocular vision

Cyclops was a clumsy one-eyed monster. The clumsiness was in part a consequence of his single eye. There are a number of ways in which we can demonstrate our binocular vision.

What the boy saw

'Have you seen this, sir?' asked a third-form boy. He had placed two rectangular mirrors side by side on the bench. Looking down, he could see the whole of his face;: he could still see the whole of his face when he drew the mirrors apart. He wanted to know why. I told him to shut one eye. The gap between the mirrors now showed up as a gap in the image of his face. Next I told him to look at the gap between the mirrors: his face disappeared. If only one mirror is available, a strip of paper can be placed down the middle of the mirror in place of the gap.

Seeing double

1 Make two holes in a card and cover them with gauze. Look at a torch bulb through the holes. If the card is held in the right position, two lamps shine out – not just one. Figure 3 shows how this comes about and how suitable distances can be chosen. When two lamps can be seen, close each eye in turn. Only one lamp will be seen at a time: each eye sees its own lamp.

In this demonstration, one bright light at the back is turned into two at the front. In the next demonstration, one dark spot at the front is turned into two at the back.

2 Make a black dot on a sheet of glass. Hold the glass near your eyes and look through it at a distant wall. You will see two dots (Figure 4). Close each eye in turn. Each eye has its own dot, the left eye being responsible for the right dot.

Next draw a simple face on a sheet of paper but do not draw the eyes. Look at this face through the glass sheet with the black dot. When the distances are just right, the face will acquire two eyes (Figure 5). By moving your head or the sheet of glass the eyes can be made to roll about in an amusing way.

Two eyes: the decider eye

By unkind usage 'one-eyed' is an adjective of disparagement, e.g. a 'one-eyed town'. One great benefit of our two eyes is that they enable us to judge distances. Put a small coin on the table. Close one eye and with a pointer try to touch it quickly: try again with both eyes.

For some purposes, only one eye can be used at a time. Both eyes may be equal but one is more equal than the other. It used to be called the 'master eye' but perhaps the 'decider eye' is more in tune with modern attitudes. When you fix a magnifying glass into the socket of your eye, it is into that of the decider eye. When you look down at a microscope or through a telescope you use your decider eye.

Just as nature or custom has decided that right is right (that it is right to write with your right hand) so the army has decided that your right eye should be the decider eye – rifles are made for right-eyed people (or they were forty years ago). Left-eyed people are at a disadvantage: the cocking piece is on the wrong side for them. It is well known that if you hold a finger up in front of you and look past it at a distant wall the finger looks transparent. But there is a difference between the two eyes here. If instead of shutting your decider eye you shut your other eye, the vague shadowy finger becomes a real solid one *in the same place*. But if you shut your decider eye the finger becomes a real solid one as before but *moves to the side*. If the decider eye is the left eye, the movement is to the left.

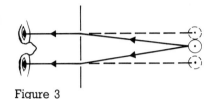

Figure 3

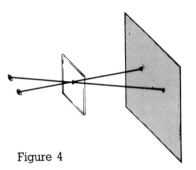

Figure 4

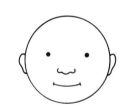

Figure 5

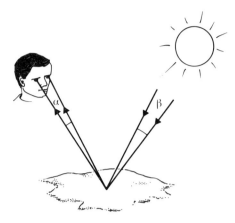

Figure 6

A snowflake on the ground

One day I was looking at snowflakes lying on the ground. The sun was shining. I directed my attention to a particular flake and noticed that I could position my head so that the bright flake was visible with one eye but not with the other.

Had I been younger, I would have quantified this observation to measure the angle subtended on the flake by the sun's disc. There will be a critical distance for this effect. If α (Figure 6) is greater than β, the flake can only be seen by one eye at a time.

Persistence of vision

It requires imagination to work out what would happen to modern life if vision did not persist: there would be neither cinema nor television. The effects of the persistence of vision can be opposites: it can make stationary pictures move, as in the cinema; it can make rotating objects still, as in the stroboscope.

In the early days of the cinema only 18 frames a second were shown. In consequence, the actors and actresses moved about jerkily. There was still a perceptible flicker; an early slang name for the cinema was the 'flicks'. Later the number of frames was increased to 25 a second and the flickering practically disappeared. If there is a lot of background lighting in the cinema, a slight flickering can still be noticed.

A comrade of my REME days had been a projectionist in a big London cinema. He told me of the long tussle between the cinema managers and the Watch Committees which at that time controlled cinemas. The Watch Committees, concerned with both public safety and public morals, wanted relatively high background lighting. The managers, knowing that there were other reasons for going to the cinema than watching the film, wanted less. An inspection would take place and the lighting would be increased, but in the following weeks it would slowly sink back to normal.

Hand stroboscopes

The hand stroboscopes provided for making ripples stand still can be used in places other than the physics lab. It would be interesting to take one into a cinema, but it would distract the attention of other cinema goers. If a strobe is used to view a television screen, what is seen depends on where the strobe is held and the speed of rotation. When the strobe is held near the eye, we look at the screen; when it is held at arm's length, we tend to look at the strobe itself.

If we look through a rotating strobe at a mirror, we see a stationary strobe. Here it is helpful to use only one eye at a time and to see what happens when we change eyes.

A rotating hand strobe can be used as a dazzle diminisher. Only about 5% of the light passes through it. With a strobe, look at a bright pearl lamp: the writing will become legible. If the edge of a cloud catches too much sunshine, neither the cloud nor the blue sky beyond can be clearly seen. Looked at through a strobe, the dazzle is diminished and the blue sky makes a beautiful contrast with the white cloud.

Colour blindness

John Dalton was colour blind but at first he did not realise it. On one occasion, he unwittingly caused great offence by turning up at a Quaker Meeting wearing a vivid red waistcoat, thinking it was a grey one.

I have colour deficiency but it is by no means as great as Dalton's. When my wife asked me to bring down from the wardrobe a beige or fawn dress for one of my young daughters, I would not know which one was meant. So I took down all their dresses.

For some years I taught chemistry as well as physics and then I did have colour problems. On one occasion, I had changed the colour of a potassium dichromate solution with sulphur dioxide. I could not name the new colour. I asked Silas, a farmer's son, to do so. 'Zurr, it be colour of zour zyder', and that was its name ever after.

Sometimes pupils have pointed out colour effects which had escaped me. A third-form girl had used a convex lens to focus a bright image of a 12 V lamp on to a white card. She shyly showed me that the image was white at the front, and yellow at the back.

Once I was showing an experiment with shadows to some non-science sixth-formers. A 150 W filament lamp threw a shadow (Figure 7). Sunlight came in through a window, making a second shadow. The sixth-formers pointed out that the shadow at A looked blue, whereas that at B looked yellow; elsewhere the screen was whitish.

It is hard for people with normal vision to imagine colour deficiency. I used to show children the Ishahara chart and tell them that I could not pick out the number amongst the dots. Some of them, I gathered from the tone of their voices, thought that I was joking. When I looked through a red filter, the number stood out clearly.

There is one slight advantage in colour deficiency. I am not worried by the need to make colours match – ties with shirts, jackets etc. For some people colour matching becomes a real tyranny.

I wanted to show fluorescence, so I set up a spectrometer and grating, illuminated by an ultraviolet lamp. I saw only a single violet line, 4.05×10^{-5} cm. I sprinkled a little zinc sulphide on to the cross-wires graticule and now saw a second line: it was produced by fluoresence at 3.66×10^{-5} cm. I showed this to the sixth form. They reported that they could see the second line without the fluorescence. Different eyes see different spectra.

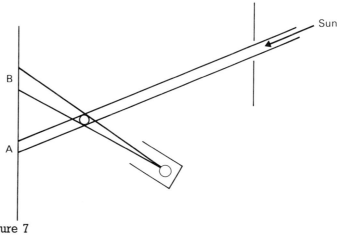

Figure 7

Electroscopes

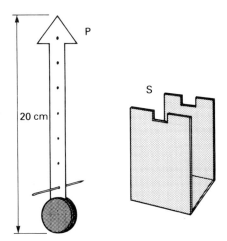

Figure 1

We talk about electrostatics – electricity at rest – but actually electric charges are mobile (sometimes too mobile). For example, humid days are bad for electrostatics – the charges run away too soon. I once tried to give an electrostatics lecture during a thunderstorm. Not a single experiment worked. For an electrostatics lecture, it is a wise precaution to have a hygrometer to hand. If the humidity is above 80%, don't try – do something else instead.

A cardboard electroscope

Figure 1 shows a cardboard electroscope suitable for demonstrating to a large class. The pointer P is free to turn about the needle which is placed in the support S. Coins are used to bring the centre of mass below the needle: if it is too far below, the pointer is not sensitive enough; if it is too near, the pointer is not stable.

Stand the electroscope on a suitable surface (one that is not highly insulating). To find out which bodies become charged after rubbing, bring each body in turn near the top of the pointer. If attraction takes place, the body is charged. At one time, polythene detergent bottles charged well; now they don't. Perhaps they were attracting dust and looking dirty – not a recommendation for detergents. Transparent soft drinks bottles (polyvinyl chloride) charge well.

Charge the bodies by rubbing them with a 'silk' scarf. Not all 'silk' scarves are suitable as rubbers – the only way to find out is by trial. Cylindrical ('sausage') balloons charge well. Indeed merely blowing them up seems to charge them. Some glass bottles charge – others don't. I find that pyrex glass beakers can generally be relied on: fix a cuphook as shown in Figure 2 so that the glass need not be handled by fingers.

Figure 2

Some people are better at electrostatics experiments than others: people with dry skins can charge objects such as polythene strips merely by rubbing them. Before asking a pupil to help me with an electrostatics experiment, I would shake him or her by the hand. Those with damp hands I would turn down, 'No, not you.'.

Electrostatic attraction is quite common. Any body if it is light enough or easily moved will respond to a charged rod. Thus if such a rod is brought up to a fine stream of water, the stream will curve out of line (Figure 3). It is an 'electrostatic deflection'. A metre stick is, of course, much heavier than cotton threads or pith balls but if it is balanced on a watch glass and a charged rod brought alongside it

Figure 3

Figure 4

there will be sufficient attraction to bring about rapid rotation (Figure 4).

A feather electroscope

From the *uncharged* cardboard electroscope we move on to a *charged* electroscope.

On a good dry day a pheasant feather, rubbed with silk, will become charged. Figure 5 shows the active part of a feather electroscope. A nail pushed up the hollow stem of the feather acts as counter-weight; a fine needle as axle. The needle is placed on a support like that shown in Figure 1.

If a hand is brought near the charged feather, attraction takes place and the feather quickly jumps to it. With the cardboard electroscope it is the uncharged body (the cardboard) that moves: with the feather electroscope it is the charged body (the feather).

What happens when one charged body is brought up to a second charged body? As Figure 6 shows, two charged feathers will repel each other. Figure 7 shows a method of mounting a sausage balloon so that it is free to rotate. Charge one end of a balloon, mount it as shown and bring up a second charged balloon. Repulsion is clearly shown: the mounted balloon frantically tries to get out of the way of its repulsive fellow.

Next, fasten two strips of thin polythene to a piece of card (Figure 8). Charge them and hold them up. Because the polythene strips are so light, their mutual repulsion causes them to spring apart.

Figure 5

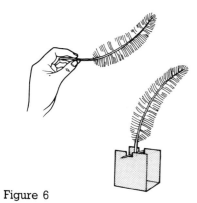

Figure 6

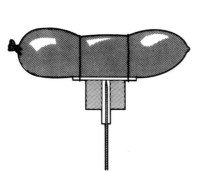

Figure 7

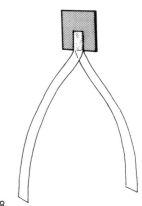

Figure 8

Like charges

Charged feathers repel charged feathers; charged balloons repel charged balloons; charged polythene repels charged polythene.

● Like charges repel

Conversely, if repulsion occurs the two charges must be 'like'. Attraction is not quite so simple.

I showed the experiment with the repelling feathers in the

Members Exhibition of the Assocation for Science Education in Manchester in 1983.

Television reporters were present: they saw feather repelling feather, and since it made good telly, they filmed it. The following dialogue (or something like it) took place:

TV	What does the experiment show?
CS	That like charges repel.
TV	Why do like charges repel?
CS	It is fundamental fact.
TV	There must be an explanation.
CS	No, it's a fundamental fact that we accept.
TV	But there must be an explanation; isn't it due to electrons?
CS	(Slightly rattled) Nonsense!

A more philosophical reply could have been to ask the television men to try to envisage a universe in which like charges *attracted*.

My demonstration with pheasant feathers caught the attention not only of the television men but also of the versatile scientist–mathematician Jean-Pierre Petit who was on a visit from France. He drew the sketch shown in Figure 9 there and then.

Figure 9

Unlike charges

Make a polythene electroscope similar to the cardboard electroscope of Figure 1. Charge it and test that a similar piece of charged polythene will bring about repulsion.

Now try the effect of a charged feather on the pivoted polythene: they are attracted. Then try the effect of charged polythene on a pivoted feather: they are again attracted.

There are two classes of charged bodies: the charged polythene class which for the moment we will call class A and the charged feather class which we will call class B. Glass is in Class B.

Bodies in class A repel each other; bodies in class B repel each other. But bodies in class A attract and are attracted by bodies in class B.

- Unlike charges attract

The converse statement – that attraction denotes unlike charges – is not necessarily true. Attraction also takes place between a charged body and an uncharged body (apparently uncharged, anyhow).

Place on the bench the three pivoted electroscopes (the feather, the cardboard and the polythene) keeping them some distance apart. Test different kinds of charged bodies on the three electroscopes in turn, starting with the cardboard electroscope to make sure that the body is charged. Each charged body can be allocated to its class, A or B.

Naming the two classes

We all *know* that the two classes are named positive and negative, and it may seem to be pushing an open door to spend time justifying the two names. Electrostatics has had a long history. Dr Gilbert, Queen Elizabeth's physician, showed her electrostatics experiments which were weird, wonderful, unpredictable and inexplicable. A century and a half had to pass before Benjamin Franklin realised what the relation was between the two classes, i.e. before 'the separation of charges' was discovered.

With careful preparation the separation of charges can be demonstrated in the following way: a plastic bottle is to be rubbed with a silk scarf made into a pad. The three electroscopes (suitably placed) are in readiness, the feather and polythene electroscopes being charged. Before rubbing takes place, the scarf and the bottle are tested with the cardboard electroscope to make sure that they are not charged. The bottle is then briskly rubbed with the silk pad and tested with the polythene electroscope; the silk pad is tested with the feather electroscope. If things have gone to plan, both bottle and pad will be found to be charged but one will have a class A charge and the other a class B charge. From two uncharged bodies, two different charges have been obtained.

The silk has to be chosen the day before: some silk pads will charge bottles but will not hold their charge for long. When a satisfactory one has been found, it has to be left to lose its charge.

To Benjamin Franklin belongs the great honour of grasping this idea of the separation of charges. He saw too that since a positive quantity added to a negative quantity in the right proportions will leave no quantity at all, the two classes of charge are justifiably called positive and negative.

But which is which? As far as I know, nothing is known about how Franklin made his choice. When he made it there was no reason for one choice rather than the other. Let glass, he said, when rubbed be considered the positive class, making the other class the negative one. This was the ebonite class; ebonite rubbed with fur or flannel was negatively charged.

For a hundred years and more it was not realised that Franklin

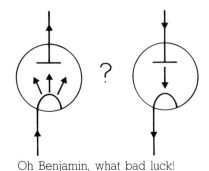

Oh Benjamin, what bad luck!

Figure 10

had made an unfortunate choice. When the electron was discovered, by Franklin's definition it was negatively charged. This does not matter much if we deal only with currents along wires: negative charges moving to the left are easily mentally changed into positive charges moving to the right. But after the thermionic effect was discovered thermionic valves were invented. Inside the valve the movement can only be from the hot cathode where electrons are liberated to the cold anode where they are collected. The 'current' however flows from anode to cathode (Figure 10).

On more than one REME radio mechanics course I witnessed the 'which way' controversy getting heated. On one occasion, indeed, fists were about to flash. I interceded on behalf of peace. Franklin, who was a Quaker, would have appreciated this even if I did lay the blame on his broad shoulders.

Polythene and perspex

Cut perspex strips similar in size to the polythene strips shown in Figure 8. Charge both the polythene strips and the perspex strips, keeping them well apart. Charged polythene repels charged polythene; charged perspex repels charged perspex. Bring the perspex and the polythene together slowly. The two inner halves begin to seek each other out; eventually they will, as it were, embrace (Figure 11). Since polythene is negatively charged, the perspex strips must be positively charged.

I had done this simple demonstration many times but it was left to a student teacher to point out to me that when the two inner strips have become entwined the two outer strips hang straight down. The fields due to the two inner charges have cancelled each other out as positive does to negative.

Attraction turning to repulsion

A piece of tissue paper will jump up from a table to a charged rod, stay there and (sometimes but not always) jump off. This change from attraction to repulsion was very puzzling to the early experimenters.

Stand a cardboard electroscope on a good insulator, e.g. a polystyrene box. Bring a well-charged bottle up to its head (Figure 12(a)): attraction ensues. Leave the head in contact with the bottle

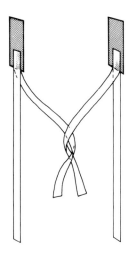

Figure 11

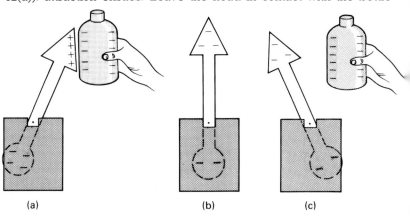

(a)   (b)   (c)

Figure 12

for a short while, then remove the bottle. With an insulating strip, stop the cardboard swinging (Figure 12(b)). Slowly bring up the bottle a second time. On a good day the head will be repelled (Figure 12(c)).

This change of attraction into repulsion is due to leakage of charge from the bottle to the arrowhead while the bottle is in contact with the head. This leaves the cardboard with an overall negative charge.

If the bottle is brought still nearer, positive charge is again induced in the head and attraction returns.

attraction → repulsion → attraction

No wonder that the early experimenters were puzzled!

The can electroscope

Figure 13

There are disadvantages in the use of the gold-leaf electroscope in school: the leaf can only be seen by a small number of children; it is fragile. If a dozen gold-leaf electroscopes are put out for use, after 5 minutes only six will be working; after 10 minutes, only three of them will work. The half-life is therefore 5 minutes. Once broken they cannot be repaired by the children.

In contrast, a can electroscope is visible by the whole class, is robust and easily repaired, can show new effects and costs nothing so it will never appear in manufacturer's catalogues. Perhaps that is why a manufacturer, viewing a can electroscope at work, asked me in all seriousness if children would believe in anything it did. After all, he said, it was only an old can.

A can rests on a clean, dry, highly insulating plastic tub (Figure 13). Two arms hang from its sides. They must be free to swing outwards. A satisfactory way of doing this is to hang each arm from a pin, the pointed end of which is pushed into a blob of Blu-tack. There will be no leakage from the round head at the other end of the pin.

The arms can be of tissue paper or 'silver paper' – the wrapping paper from bars of chocolate. Normally, tissue-paper arms are satisfactory, but on very dry days these arms become such good insulators that they will not charge up. They are an exception to the general rule that humidity is bad for electrostatics. To make the arms more visible they are provided with hands.

Uses of the can electroscope

1 Charge detector

Figure 14

If a container half-filled with the cake decorating beads known as 'hundreds and thousands' is shaken vigorously, the beads dance about in a lively manner. Empty some of the beads into a small can electroscope. To the delight of the class, the arms rise. Grains of rice and doubtless other foodstuffs can be used in place of hundreds and thousands (Figure 14).

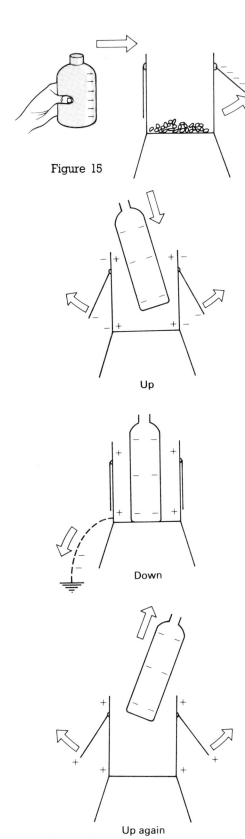

Figure 15

Up

Down

Up again

Figure 16

2 Sign finder

The cake beads transfer their charge to the can. To find the sign of this charge, bring up first a positively charged body such as a pyrex beaker and then a negatively charged body such as a polythene bottle to the can. The charge that *repels* the near arm is the like charge (Figure 15). The deflection of the far arm will increase.

For the experiment with the cake beads, a small can (e.g. of capacity 250 cm^3) is suitable. For other experiments a can big enough to take a plastic bottle is required.

3 Testing for good insulators

Charge a plastic bottle or pyrex beaker and put it into the electroscope: the arms deflect. Then touch the can with a wooden rod: the arms drop – wood is *not* a good insulator.

If instead of a wooden rod the charged can is touched with a polythene rod, the arms stay deflected – polythene is a good insulator.

The electroscope does not differentiate between insulators and conductors; it differentiates between good insulators and poor insulators. If a charged can is left untouched, the deflection of the arms decreases but only very slowly. (After perhaps 10 minutes, the drop is noticeable.) Thus both the plastic tub on which the can is resting and the air which surrounds it are good insulators.

If a burning match or a lighted taper is held near the charged can, the deflection quickly decreases. It is rather an exaggeration to say that flames make air conduct, but they do make it a poor insulator.

4 To demonstrate induction

Put a charged bottle into the can: the arms deflect. Ask a pupil to touch the can and then to remove her finger: the arms drop. The girl, if not a good conductor, is a poor insulator. She has discharged the can. Or so it appears.

Now remove the charged bottle from the can. To general amazement and amusement the arms rise again as the bottle is removed. You pretend to be cross: 'I told you to discharge the can'.

To find out what has happened, repeat the procedure but this time find the sign of the charge each time the arms deflect. If it is negative the first time, it will be positive the second time.

When the negative bottle is placed in the can, it *induces* a positive charge on the inside of the can. The can stands on an insulator so the positive charge on the inside of the can must be balanced by a negative charge on the outside. Touching the can lets the negative charge escape to earth. Removing the bottle allows the positive charges on the inside to flow by mutual repulsion to the outside (Figure 16).

5 To demonstrate leakage

This demonstration is so similar to the previous one that, to avoid confusion, it had better be done on a later occasion.

Metal arms are required. Put a *negatively* charged bottle in the can: the arms deflect. Remove the bottle *without touching* the can: the arms begin to fall, but before they have fallen far they rise again.

Testing shows that the can is now *positively* charged.

The metal arms have fine edges. When the bottle is put into the can, some of the strong negative charge in the edges leaks away so that there is now more positive charge inside the can than there is negative charge outside it.

6 To demonstrate differential leakage

Put a negatively charged bottle into the can: the arms are negatively charged. Estimate the angle of deflection. Then touch the can and remove the bottle: the arms are now positively charged. Estimate this second angle of deflection; it will be greater than the first.

When a positive charge, e.g. the charge on a pyrex beaker, is used in place of the negative charge, the first deflection (a positive one) is greater than the second deflection (a negative one).

From estimates, I went to measurements. With the arrangement shown in Figure 17, I measured the four angles of deflection (Table 1).

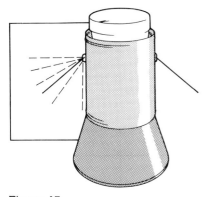

Figure 17

Table 1

Charger	First deflection	Second deflection
Negative bottle	35°	55°
Positive beaker	55°	35°

It is tempting to say that these figures show that negative charges leak away more quickly than positive charges. But positive charges cannot leak away; only negative charges can do this. Correctly interpreted, the figures show that negative charges can leak away from the metal arms more quickly than they can leak back.

7 An electrostatic courtship

The final demonstration with the can electroscope is a light-hearted one, a courtship.

Two cans are needed: Jack has metal arms, Jill has tissue-paper ones. For ease of movement, one of them stands on a light board. One is charged negatively, the other positively. Start with them at some distance apart.

Slowly bring the can on the board up towards the other can. As expected, the two inner arms approach each other (Figure 18). As soon as they touch, they very quickly drop. The path of true love has not been smooth. Slowly the arms rise again to touch a second time, to drop a second time and so on. I have counted this happening up to 14 times before eventually true love prevailed and Jack and Jill held hands.

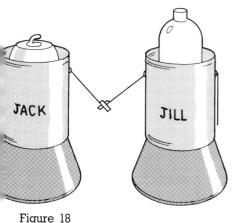

Figure 18

A pulse electrometer

A can electroscope may be converted into a measuring device – an electrometer – by fixing an earthing strip as shown in Figure 19. A charged body is lowered *slowly* into the can and the number of

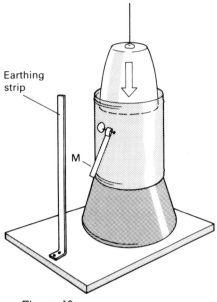

Earthing
strip

M

Figure 19

Figure 20

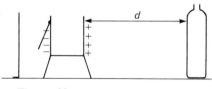

Figure 21

pulses of the arm M against the earthing strip is counted. This number is a measure of the charge on the body.

As the charged body is lowered, M deflects – slowly at first. Eventually it becomes unstable, jumps to the earthing strip and so discharges the can. M then falls back. Each pulse represents a definite quantity of charge on the can.

The pulse sensitivity can be controlled. It depends on three factors: the length of the arm, the position of the earthing strip and the mass-to-area ratio of the arm. I used aluminium cooking foil for the arm, its mass-to-area ratio was 4.7×10^{-2} kg/m^2. The other factors were adjusted so that by the time the charged body (for example, a pyrex beaker) had reached the bottom about 10–20 pulses had taken place. When the charged body is removed, the number of pulses is again counted; within one or two is should be the same as before.

Students can make their own pulse electrometers for practically no cost! They can then carry out the following investigations.

1 How does the maximum charge obtainable vary from one body to another?
2 For a particular substance, how does this charge depend on the superficial area?
3 How does the pulsing rate depend on the mass-to-area ratio of the material of the arm? (Theory says that the number of pulses for a given charge should be inversely proportional to the square root of the mass-to-area ratio).
4 Find how the charge on a body decays with time.

Ideas from Hungary

A Hungarian physicist József Öveges wrote a book whose title when translated was *Playful Experiments in Electrostatics*. Published in 1981, it has plenty of diagrams and so the language barrier can be crossed. Figure 20, which is taken from the book, needs no explanation. The pulse electrometer shown in Figure 19 was adapted from *Playful Experiments*, so also was Figure 21 which shows the use I made of a pulse electrometer in an experiment on Coulomb's inverse square law.

The first pulse took place when the near side of the charged bottle was 30 cm away from the near side of the can. Three more pulses took place when this distance was reduced to 15 cm. Thus in all four pulses had occurred. At *half* the distance, the field was *four* times as great. I decided that this was too good a result to spoil; I did not reduce the distance by a further 5 cm to see if there were a further five pulses.

Bigger and Better Sparks

Figure 1

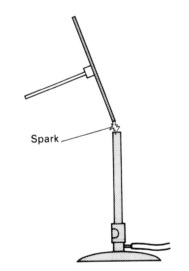

Spark

Figure 2

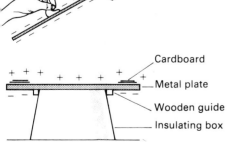

Figure 3

The electrophorus

Volta's electrophorus

The purpose of an electrophorus is to transfer an electrostatic charge from an insulator, where it is fixed, to a conductor where it is free to move. This freedom allows new experiments to be performed. Volta, of course, is rightly famed as the scientist who with Galvani made currents flow from the cells which bear his name. By freeing charges from insulators, the electrophorus was a link in the chain between static and current electricity.

Figure 1 shows a typical Volta electrophorus. B is a cake of resin, to be charged by friction. A is a metal plate held by a glass handle. Today, in place of unreliable glass, we use ebonite or perspex. The plate is placed on the resin, touched for a moment and removed. A spark can then be obtained by bringing a knuckle up to the edge of the plate, as the figure shows.

An experiment that used to bring delight to the class was to light a bunsen burner with the spark (Figure 2). As long as we were using coal gas and the metal plate was big enough (30 cm in diameter) the experiment generally worked. With North Sea gas, however, it never succeeded.

Upside down

In Volta's model the charged insulator is below, the conductor above. These positions can be reversed as Figure 3 shows. As an insulator, I used a 30 cm gramophone record made in 1930 whose music days were over. To handle it, I fitted it with a stick-on cuphook. When rubbed briskly with a silk scarf or pad it acquires a charge of about $\frac{1}{2}$ μC. The metal plate is supported on a plastic box of suitable dimensions and good insulating power. Wooden guides are fitted to the underside of the plate so that it can be lifted by the plastic box without slipping. Small thin cardboard circles glued to the top side of the plate cut down loss of charge by leakage.

The negative charge on the record induces a positive charge on the top side of the plate, but this is balanced by an equal negative charge on the bottom side of the plate. Touch the edge of the plate for a moment. (If you do this by bringing your knuckle near you will get a spark.) This enables the negative charge to flow away to earth. The positive charge is held in place by the negative charge on the record. Remove the record. The positive charge on the plate will remain but will be shared between the top and bottom surfaces.

In Figure 3 labels:
Record
Cardboard
Metal plate
Wooden guide
Insulating box

Levitation

To show levitation, have in readiness a strip of dutch metal about 30 mm long and 4 mm wide. (By force of habit such a strip is referred to as a gold leaf.) With one hand lift the plate by its plastic base; with the other, using tweezers, drop the gold leaf on to the plate. It will jump off. By gentle movement of the box, electrostatic repulsion will hold the gold leaf in space by levitation.

Occasionally a cheeky pupil would suggest that the leaf was held up not by electrostatics but by air currents. The answer to this objection is simple. Bring the gold leaf (and the pupil) down to earth by touching the plate.

There is more to this experiment than electrostatics. Strips of aluminium foil will also jump off the charged plate, but they cannot be held in space. The gold leaf is considerably lighter than the aluminium strip. Therefore it has a smaller 'terminal velocity' for free fall and is easier to control.

Students can make their own electrophoruses. For a metal plate, cooking foil wrapped around a sheet of cardboard will do. It need not be circular in shape. Since gold leaf is not available to students, I recommend them to use dandelion 'parachutes'. On to a well-charged plate, tip a lot of such parachutes. It is a fascinating sight to see parachutes rising.

Sparks

Once the charged record has been removed leaving behind a positively charged plate, a second spark can be obtained. Holding the plastic box, I bring the plate to the tip of a volunteer's nose (Figure 4). I ask the class to watch his eyelids as I bring the plate nearer and nearer. (I write 'his' because this is no experiment for long-haired girls.)

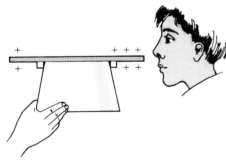

Figure 4

If conditions are right, a spark will take place – it can be heard and the volunteer's eyelids will flicker. On one occasion I showed the experiment to about 200 middle-school children. As I brought the plate nearer to the boy's nose the tension became too great for a boy standing at the back – he let off a noisy fart. A great roar of laughter went up: if looks could kill, those of the teachers would have put an end to the offender. I waited for the laughter to die down, said not a word and repeated the experiment.

Sometimes, although the plate is charging up well, no spark takes place. With long-haired girls the reason is that their hair is attracted to the plate and discharges it. With boys, it is a good idea to ask if they have had pickles for breakfast. Pickles make breath conductive and so cause the charge to leak away.

The noise made by the spark is feeble. It can be greatly increased if a radio receiver at full volume but off station is placed nearby. In this case, not only is there a loud click when the spark occurs, but there are other rustling sounds as well. The first transmission of radio waves was made by Heinrich Hertz in 1886. They were sent out from electric sparks.

When the electrophorus is giving good sparks, ask the receiver of them if he can smell anything. Sometimes he can and reports a faint pungent smell – perhaps ozone, perhaps an oxide of nitrogen.

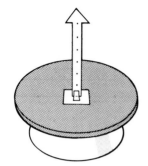

Figure 5

Figure 6

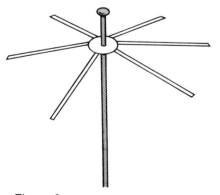

Figure 7

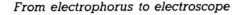

Figure 8

From electrophorus to electroscope

Before placing the charged insulator on the plate put on it a tissue paper arrow fixed at the bottom end so that it can stand up. When the plate is then charged the arrow will stand upright by electrostatic repulsion (Figure 5). How long it stays upright depends on the atmospheric conditions: on poor days, for only a few seconds if that; on good dry days, for an hour or more.

On good days, the arrow on its charged plate can be used to test for good insulators. Touch the plate with a rod or strip of the material under test. If the arrow stays up, the material is a good insulator. If a burning taper is brought close to the erect arrow, the arrow collapses immediately.

The arrow is charged positively. A positively charged body will repel the arrow; a negatively charged body will attract it.

In these ways the electrophorus can be used to test for insulators and to distinguish between positive and negative charges. Thus the upside-down electrophorus functions as an electroscope: this is another advantage of turning it upside down.

Electrostatic machines

Figure 6 shows a machine made for John Tyndall in 1875. Stimulated by this picture I made a modern version, using for the cylinder a large polythene detergent bottle (Figure 7). If necessary, to ensure that it charges, the cylinder can be coated with a thin perspex sheet. As a 'rubber' I used a pad made from a silk scarf. The pad has to be pressed with sufficient pressure. If the silk is too good an insulator, it is of no use. In place of the silk pad I could use my hand. It is a simple business to drill a hole in the base of a polythene bottle – not so with a glass one. As an axle I used a No.8 knitting needle; this fits the hole in a Meccano faceplate. At first I used a line of pins, as Tyndall had done, but I found that a thin wire parallel to the cylinder was just as successful and less trouble. The collector wire leads to the apparatus to be tested which must stand on a good insulator.

A maypole

Make a maypole from strips of tissue paper about 0.5 cm wide and 20 cm long by hanging them from a knitting needle. When the machine is working, the cylinder charges up, the charge flows along the wire, the strips stand out as shown in Figure 8.

An inherent contradiction of this machine is that the charge is collected by the fine wire as long as the cylinder is rotating, but as soon as the rotation stops the charge leaks away backwards through this same wire. The maypole therefore does not remain charged for long.

Figure 9

A mill

Figure 9 shows a simple 'Hamilton' mill made from a press-stud and two sharp pins. The charged air particles leak from the points and are driven away by electrostatic repulsion. Reaction causes the mill to rotate backwards.

Levitation

To show levitation, place a metal disc on an insulating tub. Lay a gold leaf on the disc. Charge the disc using the machine. The leaf will rise and float away. Longer strips rise more elegantly. Next cover the plate with dandelion parachutes. They float away in an entertaining fashion.

Sparks

Stand a tin can on the insulating tub. Charge it up. Bring up a suitable discharging knob: a stream of sparks a few millimeters long can be obtained. They are not at all impressive: these days we have been spoiled by the Van de Graaff machine.

Two maypoles

To show that in charging by friction a 'separation of charge' takes place, fix the silk pad to an insulating tub held by the hand. A wire is connected to the pad and leads to a second maypole (Figure 10). When the cylinder is rotated, both maypoles charge up. Testing will show one to be positive, the other negative.

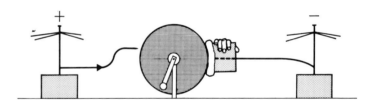

Figure 10

Simple electrostatic machines today are made only for entertainment purposes: but this has always been one of their uses. Pieter van Musschenbroek discovered the Leyden Jar, the first capacitor, in 1746. With these jars charged by machines such as Franklin's, wonderful and frightening experiments were demonstrated by travelling showmen. One such, in the presence of the King of France, passed a discharge through a line of 180 guards. At the Convent of Paris a line of Carthusian monks 900 ft long all sprang into the air at the same moment on the discharge of the jar. I have never had much success in getting a line of pupils to take a Van de Graaff shock: two, at least, would only pretend to be holding hands.

Sparks and lightning

Franklin saw the resemblances between the sparks from his machine and lightning flashes. In November 1749 he listed 12. 'Electric fluid agrees with lightning in these particulars: 1) giving light; 2) colour of the light; 3) crooked direction; 4) swift motion; 5) being conducted by metals; 6) crack or noise in exploding; 7) subsisting in water or ice; 8) rending bodies it passes through; 9) destroying animals; 10) melting metals; 11) firing inflammable substances and 12) sulphurous smell.'

There were sound practical reasons for fearing thunder and lightning as well as superstitious ones. Big buildings were often destroyed by lightning – the St Mark's Campanile in Venice had been badly damaged nine times in 300 years. In a famous but dangerous experiment, Franklin showed that he could 'draw down' the lightning by using a metal wire attached to a kite. He showed how damage could be avoided by means of lightning conductors. Some people objected: if God had decided to punish us, we should accept his punishment.

The design of lightning conductors led to a furious controversy: should the end of the conductor be a point or should it be a globe? By this time Franklin had become a politician. He had led the American Colonies out of the rule of Great Britain. The scientific dispute led to a political one. Franklin was for points, therefore loyal subjects of the British crown were for globes.

The Van de Graaff generator

A small Van de Graaff is undoubtedly one of the showpieces of physics (Figure 11). If a Franklin generator can be likened to a churn, the Van de Graaff generator can be likened to an escalator. Passengers are picked up at the bottom and carried to the top where they step off; other passsengers are picked up and taken down.

Children will have heard about its famous sparks before they meet it in their school physics. When one day they come into the lab and see the huge metal globe there, sitting on the bench 'beaming at them', they will not be content until they have seen a spark, and a volunteer has gained glory by taking a 10 cm one without wincing. After that, other demonstrations can be shown. First, two demonstrations that do not require the discharging sphere.

Positive or negative?

The first thing to find out is the sign of the charge. Hold a charged feather on a thread near, but not too near, the sphere. Switch on. If the feather is repelled, the sphere is positively charged; if the feather is attracted, the sphere is negatively charged. Confirm this by using a negatively charged polythene strip. We will suppose that the generator is charged positively.

Paper strips and cotton threads

Fasten one end of a strip of tissue paper to the top of the generator. Switch on. The strip will stand straight up. Electrostatic repulsion causes it to set along the electrostatic field lines. If several strips of paper are used, they give a vivid demonstration of a radial field (Figure 12).

The field can be detected at a considerable distance by mounting a 'compass' of thin cardboard, using a press-stud to support it (Figure 13).

Much entertainment and at least some instruction can be had if cotton threads are used in place of paper strips. Lay a long thread

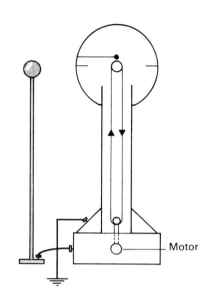

Figure 11

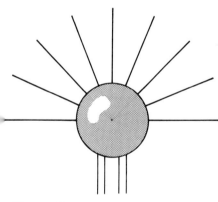

Figure 12

Figure 13

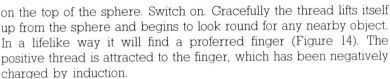

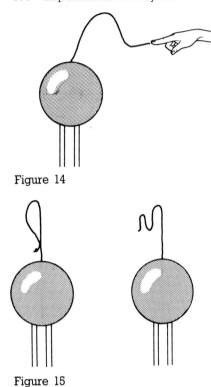

Figure 14

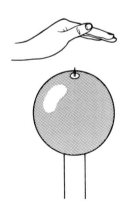

Figure 15

on the top of the sphere. Switch on. Gracefully the thread lifts itself up from the sphere and begins to look round for any nearby object. In a lifelike way it will find a proferred finger (Figure 14). The positive thread is attracted to the finger, which has been negatively charged by induction.

Hold the end of the thread by two fingers for a few seconds, then release it. A crook may be formed: it may be a closed one or it may be a double one (Figure 15). It depends on the length of the cotton and the length of time it was held. Cotton is a very poor conductor. When the end of the cotton is held, the charge from the negative fingers slowly creeps down it. When the thread is released, the negative end is attracted to the rest of the thread which is positively charged.

When the thread is a crook, switch off the generator. The sphere gradually loses its charge. The end of the thread is slowly and gracefully pulled down to the sphere but, as soon as it touches, it goes beserk. It springs up, then falls down immediately to spring up again and so on. I have counted up to a hundred of these ups and downs before the thread finally wearies of the game.

From cotton threads move on to a long strip of aluminium foil. Before switching on, ask the class to predict what will happen. In marked contrast to a paper strip, a metal strip waves about wildly.

Other experiments require the discharging sphere.

Insulators

Switch on. Bring up the discharging sphere until there is a steady stream of sparks. Touch the main sphere with a wooden rod held in your hand: the sparks stop. Wood is not a good insulator. Next try a perspex rod: the sparks continue unabated. Perspex is a good insulator. (The transparent column on which the sphere rests is generally made of perspex.)

The action of points

Position the discharging sphere so that there is a steady stream of sparks. Switch off. Put a drawing pin point upwards on top of the sphere. Switch on. There will be no sparks. With a ruler or – if you are brave enough – by hand, remove the pin. The sparks start again. Replace the pin. Cup your hand and hold it above the pin. A strong rush of air will be felt (Figure 16).

Hold an ordinary pin, point outwards, some distance away from the sphere. Sparks take place. Bring the pin nearer. Suddenly the sparking stops. If you are in a playful mood, try this trick. Hidden in your hand and so held that it does not stop the sparks, you have a pin. Ask a boy or girl to walk towards the generator. The class watches their fellow pupil, not you. As he or she gets near the generator, the sparks suddenly stop as if by magic. Then you own up: by the movement of the pin you had stopped the sparks.

The vicinity of the generator must be cleared of threads, wires, metal foil etc. Like sharp finger nails, these will stop the sparks. The big Van de Graaffs could be put out of action by a single gnat alighting on the surface. This poses an interesting puzzle: is there any limit to the smallness of the gnat below which it would have no effect?

Figure 16

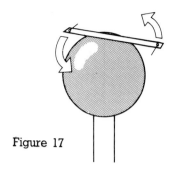

Figure 17

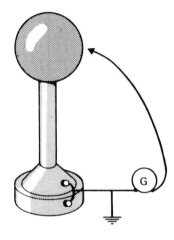

Figure 18

A whirl can be made from a stick and two pins as shown in Figure 17. The streams of ions shooting from the points produce sufficient reaction.

Bring your nose near to the end of a stick resting on the dome. What was barely noticeable with the spark from the electrophorus now becomes a pronounced effect – there is a pungent odour. Ozone? Oxides of nitrogen? Has lightning been responsible for life on earth? There are, after all, at any moment hundreds of thunderstorms taking place on the globe.

A steady current

Connect one terminal of a scalamp galvanometer to the earth terminal of a Van de Graaff. Fasten a length of wire to the other terminal and bring this wire near to the sphere (Figure 18). A steady current of several micro-amperes flows through the meter. The Van de Graaff not only generates static electricity: it generates direct current too.

Surprisingly the current is almost independent of the size of the gap between the wire and the sphere. Even more surprisingly, if a wooden half-metre stick fills the gap, the current hardly drops.

What decides the current is the rate at which charge is being carried up the rubber belt: an increase in motor speed increases the current. Static electricity is a matter of very high voltages, even higher resistances and so very small currents.

The sparks

If the spark gap is narrow, the sparks are frequent, regular and quite pleasant to hear. As the gap is increased, they become less frequent, irregular and frightening. I found that with a gap of up to 6 cm they came at regular and measurable intervals. The most fascinating sparks are, of course, the longest ones; they are also the least regular. Every lesson with a Van de Graaff generator should spend a few minutes at least finding the longest spark for that day and putting it in the record book.

At Thornton I was fortunate to have a Nicholson Van de Graaff. The diameter of the sphere was 30 cm. The longest spark I recorded was 15 cm. If we accept the 30 000 V/cm figure for the breakdown of the resistance of air, i.e. the limit of its field strength, that makes the voltage no less that 450 000 V.

Children are very impressed if their teacher acts as the discharging sphere and takes the spark with his or her knuckles. Generally there is no lack of volunteers to take over. Doing experiments near the generator, one sometimes takes a spark unintentionally. These sparks do indeed give a shock. The answer to the riddle, 'When is a shock not a shock?' is 'When you are expecting it'.

The voltage obtainable is roughly proportional to the diameter of the sphere. A Van de Graaff big enough to hold a man or woman would need a diameter of 3 m and would produce voltages of about 5 MV. Generators of this size were used for nuclear research.

An interesting feature of long sparks is that they seemed to have a break in the middle. I took the generator into a dark cellar and photographed the spark: sure enough the photos showed a break. Also on the photos appeared a long light band. It was traced to a fluorescent lamp in the ceiling. It had lit up, even though it was not switched on.

The generator is as interesting in a dark room as in a lab. Neon bulbs, fluorescent lamps and Geissler tubes all light up if they are near enough. Finger nails glow. The electric whirl becomes an illuminated roundabout.

The electromagnetic waves sent out by the spark can be detected some distance away. Send a volunteer armed with a radio receiver at full volume but off station a known distance away. You then make a counted number of sparks. The volunteer returns and is asked how many sparks he or she has heard.

Rote learning

To judge by appearance Pinnock's *Made Easy* series of booklets was published early in the 19th century. One booklet is entitled *Astronomy* but the last chapter (Chapter XXX) deals with thunder and lightning. It comprises 33 numbered statements.

13 When a person is killed by lightning his shoes are generally burst to pieces.
14 When it falls on a wet surface, it spreads along it.

There are 33 questions at the end of the chapter.

13 What happens to a person's shoes when he is killed by lightning?
14 What does the lightning do when it falls on a wet surface?

Mnemonic

The Van de Graaff is a problem for weak spellers: I suggest a mnemonic:

To spell Van de Graaff
there's only one way
use a couple of effs
and double the a.

_____ *Chapter 16* _____

Calculations?
Not Today, Please!

In my experience some pupils enjoy physics as long as they are doing experiments but lose interest when they come to calculations. It is also my experience that their dexterity in mathematics decreases considerably when they come into the physics lab; it is almost as if they resented having to use their mathematical abilities. Sometimes in the sixth form, when the mathematical content of physics increases, impudent students have expressed surprise that I could differentiate. 'That's nothing,' I would say, maintaining the mockery. 'Wait until you see me integrate'.

At the other end of the intellectual scale I remember an incident in the Cavendish lab in the early 1930s. I was attending a short series of lectures on the discharge of electricity through gases: one of them was given by Rutherford himself. He had done an impressive experiment: he was looking at the theory of it and had derived an equation which required integration. He tried to do the integration but apparently could not: he turned to his audience (a small one) and asked us for help, which we joyfully gave. I was astounded – the great Rutherford himself stumbling over a petty integration! I found out that he had only been pretending – indeed, he had begun his university days in New Zealand as a professor of mathematics.

Pocket calculators should help. Previously this would happen; a demonstration experiment involving measurements had been done. Before the result could be found, a had to be multiplied by b then divided by the product of c and d. Today no sooner is d written down than somebody has the answer.

Calculators

Having retired from classroom teaching before calculators came in, I first encountered them in the physics lab at Bradford University where I was assisting first-year students. From measurements of three or even two significant figures results were calculated to *eight* digits. I explained the absurdity, I pleaded for an end to it, but still the eight digits appeared. So I hesitated about buying a calculator for myself.

On a visit to my son, a chemical engineer in Zambia, I had taken with me some problems and my log tables. He was appalled when he saw me grappling with the problems. He urged me to throw the tables away and to buy a calculator.

'When you show me something that I can do with it that I can't do with tables, then I will.'

'What was your army number, Dad?'
'10542619'
'And you never found out if it was a prime number?'
'No.'
He went off to work. Before many minutes had passed, he phoned. 'Try 3109.' I did.

As soon as I got back home I bought a calculator and would not be without it now.

Calculation problems are more interesting if they relate to real practical situations such as the following.

1 To find the voltage of an electrostatic machine

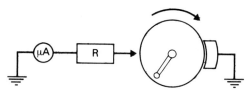

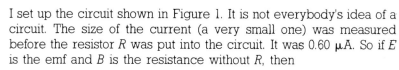

Figure 1

I set up the circuit shown in Figure 1. It is not everybody's idea of a circuit. The size of the current (a very small one) was measured before the resistor R was put into the circuit. It was 0.60 μA. So if E is the emf and B is the resistance without R, then

$$E = 0.60 \times 10^{-6}B$$

When a very large resistance – no less than 10^5 MΩ – was included, the current dropped to 0.10 μA. In this case

$$E = 0.10 \times 10^{-6}(B + 10^{11})$$

Therefore

$$0.60B = 0.10(B + 10^{11})$$

and

$$B = 2.0 \times 10^{16}$$

Therefore

$$E = 0.60 \times 10^{-6} \times 2.0 \times 10^{10}$$
$$= 1.2 \times 10^4$$

Thus the resistance of the circuit was 2.0×10^{10} MΩ and the emf was 12 kV.

2 To find the voltage required for a 5 cm Van de Graaff spark

If i is the current taken up to the sphere and t is the time between sparks, the quantity Q of electricity discharged at each spark is

$$i \times t$$

If the capacitance of the sphere is C, this quantity raises the potential of the sphere to V where V equals Q/C. So

$$V = \frac{it}{C}$$

The capacitance of an isolated sphere of radius r is $4\pi\epsilon_0 r$ and so

$$V = \frac{it}{4\pi\epsilon_0 r}$$

The main sphere was separated from the discharging sphere by a

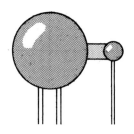

Figure 2

card (Figure 2). The current measured by the method shown in Chapter 15, Figure 18, was 5.5 μA. The sparking began as soon as the wire shown in the figure was moved back. Twenty sparks were counted, regularly spaced in time. The average time between the sparks was 0.48 s. The radius r was 0.15 m. ϵ_0 is 8.85×10^{-12} F/m. Thus

$$V = \frac{5.5 \times 10^{-6} \times 0.48}{4\pi \times 0.15 \times 8.85 \times 10^{-12}}$$

$$= 0.16 \times 10^6$$

To get a 5 cm spark, the voltage required was 160 kV. This agrees with the figure of 30 kV/cm usually quoted. It is, however, a considerable overestimate: since the sphere is not isolated, its capacitance will be greater than that of an isolated 30 cm sphere.

3 The electrophorus: theory

The electrophorus is generally regarded qualitatively but there is a quantitative side to it. We have seen that it will make tissue-paper arrows stand upright and dutch metal strips levitate by the electrostatic force of repulsion. What is the size of this force? A full treatment of the problem is given in Jean's classical *Electricity and Magnetism*.

Consider a metal strip of area δA resting in a recess in the surface of a conductor (Figure 3).

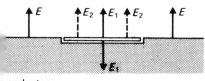

onductor

Figure 3

Above this strip there will be an upward field E_1 due to the charge on the strip, and below it there will be an equal downward field.

Above the strip there will be another field E_2 due to the charges which surround the strip. The sum of E_1 and E_2 will equal the field E above the conductor

$$E = E_1 + E_2$$

There can be no field within the metal below the strip, because it is a conductor. The field E_2 is upwards everywhere; the field E_1 changes sign from the top of the strip to the bottom. Since there is no field below the strip,

$$0 = -E_1 + E_2$$

and

$$E_1 = \tfrac{1}{2}E$$

So half the field E above the strip is due to the strip; the other half is due to the surrounding charges.

The strip cannot exert a force on itself. (It is the field due to the surrounding charges which produces levitation in the gold-leaf experiment.) Thus for the strip

the upwards force = the charge on the strip $\times \frac{1}{2}$ the field

If σ is the surface density of the charge on the conductor, the charge on the strip is $\sigma \times \delta A$. By electrostatic theory, E equals σ/ϵ_0 and so the force F of repulsion on the strip is

$$F = \frac{1}{2}\sigma \times \delta A \times \frac{\sigma}{\epsilon_0}$$

$$= \frac{1}{2}\frac{\sigma^2 \, \delta A}{\epsilon_0}$$

If Δ is the superficial density (mass/area), the force of gravity on the strip equals $\Delta\delta Ag$. When F just exceeds the force of gravity, the strip will rise. In the critical case

$$\frac{1}{2}\frac{\sigma^2 \, \delta A}{\epsilon_0} = \Delta\delta Ag$$

and

$$\sigma^2 = 2\Delta g\epsilon_0 \tag{1}$$

The electrophorus: practice

In Chapter 15 I described how to levitate dutch metal strips using a homemade electrophorus. As the strip is not held up but thrown up, the charge density given by equation (1) is well below the real value. Since for dutch metal Δ equals 4.8×10^{-3} kg/m^2 the equation gives $\sigma = 0.90$ μC/m^2. If the strip is levitated, we can say that the charge density is at least 0.90 μC/m^2.

I found that the superficial density of some tissue-paper was 1.9×10^{-2} kg/m^2; that of newsprint was 5.0×10^{-2} kg/m^2. I cut rectangular strips $13\frac{1}{2}$ cm $\times$ 1 cm of both tissue-paper and newspaper, and mounted them in turn on the metal plate of an electrophorus, as shown in Chapter 15, Figure 5. Only when the humidity was below 45% would the newsprint stand up; only when the humidity was high (about 85%) did the tissue-paper fail to stand up.

At the stage when the strip is about to stand up (Figure 4) all the charge on the metal plate will be on its top side. Moreover, like the charge on the record, it will be uniformly spread. σ is equal to this charge divided by the total area. As the record is lifted, charge will flow to the bottom side of the plate, thus reducing the surface density. But since the paper strip has begun to rise, extra charge will flow to it. This explains why once the strip has stood up it remains standing.

Substituting the value for Δ in equation (1) gives a value of 2.9 μC/m^2 for the charge density on the plate.

On a day when the newsprint would just stand up, I measured the charge on the plate with an electrometer. Taking the average of six readings, I obtained a value of 0.20 μC. The area of each side of the plate was 7.1×10^{-2} m^2 and so, when all the charge was on one side, the charge density was 0.20 $\times$ 7.1 $\times$ 10^{-2}, i.e. 2.8 μC/m^2, in agreement with the other value.

There is a different way of looking at these results. If equation (1) is transposed, it becomes

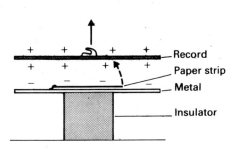

Record
Paper strip
Metal
Insulator

Figure 4

$$\epsilon_0 = \frac{\sigma^2}{2\Delta g}$$

The value of σ found from the electrometer measurements can then be used to obtain a value for ϵ_0.

$$\epsilon_0 = \frac{(2.8 \times 10^{-6})^2}{2 \times 5.0 \times 10^{-2} \times 9.8}$$

$$= 8.0 \times 10^{-12} \text{ F/m}$$

Epsilon nought is a difficult idea to grasp: to some it is remote and unreal. Perhaps the fact that this simple experiment with a gramophone record, a strip of newsprint and a metal disc will give a value for it (even though only a rough one) will help to make it more real.

A parallel-plate capacitor: practice

From the single plate of the electrophorus we move to parallel plates. With the extra-high-tension voltages now available, it is possible to lift small tissue-paper squares from the bottom plate.

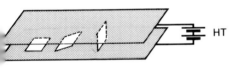

Figure 5

If the side of the square is less than the separation of the plates, then as the voltage is increased the square will eventually stand up along one edge (Figure 5). A further increase in voltage will cause the square to jump up to the top plate and to stay there for a few seconds before falling down.

From the superficial density of the tissue-paper it is possible to calculate the critical voltage. For small squares the critical voltage should be independent of the area. I found, however, that the larger – though still small – squares were lifted by slightly smaller voltages. The reason is that a lack in flatness has a greater effect with them.

The plates were separated by small perspex blocks (thickness, 3 mm). When 2, 3 and 4 blocks were piled up in turn, I found that the lifting voltages were 1400 V, 2100 V and 2900 V respectively. Thus the field strength between the plates depends on the ratio of voltage to separation.

If squares cut from thin metal foil are used, sparking takes place and there is no regularity of behaviour.

Theory

For a given separation d of the plates and a given superficial density Δ of the tissue-paper, find the critical voltage for lifting.

Equation (1) above has to be adapted. Electrostatic theory shows that the capacitance of a parallel-plate air capacitor is $\epsilon_0 A/d$, where A is the area of each plate. Thus

$$\frac{Q}{V} = \frac{\epsilon_0 A}{d} \quad \text{and so} \quad V = \frac{Q}{A} \times \frac{d}{\epsilon_0}$$

Q/A equals the surface density σ of charge and so

$$V = \sigma \frac{d}{\epsilon_0}$$

Using equation (1) for σ^2, we find that

$$V^2 = \frac{\sigma^2 d^2}{\epsilon_0{}^2} = \frac{2\Delta g \epsilon_0 d^2}{\epsilon_0{}^2}$$

and so

$$V^2 = \frac{2\Delta g d^2}{\epsilon_0} \tag{2}$$

For a sheet of tissue-paper, Δ equalled 1.86×10^{-2} kg/m^2. I checked the sheet for uniformity of Δ by cutting several $\frac{1}{2}$ cm squares: they all lifted at practically the same voltage, 1300 V. The separation d was 6.5×10^{-3} m. Substitution in equation (2) gives a value for V of 1400 V, satisfactorily near the voltmeter value of 1300 V.

The experiment can be regarded as a method of checking the calibration of a voltmeter. Thus it is an electrostatic method of checking an electromagnetically calibrated instrument. It provides a link between electrostatics and electromagnetism and so it will give another value for epsilon nought!

Re-arranging equation (2) we find that

$$\epsilon_0 = \frac{2\Delta g d^2}{V^2}$$

Substituting the values for Δ, d and V from the experiment, we find that the experiment gives

$$\epsilon_0 = 9.1 \times 10^{-12} \text{ F/m}$$

Ancient history

Once upon a time there were two systems of electrical units, the electromagnetic and the electrostatic. (The electrostatic unit of charge was that point charge which placed 1 cm from an equal charge would repel it with a force of 1 dyne.)

The capacity of a parallel-plate capacitor could be calculated in electrostatic units from its dimensions. The capacity could be measured using electromagnetic methods.

Maxwell showed that the two values of the capacity, the electromagnetic and the electrostatic, were connected by the velocity of electromagnetic waves in general and light in particular.

Thus, in the 1920s, experiments to measure capacities were sometimes called experiments to measure the velocity of light. As schoolboys, we were delighted to think that we were measuring this fundamental quantity but some of us did wonder just where light came in.

Figure 6

The Van de Graaff blows its top

Practice

If a small cardboard or metal cap is placed on the dome of a Van de Graaff generator and the spark gap is slowly increased, the cap will eventually be blown off, to the delight of juvenile beholders (Figure 6).

Testing with cardboard circles of diameter 1, 3 and 5 cm showed that the spark gap needed was independent of diameter up to a diameter of 5 cm.

A square cap made from aluminium tape required a gap of $2\frac{1}{2}$ cm. A longer strip of the same tape folded so that it was four pieces thick required a gap of 5 cm. A *fourfold* increase in mass requires a *doubling* of the gap.

As theory predicts that the force of repulsion is proportional to the square of the voltage, the fourfold increase in mass means a doubling of voltage. Thus the voltage is proportional to the width of the gap.

A thin cardboard cap with a mass-to-area ratio Δ of 0.11 kg/m^2 required a gap S of $2\frac{3}{4}$ cm; a thicker cap with a mass-to-area ratio of 0.53 kg/m^2 required a gap of 6 cm. For the first cap S^2/Δ is 690; for the second cap it is 680. This confirms the idea that the voltage is proportional to the gap.

Theory

From equation (1), derive the connection between voltage V, radius r and mass-to-area ratio Δ.

Electrostatic theory tells us that the charge density

$$\sigma = E\epsilon_0$$

where E is the field strength, and that the field strength just outside a sphere equals V/r. Thus

$$\sigma = E\epsilon_0 = \frac{V}{r}\epsilon_0$$

But

$$\sigma^2 = 2\Delta g\epsilon_0 \tag{1}$$

Therefore

$$\frac{V^2}{r^2}\epsilon_0{}^2 = 2\Lambda g\epsilon_0$$

and so

$$V^2 = \frac{2\Delta g r^2}{\epsilon_0}$$

The radius of the dome was 0.15 m. Substituting, we find that the voltage required to blow the lighter cap off is 74 kV; that required to blow the heavier cap off is 160 kV:

$$\frac{74}{2\frac{3}{4}} \approx 27 \qquad \frac{160}{6} \approx 27$$

The figure usually quoted is 30 kV/cm. A weakness in this calculation is the neglect of the effect of the nearness of the discharging sphere. The capacitance of the main sphere will certainly be increased by the presence of its small neighbour.

Why is the spark safe?

Children who have been taught that voltages of 240 V are exceedingly dangerous want to know why it is safe to take the much, much higher voltages of the Van de Graaff generator.

The reason lies in the very low capacitance of the sphere. The capacitance of an isolated sphere is $4\pi\epsilon_0 r$ and so for a dome of radius 15 cm it is only 17×10^{-12} F. The charge stored on the dome is in consequence very small indeed and is very quickly conducted away through the human body to earth. Experience shows that the human body can take this short-lived current without harm.

The Van de Graaff replaced the Wimshurst machine. It is more reliable, gives longer sparks and is much easier to explain. The capacitance of the Leyden jars of the Wimshurst was far greater than that of the Van de Graaff dome. A shock from the Wimshurst machine could be most unpleasant, even dangerous.

What has maths to do with it?

There is a game called the *The Tower of Hanöi*. Six discs of decreasing size rest on one of three pegs (Figure 7). They have to be moved one at a time from the first peg to the second peg, making use of the third peg in such a way that a bigger disc is never on top of a smaller one. The object of the game is to do this in the minimum number of moves.

This game came into our sergeants' mess in Braunschweig. The RSM tried his hand and declared that he could do it in 57 moves. I went into a corner and wrote some numbers down.

'No, sergeant-major, with all due respect you did not do it in 57 moves. The minimum number is 63.' The other sergeants gasped: Sgt. Siddons had gone too far this time. The RSM fumed and blustered. I stood my ground. '57', he repeated. '63', I replied.

So we put it to the test. Every move he made was watched with eagle eyes and carefully counted. To give the RSM his due, he did not make a wrong move: he did it in 63. He said nothing, and stalked out of the mess. The other sergeants, relieved for my sake, wanted to know how I had done it.

'By maths.'
'What has maths to do with a game?' They persisted, 'How had I done it?'
'$2^n - 1$' , I replied.

Like Hooke, centuries before, I wanted to keep the secret to myself. The numbers that I had written down were 1, 3 and 7, the number of moves required with 1, 2 and 3 discs. With 4 discs, 3 discs would first be moved (7), then the 4th disc itself (1), then 3 again (7).

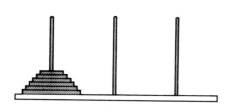

Figure 7

$$7 + 1 + 7 = 15 \quad 15 = 2^4 - 1$$

For six discs,

$$2^6 - 1 = 63$$

I later relented, explained how I had done it and urged them, as I have so often urged my students, not to be afraid of calculating.

Chapter 17

Electromagnetism

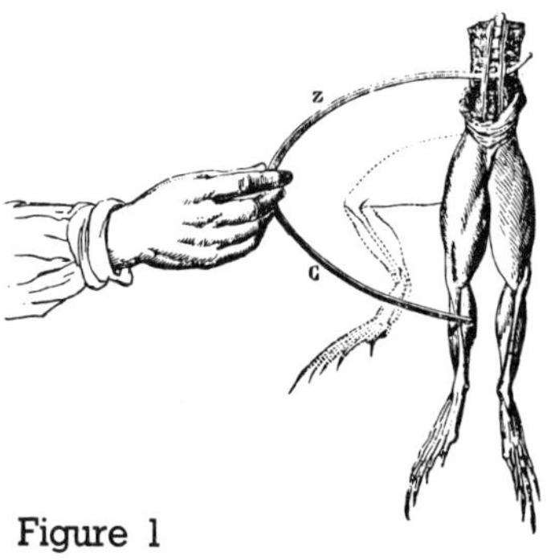

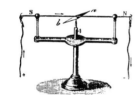

Figure 1

Figure 2

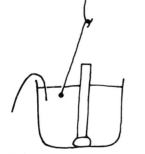

Figure 3

Figure 4

Two ifs

Luigi Galvani, Professor of Anatomy in Bologna about 1780, investigated the effect of static electricity in frogs. He found that when the lumbar nerves of a dead frog were connected with the crural muscles by a metallic circuit the muscles contracted briskly. This was the starting point of the discovery of galvanic electricity.

Figure 1 is from Ganot's *Physics*. The Italian frog is huge in comparison with an English one. Saint Patrick is reputed to have banished all the frogs (as well as all the snakes) from Ireland. *If* he had banished them from Italy as well, when would currents of ampere strength have started to flow? When the frog legs twitched on Galvani's table, we jumped into the modern era – the age of electricity.

Hans Christian Oersted in 1819 discovered (some say accidentally) that when the current from a galvanic battery flowed along a wire a neighbouring magnetic needle was affected. Electromagnetism had begun. *If* the earth itself had not been a magnet, how could electromagnetism have been discovered?

Oersted's experiment

Figure 2, also from Ganot, shows an early version of the Oersted experiment. It is a simple experiment to repeat in school.

Start with a magnetised needle balanced on a watch glass, and a small current. Then try a large flat magnet and a strong current; finally, use a big U magnet (taking care not to crush the watch glass) and a still stronger current (Figure 3).

Faraday's experiments

Two years later, Faraday repeated and extended Oersted's experiment. Oersted had used a fixed wire and a movable needle. Faraday showed that if the magnet was fixed it could make a wire move. More precisely, he made the wire rotate. Figure 4 is taken from Faraday's diary. The magnet is loaded with platinum so that it floats upright in the mercury.

Faraday reasoned that the magnetic field due to the earth, though very weak, might still be strong enough to make a wire

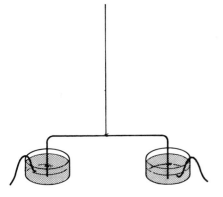

Figure 5

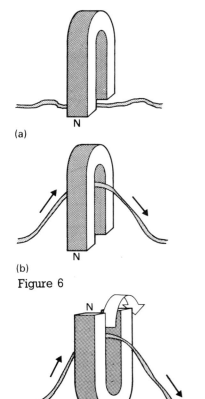

(a)

(b)

Figure 6

Figure 7

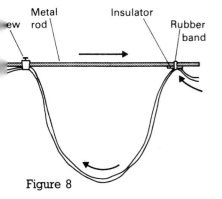

Figure 8

move. Figure 5 shows how he succeeded in doing this. The wire is suspended by a long silk thread. The ends of the wire dip into a basin of mercury. They were great users of mercury in those days; it must have been cheaper than it is now, and its poisonous properties were not suspected. A solution of copper sulphate can be used instead. When the circuit was completed, the wire moved sideways as far as the basin would allow.

In Faraday's footsteps

Aluminium, though common enough in compound state, was still a rare metal in Faraday's time. Because it is so light and can be obtained in the form of thin strong tapes, aluminium can be used for vivid demonstrations of electromagnetism. Faraday would have loved to have used it.

A common type of aluminium tape has a thickness of about 0.02 mm, a breadth of 1.3 mm and a mass of 0.8 g/m. Lay a length of such tape on a table, leaving plenty of slack. Straddle it with an inverted U magnet as shown in Figure 6(a), and switch on a direct current through the tape. The tape may jump up as shown in Figure 6(b). If it does not, either turn the magnet round or reverse the current – then it will jump up.

If the magnet is turned upside down, great fun can be had by making the tape jump right out of the U and then back again (Figure 7). These experiments correspond to Faraday's experiment in which a fixed magnet moved a current-carrying conductor (Figure 4).

The field strength inside the U magnet is a thousand times greater than that of the vertical field of the earth. For a current to make a tape move in the earth's field, lighter tape is required. I obtained a reel of tape 0.50 cm wide, 0.01 mm thin and with a mass of 0.12 g/m. With this, I was able to demonstrate terrestrial electromagnetism; this experiment corresponds to another of Faraday's experiments (Figure 5).

I hung the tape so that it had a span of 40 cm with a drop of 30 cm (Figure 8). The current returned along the metal rod. With a current of 7 A, a deflection was noticed – at the bottom it was about 5 cm. By suitable timing of repeated reversals, big swings were built up.

Some years ago, a student teacher and I were showing this experiment to a class. The tape chanced to be in an east–west direction. Up until then I had thoughtlessly assumed that the orientation would have no effect. The student pointed out that the deflection to the north was slightly greater than the deflection to the south. Only when the tape is hanging straight down does the horizontal component of the earth's field have no effect.

It is necessary to keep an eye on the ammeter. Too big a current will fuse the tape. Explain this to the class. They will urge you to step up the amps: make them wait until the lesson is nearly over. Or, better still, ask them to predict what would happen if the experiment were performed near the equator, and to explain why. Let the first person to get the right answer be the one to step up the amps.

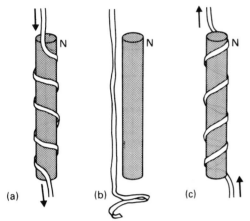

(a)   (b)   (c)

Figure 9

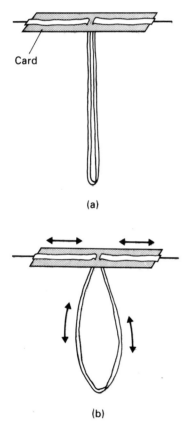

Card

(a)

(b)

Figure 10

More tape experiments: the grape vine

Hold a long cylindrical magnet vertically by the middle. Hang a length of aluminium tape alongside it, making sure that the tape has plenty of slack (Figure 9(a)). Ask the class to predict what will happen when a current is switched on through the tape. Some of them may think that the tape will be repelled; others that it will be attracted. One or two may even get the right answer (see Figure 9(b)).

The tape twists round the magnet to form a coil – indeed, a solenoid. It has become an electromagnetic grape vine. Reverse the current. The effect is quite eerie (Figure 9(c)). The coil quickly untwists and then hurriedly twists again in the opposite direction.

If the experiment shown in Figures 6(a) and 6(b) is repeated using a powerful alcomax magnet and thin tape with lots of slack, then if the current is flowing in the correct direction the tape will first jump out of the magnet and then coil itself around one limb of the magnet.

The elbow effect

Each part of any circuit is in the magnetic field produced by the rest of the circuit. If an aluminium tape is in the shape of a steep V and a current is sent up and down it, each half of the tape is in the field due to the other half.

Set up a length of very thin tape with a drop of 30 cm (Figure 10(a)). To avoid a complicating secondary effect, pass an alternating current through the tape; use as big a current as the tape will take without fusing (e.g. 8 A). The tape opens up as shown in Figure 10(b)). Each half of the tape has 'elbowed' away the other half. The separation in the middle will be about 7 cm.

The size of the force on a length of current in a magnetic field is proportional to the product of the current and the strength of the field. In this case, the field is also proportional to the current, so when the current is doubled the field strength is doubled also. The force will therefore be increased fourfold. Thus the force depends on the square of the current; a bigger current produces a much bigger effect.

In this experiment, electromagnetism is demonstrated with only 60 cm of aluminium tape and no iron or steel. Faraday would have loved it, for his aim always was to reduce every effect to its simplest manifestation.

Experiments with flat coils

Oersted used a long straight wire but if a coil of many turns is used instead the electromagnetic effects will be considerably enhanced.

Some thought is required in winding a coil: the internal resistance of the power supply unit has to be taken into account. The best effects will often be obtained when the resistance of the coil equals the internal resistance of the supply unit.

The bigger the current, the stronger the magnetic field – but the hotter the wire gets. Use big currents for a short time.

1 Iron filings

Figure 11

Wind a flat circular coil with 200 turns of 24 or 26 swg cotton-covered copper wire. Lay it down on a bed of iron filings. Switch on a big direct current. Near the centre of the coil, the filings stand up; near the edge, they curl round the coil. Ask the class to predict what will happen if alternating current is used instead of direct current.

Figure 11 shows how to obtain the field-line diagram for a flat coil. Patience is required in winding the coil: the enamelled copper wire has to be pushed up one hole and then brought down through the other.

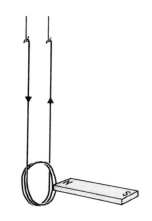

Figure 12

2 A bar magnet

Suspend a coil as shown in Figure 12. Bring a bar magnet up to the coil. One end of the magnet will attract the coil; the other end will repel it. When repulsion occurs, the coil will jump away and then turn round. The coil is behaving like a flat-faced magnet.

3 A second coil

Hold one coil and bring it up to the suspended coil (Figure 13). Switch on the current. One way, attraction is shown; the other way, repulsion. Thus here we have attraction and repulsion without the presence of iron or steel.

4 The earth

Suspend a flat coil with the two supporting wires close together and with the coil facing east–west. Switch on a direct current. Watch for a slight twist. The coil, which in effect is a flat-faced magnet, responds like a compass. The small twist can be built up into a big swing by switching the current on and off in time with the movement of the coil.

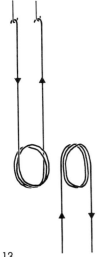

Figure 13

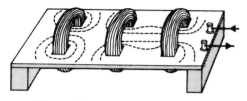

Figure 14

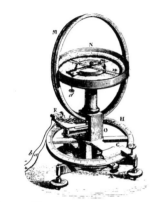

Figure 15

We can see from this experiment why it is advisable to use alternating current in the experiment shown in Figure 10. When the tape opens up, it becomes a coil. If direct current is used, except in just one position, the coil will twist so that there will be a short-circuit near the top; the tape will fuse. The class of course enjoys this, but it holds up the lesson while a new tape is prepared.

Flat coils provide one possible answer to the second 'If' question: they show attraction and repulsion even in the absence of iron and steel.

Figure 14 shows how the field lines for various arrangements of flat coils can be obtained. In the case shown, the currents through the two outer coils are in opposite directions. The inner coil is attracted by one coil and repelled by the other coil. This is an important arrangement: it is that of an ampere balance.

The tangent galvanometer

The tangent galvanometer, now a museum-piece, was an important part of the school physics lab up to the end of the 1930s (Figure 15). At the centre of a circular wire coil of 2, 10 or 500 turns, a needle was mounted. The plane of the coil was in the meridian. The current deflected the needle; the angle was measured. Its tangent was a measure of the strength of the current.

Measuring the angle was a solemn ritual. The angle was read at both ends of the needle – two readings. The current was reversed – four readings. But the needle might not have been symmetrically magnetised, so it had to be remagnetised in the opposite direction. Another four readings were then taken, making eight readings in all.

From the tangent of the average of these eight angles the current was found, assuming a value of 0.18 oersted for the horizontal component of the earth's field. (The ghost of Hans Christian must think that fate has been unkind to him: a unit – that of magnetic field strength – was named in his honour and then it was MKSed out of existence.) However, physics labs were often heated by great *iron* hot-water pipes; 0.18 oersteds was not a constant constant.

The advantage of these galvanometers was their indestructibility: there was no possibility of their coils burning out (those of moving-coil milliammeters frequently did).

Galvanometers were made to last for ever. The current that flowed (or trickled) through them was provided by enormous Leclanché cells. Only a determined emf could force a current to flow through the barricade of the porous pot. Leclanché cells too lasted for ever, unlike those 'dry' cells (which in fact are also Leclanché cells). You could get a current worthy of the name from these dry cells, but if you got a big current (as the laws of electrochemistry taught), the cells would have a limited life. New ones would have to be bought.

Money was not to be spent on science in those days. I know of one school where – suddenly and unheralded – new apparatus, new conical flasks, new pipettes and new burettes flooded into the chemistry lab. A few days later the inspectors came. The sixth-formers smiled among themselves: that was why the new apparatus had appeared. But their smiles did not last long. When the inspectors departed, so too did the new apparatus!

Stocktaking

In 1947 I shared the teaching for a term with a teacher who was about to retire.

'We shall have to do the stocktaking,' she said. 'It will take two or three weeks. We have to count everything: magnets, mirrors, watch glasses, corks.'
'It will take half-an-hour', I said. The only things I counted were the thermometers: the other things, I estimated.
'What if somebody should come from the office and check?' my worried colleague asked.
'Has anybody ever been?'
'No.'
'And if they came would they know the difference between a hydrometer and a hygrometer?'

In 1938 another physics teacher shortly to retire told me this story. He also took stock books very seriously. Many years before, he had counted the bunsen burners and found that there was one missing. A search was made but it was not found. About 20 years passed: pupils came and pupils went. Then, at the end of one lesson, a boy went up to him and said that they had a bunsen burner at home: did the teacher want it? 'Was your father a pupil at this school?' 'Yes sir.' The prodigal bunsen burner had returned to the fold. There was a problem, however: there was no column in the stock book for recording the return of stolen property.

Solenoids

We moved first from straight wires to flat coils. Now we move from flat coils to extended coils – solenoids. One great use of a solenoid is as a magnetising coil: moreover, if a solenoid will act as a magnetising coil, it will also act as a demagnetising coil.

It is a straightforward matter to make a low voltage (12 V) solenoid. The cylinder on which it is to be wound should be big enough to take a good-sized cylindrical or bar magnet, but no bigger. Brass is a suitable material for the cylinder; glass breaks and plastics melt. A solenoid that I made at Thornton and used for many years consisted of three layers of 22 swg cotton-covered wire. Each layer consisted of 170 turns and was 16 cm long. The resistance was about 2 Ω. With 12 V, 6 A flow, the wattage is therefore about 72 W. It got hot, so it was never left on for long. Figure 16 shows the field lines for such a solenoid.

Figure 16

Alternating current

In the days before low voltage supply units made life easier for physics teachers, I showed the difference between direct current and alternating current in the following way. I applied 12 V from accumulators to a Sturgeon electromagnet and placed a large 'tin' bucket upside-down underneath the magnet, leaving a short gap between the magnet and the bucket (Figure 17). When I switched on, the bucket jumped up to make a single click as it hit the electromagnet.

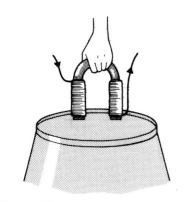

Figure 17

Then I changed over to 12 V ac: a terrific rattle was heard. If the right spot on the bottom of the bucket is found, the noise is deafening. It is an experiment that will wake up the sleepiest of pupils.

With the coming of LT supply units with both dc and ac outputs, a complication arose. When the dc output is used, the bucket does jump up as before but a humming noise is heard: the output is not completely smooth – there is a slight ripple. To begin with, use 12 V from accumulators or cells to get the click, then 12 V ac to get the rattle. Once the difference between ac and real dc has been grasped, use 12 V dc from the LPU. Ask the class to puzzle out why they now hear a hum, the notorious ac hum.

To measure ac frequency

Electrochemistry provides a simple method of measuring ac frequency.

If a current is sent through a solution of potassium iodide, iodine is set free at the anode. If starch paste has been added, a very small amount of iodine will produce an intense blue colour.

In a preliminary experiment a strip of filter paper soaked in a starch–potassium iodide solution is laid on top of a brass or aluminium base. The base is to serve as one electrode. The other electrode is a copper wire. The voltage comes from an LPU. With direct current, if the wire forms the anode, it leaves a dark line when it is drawn across the paper. With alternating current, if the wire is drawn across quickly, it leaves a discontinuous line; the wire is the anode for only half the time.

To measure the frequency, a turntable is required. (A discarded gramophone would be suitable.) A metal disc is placed on the turntable and acts as one electrode. A large filter paper soaked in the iodide–starch solution is placed on the disc. The turntable is set in motion. The wire is held so that it touches the paper and is moved outwards slowly so that the circles do not overlap (Figure 18).

The number of black sections in one complete circle is counted and the speed of rotation measured. The frequency can then be found by a simple calculation.

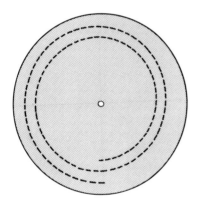

Figure 18

Uses of a solenoid

To magnetise

Before the lesson starts and the class has come in, demagnetise some steel cylinders such as needles, screwdrivers, long magnets, domestic steels (sharpeners) and files. At the start of the lesson put a needle halfway into the solenoid, held horizontally. Switch on a direct current. The class will be amused to see the needle disappear into the coil, like a rabbit diving into its warren.

Switch off. Have ready a long pile of panel pins or small tacks. Take the needle out of the coil and show that it is magnetised by putting it down lengthwise on the pile.

A junior class will be ready with questions. If the needle is kept in for a longer time, will it become a stronger magnet? If it is held

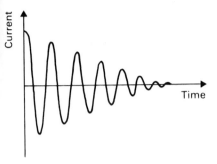

Figure 19

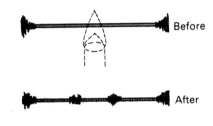

Figure 20

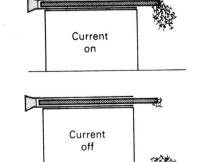

Figure 21

only half in, will only one half be magnetised? If the coil is held vertically, will the needle jump into it? If two needles are side by side, what happens?

To demagnetise

Put a magnetised needle into the coil. Switch on 12 V ac. Reduce the voltage to zero and take the needle out. It will be completely demagnetised: not a single filing will stick to it. Each time the current reverses, the polarity of the needle reverses too, but each successive magnetisation is weaker than the previous one (Figure 19).

Alternating current can also be used to magnetise. Put the needle into the coil. Switch on alternating current. Switch off and take the needle out. It will nearly always be magnetised. The polarity depends on the direction of the current at the moment of switching off. If there is no current at that moment, the needle will not be magnetised.

An ac coil can be used as a substitute for tossing a coin. Fix up a big compass needle. Put a needle into the coil and switch on the current. Switch off and take the needle out, holding the same marked end each time. Test the polarity of this end. There is an even chance that it will be a north pole.

Magnetic myths

There is a widespread idea that dropping a magnet causes it to lose its magnetism. This is certainly not the case with steel needles. I have thrown a magnetised needle down to the floor twenty times (taking care about how it bounced) and, on testing it with a search coil and a ballistic galvanometer, found no significant loss of magnetism.

Similarly, it is not possible to demagnetise a steel needle by heating it with a single bunsen burner. The poles re-appear elsewhere (Figure 20). A big oven would be required.

Older textbooks describing the magnetisation of a needle by stroking with a bar magnet recommended repeated stroking. In fact, the first stroke normally does the trick.

Some people think that magnets lose their magnetism with time. I once left a magnetised needle suspended well away from any other magnet for more than a month. Its rate of swing in the earth's field did not decrease. It did not lose any magnetism.

Are these last two ideas myths carried over from electrostatics? The charge on an ebonite rod does increase with rubbing. A charged rod, left untouched, does gradually lose its charge.

Magnetic materials

The magnetising coil shows up the difference between iron and steel. Fix an iron rod in the coil so that part of it protrudes (Figure 21). Switch on a direct current. Feed the protruding end with tacks. Junior classes are impressed by the number that stay on. Switch the current off: all the tacks fall off, except perhaps one or two.

Figure 22

Next use a steel rod of the same size. Switch on the current and feed the end of the rod with tacks. Switch off. Many tacks (perhaps half) stay on. Iron loses; steel retains (about half anyhow).

Figure 22 shows a magnetic daisy chain with which to delight young children. A layer of No.30 enamelled copper wire was wound round a 15 cm nail. The current was switched on, the nail was lowered into a bed of panel pins and then lifted.

The field of a magnetising coil is powerful enough to enforce its will (so to speak) on steel magnets, but not so with small alnico magnets. Place an alnico magnet half in and half out of the end of the coil. Switch on. It may be sucked into the coil. If so, switch off the current, take it out, turn it round and put it back again. Then switch on the current. This time, the magnet will be shot out with great speed.

Stand a small alnico magnet in the centre of a flat horizontal coil consisting of many small turns (Figure 23). Switch on a big direct current. If the current is big enough and the polarity is right, the magnet will do a somersault.

Thus alnico is harder to magnetise and demagnetise than steel. At the other end of the scale is mu-metal which is easier to magnetise than iron.

alnico → steel → iron → mu-metal

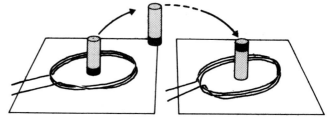

Figure 23

An experiment which depends on the properties of mu-metal is described in the next chapter.

Chapter 18

Measurements and Calculations

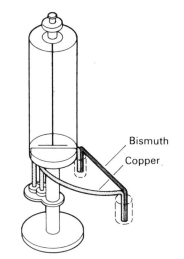

Figure 1

Ohm's experiments

Stimulated by Fourier's discoveries (1822) about the conduction of heat, Ohm set out to find the connection between the size of the current in a circuit, the driving force and the components of the circuit. The first task was to find an accurate method of measuring the current. This he did by combining a torsion balance with the Oersted effect.

The top part of Figure 1 shows the arrangement. A magnetic needle is suspended from the torsion head by a wire which has been flattened to make it more easily twisted. A current flowing along the wire underneath the needle causes the needle to deflect; torsion is applied to bring back the needle to zero deflection. A magnifying glass (not shown) was used to ensure this.

In a torsion balance, the mechanical couple is directly proportional to the angle of twist, so the angle through which the torsion head is rotated directly measures the current. The torsion head was marked off in 'centesimals', i.e. hundredths, of a complete revolution. It is a very sensitive instrument: one measurement that Ohm made was $326\frac{3}{4}$ centesimals.

When Ohm used voltaic cells he found that, as a result of polarisation, the current was not steady enough for the accuracy he required. Poggendorf, the editor of the famous *Annalen*, suggested using thermo-electric cells in place of chemical cells. This Ohm did. The emf from such cells is small (about 10^{-2} of a volt). In order to get reasonable readings on the torsion head, the resistance of the circuit had to be kept low.

The thermo-electric metals used were copper and bismuth. Copper rods were fixed to a thick bismuth rod shaped like goal-posts. The terminals of the cell dipped into cups (shown by broken lines). One cup contained boiling water, the other a mixture of ice and water. The other ends of the copper rods dipped into mercury cups. The circuit was completed by the conductor under inspection via these cups.

Ohm used in turn many metals for the conductor: copper, gold, silver, zinc, brass, iron, platinum, tin and lead. His method of experimenting is shown by the measurements he made on 8 January 1826 using different lengths of the same copper (Table 1).

Table 1

Length (in inches)	2	4	6	10	18	34	66	130
Angle (in centesimals)	$326\frac{3}{4}$	$300\frac{3}{4}$	$277\frac{3}{4}$	$238\frac{1}{4}$	$190\frac{3}{4}$	$134\frac{1}{2}$	$83\frac{1}{4}$	$48\frac{1}{2}$

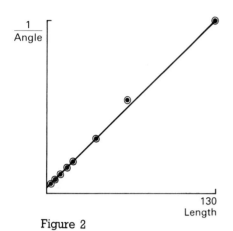

Figure 2

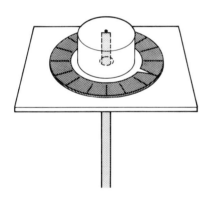

Figure 3

He concluded that the reciprocal of the angle A (the current) was equal to the sum of a constant a and a variable kL, where L is the length of the copper wire.

In Figure 2 I have plotted $1/A$ against L. The eight points, with one exception, lie on a superb straight line. (A captious critic could point out that it would have been better if the eight points had been more evenly spaced.)

Ohm declared that results like this showed that a circuit had a definite resistance which was made up of two parts, the internal resistance and the external resistance. If the same gauge of the same wire is used to complete the circuit, the external resistance is proportional to the length of the wire. Extrapolation shows that the internal resistance, mostly that of the bismuth goal-posts, equals that of 20 inches of the copper wire.

The reciprocal of the current is proportional to the sum of the internal resistance and the external resistance: the product of the current and the total resistance is constant for the circuit.

Thermo-electric cells have another advantage: the emf can be varied by changing the temperatures of the junctions. Ohm used ice and room temperature as well as ice and boiling water. The relationships still held.

In this way, Ohm established his law: he cannot of course have used the words that we now use to implant it firmly in our students' heads:

Volts equals amps times ohms

It might be thought that this law would have been recognised immediately as one of the great laws of electrical science. But the Minister of Education for the Cologne area declared that 'a physicist who professed such heresies was unworthy to teach science'. This so upset Ohm that he resigned his appointment at Cologne. For the next six years he lived in poverty. Recognition eventually came – at first from abroad, but in the end from Germany itself.

Some school experiments claim to 'prove' Ohm's law. At best, they illustrate it, using ammeters whose calibration has to be accepted. It is quite a simple matter to make a null-deflection Oersted-effect current-meter. Figure 3 shows the torsion head of one that I made from a plastic food tub (the glass case has been dispensed with).

Ohm had to make his suspension strips by beating wires; I used thin aluminium tape. I have not yet used low resistance copper–bismuth thermo-electric cells but the polarisation problems of modern dry cells are not as acute as they were. Long lengths of 40 swg copper wire can be used to provide the resistance: the sensitivity of an Oersted méter can always be reduced by increasing the separation of the needle and the wire. Perhaps the most important purpose of such a version of Ohm's experiment is to bring home to students that the meters which come to us already calibrated have had to be calibrated somewhere along the line.

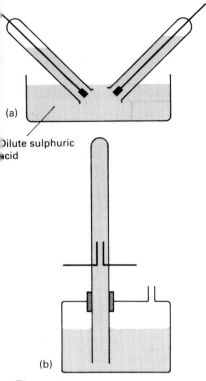

(a)

Dilute sulphuric
acid

(b)

Figure 4

Electrolysis

About the time that Ohm was finding the relation between emf and current, Faraday was carrying out very extensive measurements on the connection between the quantities of substances produced in electrolysis and the quantities of electricity required.

His method of working was to put two voltameters in series and to measure the amounts of substance liberated in each one. Thus the same quantity of electricity (current × time) flowed through each voltameter. In this way, he overcame two problems at once: the lack of ammeters at that time, and the falling off of current due to polarisation.

Figure 4(a) shows how he collected oxygen and hydrogen separately in the electrolysis of water. Figure 4(b) shows how the mixed gases were collected together.

He measured the amount of hydrogen collected and found that the size of the electrode had no effect: as much hydrogen was collected in a voltameter with a wire electrode as in one with a flat electrode.

When sulphuric acid solution was used as the electrolyte, a weak solution gave off as much hydrogen as a solution 70 times stronger.

He tried substances other than sulphuric acid: caustic soda, for example. The volume of hydrogen from the acid was the same as that from the alkali. As far as water was concerned, he had established 'the very extra-ordinary and important principle' that the same quantity of electricity produced the same quantity of substance 'notwithstanding the thousand variations in the conditions'.

Faraday then tried sending a current through a molten tin chloride voltameter in series with a water voltameter (Figure 5). A button of tin was formed in the first voltameter. From its mass and the volume of the mixed gases, Faraday calculated that 58 g of tin were liberated by the quantity of electricity that liberated 1 g of hydrogen. But the equivalent weight of tin found by *chemical* means is 58 g too. This means that there are not two kinds of atom, one in chemistry, one in electricity. We take this as axiomatic today and forget that it had to be established by – in Faraday's words – 'thousands of experiments'.

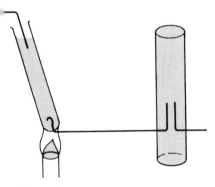

Figure 5

Lines of force: a memory

My first visit to Cambridge was in December 1931 for a scholarship examination. There was a practical physics part to it. As science teachers know, only the simplest pieces of apparatus can be used in practical examinations: the question setters have to use great ingenuity in thinking up new questions with very limited equipment.

For the question that I had to tackle I was given a bar magnet, a big sheet of plain paper and a plotting compass. The orientation of the magnet was fixed by the invigilator – probably at about 45° to the magnetic meridian. We were asked to plot the 'lines of force' (Figure 6), to find the positions of the two 'neutral points', to measure angles and so deduce the pole strength of the magnet given that H was 0.18 oersteds – a pleasant enough exercise. I had happily followed a few of the lines along their shaky paths when the invigilator came to me.

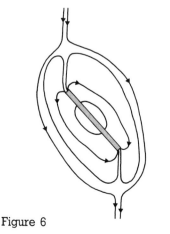

Figure 6

'Sir J.J. Thomson would like a word with you,' he said, indicating a person seated at a big desk in the far corner. It was, unmistakably, the great 'J.J.' himself: the discoverer of the electron, of positive rays, of isotopes, the Master of Trinity, a Nobel laureate and one-time Cavendish Professor of Physics.

To my astonishment, he asked me about the experiments that we did at school. I gave a wry description of pins and blocks of glass, of the variations on Kater's pendulum and of course the tangent galvanometer.

He laughed at my account. He asked me my school. 'Bradford Grammar,' I replied. 'Hmm. It has a reputation of working its students.' More than one interpretation can be put on this remark. It can mean 'getting the best out of their students'; it can mean 'cramming'. I never found out which was intended.

I went back to my plotting compass but found the shaky lines even more sinuous. How I managed to do the calculation I do not know, but I must have done it satisfactorily. I got my scholarship.

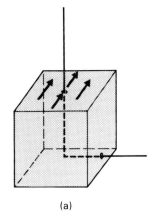

(a)

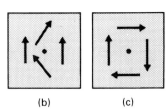

(b)   (c)

Figure 7

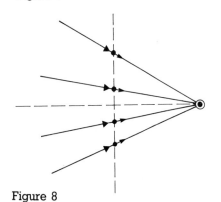

Figure 8

H, the horizontal component of flux density

Method 1

Fix a wire vertically in a box and place four plotting compasses around it as shown in Figure 7(a). Send a small current up the wire. Gradually increase the current. The compasses north and south begin to turn a little (Figure 7(b)) but at first nothing happens east and west. With further increase in current the compass east suddenly turns through 180°. Nothing happens to the compass west. The compasses north and south eventually turn through almost 90° (Figure 7(c)).

The compass east is just about to swing round when the field due to the current is equal and opposite to the horizontal component H of the flux density of the earth's magnetic field.

Put a jewel-mounted plotting compass in this position. Slowly increase the current. Read the current when the compass swings round. Slowly reduce the current. Read it when the compass swings back. The average of these two readings gives the critical value, I. If the compass is at a distance r from the wire, then

$$H = 2 \times 10^{-7} \frac{I}{r}$$

Method 2

A second method of finding H with a plotting compass and a current in a vertical wire is as follows. On a card, draw lines at 30°, 45° and 60° from the hole as shown (Figure 8). Holding the card horizontally, pass the wire through the hole in the card and send a strong current up the wire. Bring the compass in turn along each of the lines. At a definite point on each line the compass will point to the wire. Mark the position of the centre of the compass with a dot.

Join all the dots up. They lie on a straight line. The perpendicular

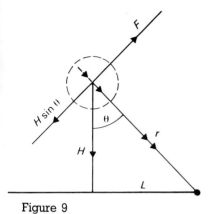

Figure 9

distance of this line from the wire gives the distance at which the field due to the current is equal to H.

Figure 9 gives the theory. When the compass points to the wire, the $H \sin \theta$ component cancels F, the field due to the current. The $H \cos \theta$ component does the pointing.

Since $\sin \theta = L/r$

$$F = HL/r$$

but

$$F = 2 \times 10^{-7}\, \frac{I}{r}$$

$$2 \times 10^{-7}\frac{I}{r} = \frac{HL}{r}$$

and

$$H = 2 \times 10^{-7}\, \frac{I}{L}$$

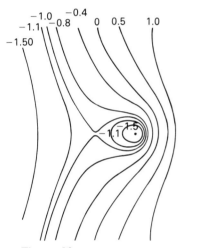

Figure 10

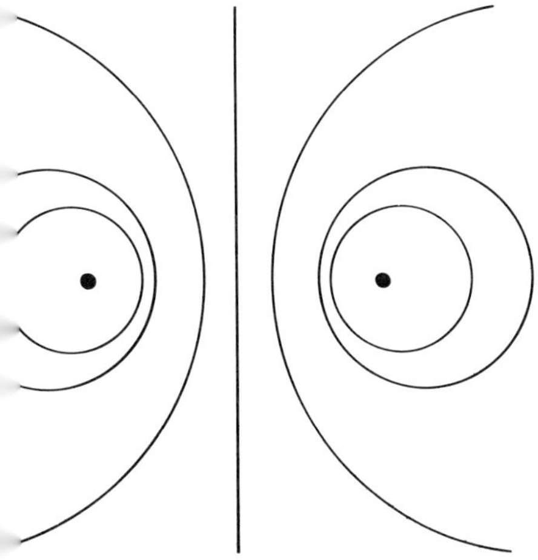

Field-line diagrams

1 The motor effect

Where field lines crowd together, the field is stronger. By giving a numerical meaning to field lines – by assuming that in air they never appear from nowhere and never disappear – it is possible to work out their shape when a wire carrying a current interacts with a uniform field. The full calculation is given in *School Science Review 149*, p.169 under the now out-of-date title 'A line of force formula'. It is the field-line diagram for the motor effect.

The shape is shown in Figure 10. The equation for the line is

$$r \cos \theta + \log_e r = -k$$

When k is greater than -1, the lines lap round the wire. Faraday would have loved this diagram; he would have pointed out that the lines are the stretched elastic bands of a catapult.

When k is less than -1, the curve is in two parts: a closed part which becomes more nearly circular the nearer it gets to the wire, and an open part which straightens out farther away from wire.

2 Two parallel wires: unlike currents

In between the wires the two fields augment each other: the lines crowd together (Figure 11). The lines are circular but not concentric; the bigger each circle is, the further away from the wire is the centre of the circle (*School Science Review 196*, p.493).

A second property which Faraday attributed to lines of force was that they pushed each other sideways. This is the elbowing effect

Figure 11

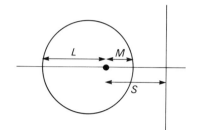

Figure 12

that we have already seen. The crowding of the lines between the wires causes the wires to be pushed apart.

Figure 12 shows one of the circles. The distances L and M are measured to the central line of the wire. The separation of the two central lines is $2S$. L, M and S are connected by an equation with a pleasing symmetry

$$S \times M + M \times L = L \times S \tag{1}$$

The circle has been drawn from this equation.

To derive this equation, I used the same idea that I used for diagram 1: I counted the field lines. The number of field lines in the length M must equal the number of field lines in the length L.

The field strength within M is proportional to the *sum* of $1/x$ and $1/(2s - x)$ where x is the distance of a point within M from the central line. If r is the radius of the wire the number of lines N_1 is therefore

$$N_1 = \int_r^M \frac{dx}{x} + \int_r^M \frac{dx}{2s - x}$$

Integration shows that

$$N_1 = \log_e \frac{M \times (r - 2s)}{r \times (M - 2s)}$$

The field strength within L is proportional to the *difference* between $1/x$ and $1(x + 2S)$.

If N_2 is the number of lines within L, integration shows that

$$N_2 = \log_e \frac{L \times (r + 2s)}{r \times (L + 2s)}$$

Equation (1) is derived by putting N_1 equal to N_2 and making r negligible in comparison with S.

3 Two parallel wires: like currents

In between the wires, the two fields oppose each other. This region is therefore thin in field lines. The field-line diagram is complicated but at big distances the lines become nearly circular.

There is a critical line within which there are two lines and outside which there is only one (Figure 13).

It is possible to count the number of lines within this critical line to the left and to the right. If L is the nearest approach of the critical line to the wire and S is half the separation of the two wires then, assuming that the wires are negligibly thin in comparison with S, integration shows that

$$L^2 + 2SL - S^2 = 0$$

and so

$$L = 0.414S$$

Drawn on the blackboard in a whimsical mood, Figure 11 can be

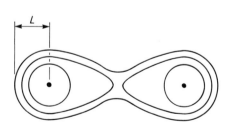

Figure 13

made to look like a slightly squint-eyed owl and Figure 13 somewhat like a frog.

'Lines of force' diagrams were more important in my early days than they are now. We were taught that a neutral point had four sides and that on opposite sides the lines were in opposite directions. Lines of force never crossed. In this connection the critical line of Figure 11 poses a problem: since the field strength at the centre point is zero, who can say whether the two curves cross over or remain separate?

The vertical component V of flux density

1 A vertical solenoid

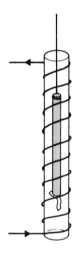

Figure 14

Mu-metal is magnetised even by very weak fields and does not show hysteresis. In consequence, a mu-metal rod held vertically in northern latitudes is magnetised by the vertical component of the earth's field. It will pick up iron filings and drop them when it is turned into an east–west horizontal position.

Mu-metal can be obtained in the form of a ribbon. From such a ribbon, I cut strips of width 2 mm and length 1 cm. A 30 cm mu-metal rod when held vertically would hold up such a strip. Figure 14 shows a mu-metal rod held by a thread inside a solenoid wound on a glass tube. The solenoid had 134 turns in a length of 50 cm: it was possible to see inside it.

When a current flows in the direction shown, the field it produces is in the opposite direction to that of the vertical component (in the northern hemisphere, anyway). Starting with a very small current, I increased it slowly. At 0.14 A the mu-metal strip fell off.

To make sure that at this current the two fields were equal as well as opposite, I sent a stronger current (0.40 A) through the solenoid. The mu-metal strip would hold on to the rod this time because the solenoid field was sufficiently stronger than that of the earth. When I now reduced the current to 0.14 A, the strip again fell off.

Thus when the current in the solenoid is 0.14 A its field is equal and opposite to that of the vertical component V. Hence,

$$\text{ampere turns / metre} = 134 \times \frac{100}{50} \times 0.14$$
$$= 38$$

In MKS units,　　　$1 \text{ A/m} = 4\pi \times 10^{-7} \text{ T}$
Hence the field　　　$V = 38 \times 4\pi \times 10^{-7} \text{ T}$
$$= 4.7 \times 10^{-5} \text{ T}$$

2 A dip-needle

Figure 15 shows how the strength of the vertical component can be measured by means of a dip-needle.

The needle is mounted at the mid-point of the central line between the two sides of the wire. The wires are in a north–south direction. In the northern hemisphere, when the current flows in the direction shown, its magnetic field is in the opposite direction to the

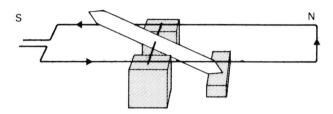

Figure 15

vertical component of the earth's magnetic field. If the two fields are equal as well as opposite, the needle rests in a horizontal position. It is held there by the horizontal component.

From the separation S of the wires and the balancing current I, the field F can be found:

$$F = 2 \times \frac{4I}{S} \times 10^{-7}$$

(there are two wires at half the distance of separation). I found that when the wires were 4.4 cm apart the current required to keep the dip-needle horizontal was 2.6 A. Thus

F (and so V) = 4.7 × 10^{-5} T

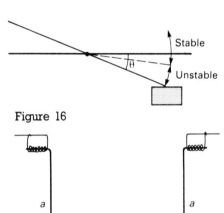

Figure 16

The advantage of using two wires is that the measurement of the separation between wire and needle is not so critical.

The stability of the needle is an interesting feature of the experiment. The stop is essential. It was placed so that the needle could not dip more than 10° (Figure 16). The current was increased slowly from a small value. Eventually the north end of the needle was lifted up. When I then reduced the current, the needle could be kept stable so long as θ was less than 5°. For angles bigger than this, the falling off of F with angle increases too much. When the current was strong enough to hold the needle in the next quadrant, the needle oscillated steadily before coming to rest. It was tilted upwards: I reduced the current until it was horizontal.

So great was the sensitivity of the balance that in place of the usual rheostat I had to use two copper plates in a solution of copper sulphate.

Calculation shows that since V is 3 times greater than H (in Britain) a variation in the current of $\frac{1}{3}$ per cent would deflect the needle by $\frac{1}{2}°$, an angle easily detected.

3 A copper tube: Faraday quantified

When a strong current is sent through an aluminium tape catenary (as we saw in Chapter 14) the vertical magnetic field of the earth causes the tape to be deflected. This can be turned into a quantitative experiment if the catenary shape is replaced by a rectangular shape.

I tried first using copper wire in the shape of inverted goal-posts (Figure 17(a)). Hooks are not satisfactory for suspension. I used instead narrow spirals of copper wire, as shown.

The thinner the wire is, the less its mass is, but also the less its rigidity is. After trials with No.24 and No.26 gauge wire, recalling what Galileo had written about the properties of tubes I sent off to Messrs Accles & Pollock. They supplied me with cold-drawn

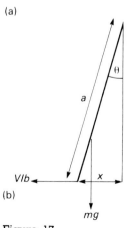

Figure 17

seamless copper tubes 0.020 inches in external diameter. The mass of a length of 120 cm of tubing was 1.42 g. The tubes kept their shape even when heated by a current of 7 A (and 7 A gave a satisfactory deflection).

A little calculus shows that for a given length of tube the value of a/b which gives a maximum deflection is $\frac{3}{4}$. I made the swing 36 cm × 48 cm × 36 cm. The centre of mass is a distance

$$\frac{a + b}{2a + b} \times a$$

i.e. $\frac{7}{10}a$, below the axis of suspension. If, at the bottom, the swing has a deflection of x, the moment of the weight of the loop about the axis of suspension will be $mg\frac{7}{10}x$ (Figure 17(b)).

Since the force on a length L of a wire carrying a current I in a magnetic field B is BIL, the moment of the force due to the vertical component V is $VIb \times a \cos \theta$, nearly $VIba$. When the swing has come to rest, the electromagnetic moment equals the mechanical moment and so

$$VIba = \frac{7}{10}\, mgx$$

$$V = \frac{7}{10}\, \frac{mg}{ab}\, \frac{x}{I}$$

By reversing the current, I obtained a double deflection which I was able to read to 0.1 mm. In one experiment, a current of 7.2 A gave a deflection x of 7.2×10^{-3} m: m was 1.42×10^{-3} kg, a was 0.36 m and b was 0.48 m. This gave a value for V of 5.6×10^{-5} T. In this way, Faraday's qualitative experiment (Chapter 17, Figure 5) has been quantified.

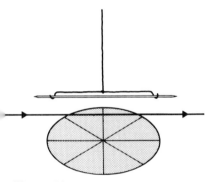

Figure 18

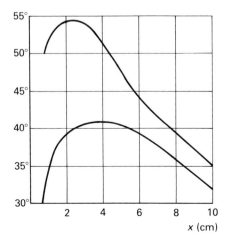

Figure 19

Measuring the Oersted effect

To show the Oersted effect to a class, the longer the needle is, the better. (A vertical version would be better still.) When a long needle is deflected, its poles move further away from the wire. In consequence, long needles are deflected through smaller angles than short needles.

With short needles, the nearer they are, the bigger the deflection is; with long needles, the deflection decreases if the needle gets too near.

For a fixed current of 7 A, I measured the angular deflection first of a needle 7.3 cm long and then of a needle 14 cm long suspended by a thread of unspun silk at varying distances above the Oersted wire (Figure 18).

With the shorter needle, the deflection reached a maximum of 54° at a distance of 2.1 cm; with the longer needle, the maximum deflection was 41° at 4.0 cm (Figure 19). These measurements confirm Ohm's wisdom in using a null method for measuring the Oersted deflection.

If we assume that the needle can be treated as having two poles a distance $2l$ apart, it can be shown (*School Science Review 232*,

p. 457) that when the centre of the needle is a distance x above the wire, the deflection θ produced by a current I is given by the quadratic equation

$$x^2 - \frac{2 \times 10^{-7}xI \cot \theta}{H} + \ell^2 \sin^2\theta = 0$$

Both H and ℓ can be found if two values of x, x_1 and x_2 which give the same deflection θ are read off from the graph.

$$H(x_1 + x_2) = 2 \times 10^{-7}I \cot \theta$$

When θ is 35°,

$$x_1 = 1.6 \times 10^{-2} \text{ m}$$

and

$$x_2 = 8.4 \times 10^{-2} \text{ m}$$

H comes to 2.1×10^{-5} T.

Substitution of this value for H in the quadratic equation gives a value of 5.3 cm for the semi-magnetic length of the 14 cm needle.

A new version of an old rhyme

It's a very odd thing
as odd as can be
Instead of an oerstead
we now say a T.

1831

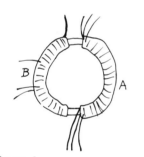

Figure 1

Figure 2

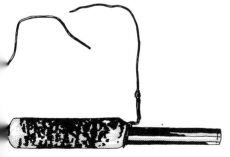

Figure 3

Throughout his long stay at the Royal Institution, Faraday entered a record of each day's work in his diary. The entry of August 29 1831 is famous. Reading the diary, it comes as a surprise – there is no hint of it in the preceding days.

> 1. Expts on the production of Electricity from Magnetism, etc. etc.
>
> 2. Have had an iron ring made (soft iron), iron round and $\frac{7}{8}$ inches thick and ring 6 inches in external diameter. Wound many coils of copper wire round one half, the coils being separated by twine and calico – there were 3 lengths of wire each about 24 feet long and they could be connected as one length or used as separate lengths. By trial with a trough each was insulated from the other. Will call this side of the ring A. On the other side but separated by an interval was wound in two pieces together amounting to about 60 feet in length, the direction being as with the former coils; this side call B.
>
> 3. Charged a battery of 10 pr. plates 4 inches square. Made the coils on B side one coil and connected its extremities by a copper wire passing to a distance and just over a magnetic needle (3 feet from the iron ring). Then connected the ends of one of the pieces on A side with battery: immediately a sensible effect on needle. It oscillated and settled at last in original position. On *breaking* connection of A side with Battery again a disturbance of the needle.

Figure 1 is Faraday's own drawing, made in the margin of the diary. It was the first experiment to show electromagnetic induction but it was not the simplest. Not only did it demonstrate the induction of an electric current from magnetism, but it demonstrated the principle of the transformer as well.

From this complex experiment, Faraday worked his way down to simpler experiments. Figure 2 was entered in the diary on 24 September. He now had only one coil but two magnets. Inside the coil there was a rod of soft iron. When the magnets were separated, a momentary current was noticed.

On 17 October he came to the basic experiment: he plunged a bar magnet into a cylindrical coil and then withdrew it. This of course is *the* school experiment on electromagnetic induction. Faraday did not leave a drawing of it but the actual coil and magnet have been preserved. Figure 3 is drawn from a photograph.

October also brought a new triumph. By electromagnetic induction, Faraday made a *continuous* current.

Arago had previously noticed an intriguing effect of magnetism.

Figure 4

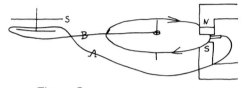

Figure 5

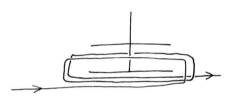

Figure 6

If a bar magnet is suspended horizontally above a copper disc and the disc is rotated, the magnet also begins to rotate and in the same direction as the disc.

A moving conductor, a magnetic field and therefore a current, Faraday argued. But a current from where to where? How could the current be led out from the disc? The diary for the end of October and the beginning of November shows diagrams of no less than 16 attempts. Figure 4 is one of them.

At last Faraday succeeded – Figure 5 shows how. The disc intercepts the field lines going from north to south. When the disc rotates, it cuts the field lines. An emf is induced between the edge and the centre of the disc. The rate at which the disc cuts the field lines is steady and so the induced emf is steady.

By repeatedly plunging a magnet into a coil and pulling it out again, Faraday had induced alternating current. From a stationary magnet and a rotating disc, he had induced direct current.

The current detectors

In 1820, one year after Oersted's discovery of electromagnetism, Schweigger invented the 'multiplier'. In place of Oersted's single wire a coil with several turns was used (Figure 6). The needle was either mounted from below or suspended from above. If it was suspended, a gap was left in the top side of the coil to allow the needle to be lowered into position.

In 1826, Nobili improved the sensitivity of the multiplier by using not one but two needles. They were mounted 'astatically' (Figure 6), i.e. with opposite and unequal polarities. The stronger needle determines which way the needles will point. The grip of the earth's field is weakened and so the Oersted effect is increased. The time of swing – important in some usages – is also increased.

In addition, if there are n turns of the coil, there will effectively be $1\frac{1}{2}n$ wires.

In the very first experiment (the ring experiment), Faraday had used a simple Oersted arrangement in spite of its low sensitivity. From this he went on to use small flat helices held near one end of the suspended needle. Finally he used a homemade astatic galvanometer.

He described the galvanometer as follows: 'The galvanometer was roughly made, yet sufficiently delicate in its indications. The wire was of copper covered with silk, and made sixteen or eighteen convolutions. Two sewing needles were magnetised and fixed onto a stem of dried grass parallel to each other, but in opposite directions, and about half an inch apart; this system was suspended by a fibre of unspun silk so that the lower needle should be between the convolutions of the multiplier, and the upper above them. The latter was by much the most powerful magnet and gave terrestrial direction to the whole.'

Many ideas that are taken for granted today had to be proved in Faraday's time. For example, he had to show by experiment the identity of electricities from different sources:

voltaic electricity
ordinary electricity [electrostatics]

magneto-electricity
thermo-electricity
animal electricity

The effects of electricity that Faraday and others studied were evolution of heat, magnetism, chemical decomposition, physiological phenomena, and sparks. If the electricity did not have 'any high degree of tension' not all the effects would be noticed. 'The spark has not been seen' by thermo-electricity.

The magnetism of the earth

By using powerful bar magnets and an iron ring, Faraday had discovered 'magneto-electric induction' (as he termed it). If there was a fundamental unity between bar magnetism and terrestrial magnetism, it should be possible (he argued) to obtain currents from the earth's magnetism. Allowance would have to be made for the relative weakness of the earth's magnetic field. Instead of using a fixed coil and a movable magnet, it would now have to be the coil that moved.

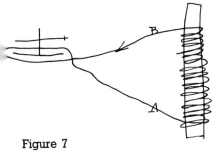

Figure 7

On 9 December he carried out the experiment shown in Figure 7. ('Helix O' refers to a particular coil.)

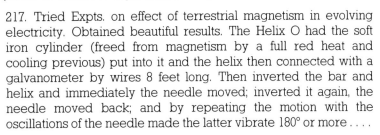

217. Tried Expts. on effect of terrestrial magnetism in evolving electricity. Obtained beautiful results. The Helix O had the soft iron cylinder (freed from magnetism by a full red heat and cooling previous) put into it and the helix then connected with a galvanometer by wires 8 feet long. Then inverted the bar and helix and immediately the needle moved; inverted it again, the needle moved back; and by repeating the motion with the oscillations of the needle made the latter vibrate 180° or more . . . .

Thus the earth's magnetism, concentrated by an iron cylinder, had evolved a current. The next step was to see if the iron could be dispensed with. He found that it could.

220. The helix O without the iron bar gave by repeated inversion a feeble and similar deflection, very distinct . . . .

The earth's magnetism, without any help from iron, had worked.

223. Found that on using thick wires in place of thin ones much greater effect was obtained at the galvanometer.

Lest with the advantage of hindsight we think this so obvious as to be hardly worth a mention, I give the conclusion of Entry 220:

. . . but putting in a copper bolt rendered it insensible or so little as not to be decided: the bolt evidently did harm yet it touched no part of the coil.

The explanation of this is not so obvious.

By repeated inversion of the coil without the iron core, he had obtained current – alternating current – from the earth's field alone. What about the rotating disc? Would this work by the earth's field alone? The last experiment that Faraday did on 14 December was to repeat the experiment of Figure 5 *without the magnet*.

He reported in Entry 226 of his diary that he had repeated

Arago's experiment with the earth magnet only. The effect on the needle was slight, but could be 'accumulated' by repeated reversal of the rotation – he was turning the direct currect into alternating current!

No iron used here, wires not more than 18 inches long and only bell wire. If had used thick wire in galvanometer and for conductors probably much more effect.

26 December

For two days, Christmas interrupted the search for the ultimate experiment in terrestrial electromagnetic induction. On 26 December, Faraday found it as Entry 274 reports.

274. Expts with a single wire – *beautiful*. A common copper wire (bell-wire) about 8 feet long, attached at each end to the wires of the galvanometer, then spread out as in the figure [Figure 8] and the loop part carried right and left over the galvanometer. Immediately the instrument needle moved, and by four or five inversions of the wire vibrated 90° or more. This effect of the earth's magnetism on moving wire ... is a truly elementary experiment.

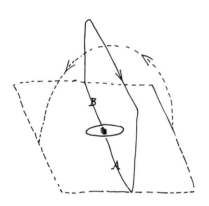

Figure 8

It would have been a niggardly mean-minded critic who would have attempted to spoil Faraday's joy by pointing out that the experiment described in Entry 220 also used only a single wire, although in that case the wire had been coiled. If each turn of that coil had had a diameter of 0.04 m and there had been 275 turns, the coils would have had the same effective area (0.36 m²) as the square with its 2 ft sides. The total flux through the coil equalled the flux through the square.

However, the big square is a considerable improvement on the coil. The distance round the square is 2.4 m (8 ft). The amount of wire in 275 turns of radius 0.02 m is 35 m (35 ÷ 2.4 ≃ 15). So to get the same flux and thus the same emf in a coil, the wire has to be 15 times longer and so its resistance will be 15 times greater.

It is no wonder therefore that with the *coil* Faraday only got a 'feeble' deflection. He was entitled to his joy in calling the experiment with the *square* beautiful. (Elsewhere he called it the epitome of his experiments on terrestrial electromagnetism.)

Later on the same day, Faraday made entry 281.

When wire is bent as in figure and *a* is made a fixed point a good exhibiting effect is produced. As both sides swing out or in together they combine to produce one strong effect on needle, for as the currents formed one in opposite directions they tend to circulate the electricity in the whole [Figure 9].

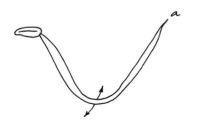

Figure 9

In neither Figure 8 nor Figure 9 does he give his usual sketch for an astatic galvanometer, though on the same day this sketch appears in four other places. The galvanometer for Entry 274 is shown as a simple squiggle. Could it be that for this 'truly elementary experiment' he had gone back to the simple Oersted arrangement with which on 29 August he had discovered electromagnetic induction?

Effort 1

I decided to investigate whether a simple Oersted arrangement would do. Faraday used 'common copper wire (bell-wire)' – the bells would be mechanical ones, requiring thick wire.

I made a square coil with 2 ft sides from No.20 swg copper wire, fixing the bottom side so that the coil could be flipped to and fro. The magnetised needle was suspended by a thread of unspun silk. It was within 3 mm of the wire.

When I flipped the coil, I could detect no motion whatever in the needle. The induced emf was an alternating one, reaching its peak as the coil went through the upright position. It is possible to calculate the peak emf from the flux density of the earth's vertical component, the area of the coil and the rate of flipping (one there-and-back flip in 3 s). It comes to 40 μV. The resistance of the wire was 0.062 Ω, and so the peak current was only 40 μV/0.062 Ω, i.e. 0.65 mA. This is too small to show the Oersted effect.

Effort 2

From copper *wire* of diameter 0.91 mm, I went to a copper *rod* of diameter 3.25 mm. The resistance of the coil dropped from 62 mΩ to 5.0 mΩ. The peak current was now 8.0 mA, which should be big enough to show an Oersted effect if the needle was within 2 or 3 mm of the rod.

First I used a needle 4 cm long, reasoning that because of its low inertia it should be easy to move. It wasn't, and it didn't. Next, not really expecting anything, I tried a longer needle – 7.3 cm long. To my delight, it moved – there was only a small swing for a single flip, and the full swing was not much more than 2° but there was, quite definitely, a swing.

Faraday did not use a single flip (inversion), he used 'four or five'. He did not think it necessary to say that the correct timing of the inversions was all-important. This timing has to be taken from the time of swing of the needle.

For the 7.3 cm needle, this time was 3.4 s. A full there-and-back flip cannot really be done in under 3.0 s. By correct timing, I was able to build up swings of 40° (full angle). (In a flippant mood, one could say that this was a flipping experiment.)

Figure 10 shows which way the current flows when the top side of the square is moving west. The Lenz force will be directed east. The earth's field lines will wrap around the wire as shown. At the top of the square, the current will flow south; on the bottom side, it will flow north. By the right-hand rule, the south end of the needle will move west. When the swings are small, it is useful to know which way to expect them. The rule is this: to an observer standing south, the near end of the needle should move in the same direction as the top side of the square.

Doubting Thomases to whom I have shown the experiment have suggested that the swinging of the needle was caused not by electromagnetic induction but by the rocking of the table. This can be neatly disproved. Set the needle swinging through a big angle and *bring it to rest* by using the opposite of the above rule. Another explanation of the swinging is that it is caused by a draught. It was

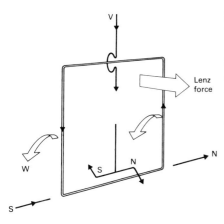

Figure 10

perhaps to rebuff this idea that, in the past, the galvanometer was generally enclosed – like a stuffed owl – in a glass case.

Having succeeded with a longer needle, I went back to the short needle whose time of swing was only 1.9 s. I cut down the flipping time by reducing the angle from the 180° shown in Faraday's diagram to 60°. The short needle now moved and, by timing, it was possible to build up big swings.

To suspend the needles, Faraday used fibres of unspun silk. I found that a single fibre of cotton separated from a thread was just as satisfactory and a lot easier to handle.

A thicker rod would have a smaller resistance and so a bigger current would be induced. However, some of the gain would be lost: the needle would now be further away from the central axis of the wire.

Effort 3

In a discussion with Mr Bernard Spurgin at the Keele meeting of the ASE, he suggested that the coil should be made of two thicknesses as in Figure 11 – the thinner rod allowing the needle to get nearer. The technical staff of the physics department at Leeds University subsequently made me a compound square. A 10 cm length of No. 10 copper rod completed a square of copper tubing which had an external diameter of 13 mm.

The mass of the tubing and rod together was 2.71 kg. From this, I calculated the resistance of the tubing to be 0.31 mΩ, and that of the rod to be 0.52 mΩ, about one-tenth the resistance of the copper rod of Effort 2.

Bigger swings were expected, and bigger swings do indeed take place. A single flip will produce a swing of 20°.

Mechanical matters have to be attended to – the bottom side of the square is fitted into a groove in a block of wood which is firmly fixed to the table. It is not necessary to make 180° flips. Smaller ones will do.

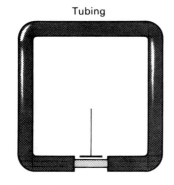

Tubing

Figure 11

Effort 4

The Members Exhibition at the ASE annual meeting is a fertile ground for new ideas. I showed the copper-rod version of this experiment (Effort 2) at the Keele Meeting in 1985. Sir George Porter, who that year was President of the ASE, came round the exhibition. The needle did swing, but Faraday had described swings ten times bigger. How had he done it? Sir George suggested that I should visit the Royal Institution. This eventually I did. There, Professor Ronald King showed me a paper that Faraday had read to the Royal Society. It contained details of the *galvanometer* that Faraday had used and which I have already quoted.

I have since made such a galvanometer. A match-stalk has taken the place of the stem of dried grass, and a cotton fibre that of the unspun silk. In place of needles, I used twist drills – the same drills that had bored the holes in the match-stalk. One drill was $\frac{3}{32}$ inches in diameter and 3.9 cm long. The other was $\frac{1}{16}$ inches in diameter and 3.0 cm long. Unlike Faraday, I put the longer stronger magnet below. The time of swing was suitable, being 2.95 s. The coil which had 16½ 'convolutions' (i.e. turns) was made with No.18 swg copper wire. It was 6 cm long and 2 cm tall. A gap was made in the top side to allow the needles to be lowered. Thinner wire would have too much resistance; thicker wire would be hard to bend into shape.

The circuit was completed with No.12 copper wire which is rigid enough not to need a supporting frame. The multiplier coil has to be held down firmly – it must not move. The resistance of the No.12 wire was 6.7 mΩ and that of the multiplier coil was 40 mΩ. A design problem arises here: the advantage of more turns has to be set against the increase in resistance. Moreover, the more turns there are, the further the outermost turns will be from the needles they have to influence.

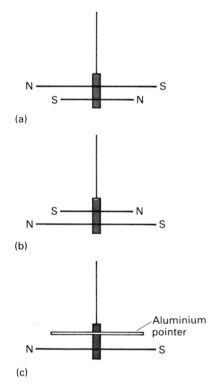

(a)

(b)

(c)

Aluminium pointer

Figure 12

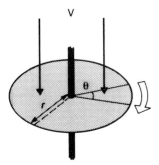

Figure 13

Some results

Faraday got 'swings of 90° or more with 4 or 5 inversions' i.e. about 20° per flip. I tried three arrangements. In Figure 12(a) the stronger magnet is on top. The swing per flip was 6½°. In Figure 12(b) the positions of the needles are reversed. The swing per flip was 19°. In Figure 12(c) only one needle is used – there is no astatic effect. The swing per flip was 11°. Thus the astatic advantage was not great: 19/11, or about 2.

These results depend on the magnetic latitude. Nearer the magnetic north pole the swings would be bigger – but not so much bigger that it would be worthwhile financing an expedition to measure them. Near the magnetic equator, there would be no swings at all.

An earth inductor used in schools has a coil with no fewer than 5500 turns. It requires an expensive galvanometer. Faraday demonstrated earth induction with a one-turn coil and a homemade galvanometer. He described his experiment as 'truly elementary'; he could have also described it as 'truly inexpensive'.

Why in the figure for the experiment did Faraday not make his usual drawing of an astatic galvanometer? Why did he draw squiggles instead? Faraday not only worked at the Royal Institution, but he lived there in an upstairs flat. Was it because Mrs Sarah Faraday had shouted down that it was Boxing Day and that it was time he came up for his goose? More seriously, was it because drawing the astatic galvanometer would have spoiled the simplicity of the drawing of his 'beautiful' experiment?

Two calculations

1 The emf induced in the rotating disc

Let r be the radius of the disc, ω the angular velocity of its rotation, n the number of rotations in one second and V the vertical flux density (Figure 13). The rotating radius uncovers an area at a rate of $\frac{1}{2}r^2\omega$. Since ω equals $2\pi n$, this equals $\pi r^2 n$. The rate at which field lines are cut is therefore $\pi r^2 nV$ and so, if e is the induced emf,

$$e = \pi r^2 nV$$

The disc that Faraday used had a diameter of 12 inches, and so r was 0.15 m. V in London is and probably was about 6.0×10^{-5} T. A rotation rate of 3 s^{-1} seems reasonable, and so

$$e = \pi \times 0.15^2 \times 3 \times 6 \times 10^{-5}$$
$$= 13 \times 10^{-6}$$

Thus the induced voltage was possibly about 13 μV.

2 The peak emf for the square coil

The emf induced across the top side of the coil is at its peak when the coil is upright. The velocity of this side is $r\omega$, the length of the side is r and so the rate at which field lines are being cut is $r^2\omega V$.

$$\omega = 2\pi n$$

so the induced emf is given by

$$e = 2\pi n r^2 V$$

V was 6.0×10^{-5} T, r was 0.61 m (2 ft) and we can take n to be $\frac{1}{3}$ s^{-1}, so

$$e = 2\pi \times \tfrac{1}{3} \times 0.61^2 \times 6 \times 10^{-5}$$
$$= 47 \times 10^{-6}$$

Thus the induced emf was about 47 μV.

Since the current round the *coil* alternates, the swings of the needles can be amplified by correct timing, i.e. by resonance. It is no wonder that the direction of the *rotating disc* had to be alternated so that the small swings of the galvanometer needles could be turned into big ones.

A riddle: when is a motor not a motor?

The mini-motors sold in model shops are easily taken to pieces and almost as easily re-assembled. This enables their construction and mode of action to be puzzled out.

To illustrate back emf, put in series a cell, a mini-motor and an ammeter. Note that, contrary to naive expectation, as the motor *gains speed* the current *drops*. When the motor is at full speed, grasp the axle to stop the rotation – the current shoots up.

These mini-motors can be used to demonstrate the counterpart of Faraday's 'truly elementary experiment' in which magnetism produces a current which in its turn produces magnetism.

magnetism → electricity → magnetism

Two mini-motors are required. To avoid problems with naming, we will call them 'devices'. The first device is connected to a 3 V cell. It is coupled to the second device by a short length of plastic tubing (Figure 14). On connecting the cell, the current through the first device makes it rotate. This device is acting as a motor.

The common axle makes the second device rotate – the lamp lights up. The second device is acting as a generator. The answer to

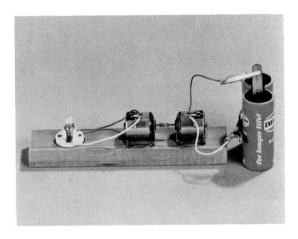

Figure 14

the riddle 'When is a motor not a motor?' is 'When it is a generator'.

The circuits can be so arranged that the cell and the lamp can be quickly interchanged. In this way, any suspicions that the two devices are not really identical can be quelled.

On the left-hand side of Figure 14, electricity makes magnets rotate; on the right-hand side, the rotating magnets produce electricity.

$$\text{electricity} \rightarrow \text{magnetism} \rightarrow \text{electricity}$$

Knowledge of this sometimes prompts the suggestion to juvenile minds: 'Why not connect the output to the input and so realise the inventors dream of dreams, to get something for nothing?'

Non-effects

We are familiar today with a word coined by journalists – 'non-event'. An effect that Faraday looked for and did not find was that of the nature of the conductor on electromagnetic induction. The distinction between emf and current, which is clear to us, was not so clear to Faraday. He did not use the word emf, but what he was really looking for was any effect of the nature of the conductor on the *induced emf.*

On 28 December he began to experiment with copper and iron. Was the emf induced in the iron different from that induced in the copper? The earth rotates, so if a wire is laid on the ground in the direction of the magnetic meridian it will cut field lines, and an emf will be induced across its ends. Faraday used two such wires – one of copper and one of iron. The circuit was completed through a galvanometer (Figure 15).

No current was found – the emf across the iron equalled that across the copper. The emf can be calculated – it is not too small. The velocity of a point on the ground in London due to the rotation of the earth is given by

$$2\pi r(\cos\theta)/24 \times 60 \times 60 \text{ m/s}$$

r is 6.4×10^6 m, θ is 52° (Figure 16). Substituting, we find that the velocity v is 290 m/s. V is 6×10^{-5} T.

Copper   Copper

Iron

Figure 15

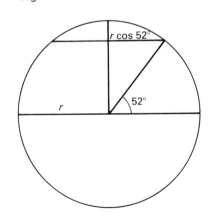

Figure 16

Since the wires were 37 m long (120 ft), the emf (VLv) was $6 \times 10^{-5} \times 37 \times 290$, i.e. 0.64 V, a far bigger emf than the one induced in the wire square.

But iron and copper are both metals. Perhaps there would be an effect with more dissimilar conductors. Faraday tried copper and water, making use of the Round Pond in Kensington Gardens. One half of the circuit (160 yards long) was the water in the pond; a copper wire on land formed the other half. This time there was a current but Faraday, careful as ever, traced it to thermo-electric effects.

He had a third try. If stationary water does not show any effect, what about moving water? Why not use the Thames itself? A copper wire 960 ft long was stretched along the parapet of Waterloo Bridge. The circuit was completed through the river. Tests were made in the morning when the tide was ebbing and again in the evening when it was flowing. The results were conflicting, and after three days Faraday abandoned the experiment.

But he continued to wonder and to speculate. From the Thames, his thoughts turned to the English Channel, whose waters flow first one way and then the other. Would a current flow along a circuit one half of which was the Channel itself, and the other half the stationary land under the Channel?

And some people think that scientists lack imagination!

A Christmas lecture

I was invited by the Head of a local middle school to give a 'Christmas lecture'. There are some problems in giving lectures in schools: the room is often available for setting up apparatus for only a short time, and would-be helpers stand about – one wishes they would go away.

The Head had informed the local newspaper of my lecture, so 10 minutes before the start, and while I was still setting up, a reporter turned up. She had been celebrating – perhaps the winter solstice, perhaps the birth of Jesus. More likely, she had just been celebrating for celebration's sake.

She asked me about Christmas lectures. In between checking the electrostatics experiments, I told her: she wrote things down. I asked her to read out what she had written. 'The Royal Institution – Christmas – famous lecturers – Mr Siddons had given lectures there together with Mr Faraday'. One has to be careful what one tells reporters, especially if they are drunk.

Electricity

When I began teaching I was occasionally asked, 'Please sir, what is electricity?' As more and more uses were found for electricity the question was asked less and less frequently.

Chapter 20

Heat, Expansion and Contraction

The expansion of aluminium tubes

Some experiments give demonstrations a bad name. I remember a chemistry experiment that I saw when I was at school. We sat in a lecture theatre, and the teacher passed hydrogen over heated copper oxide. This had been weighed beforehand and it was weighed afterwards when it was just copper. We never saw the oxide and we never saw the copper. We were remote and passive. Weighing with a chemical balance is a tedious affair: tedious for the weigher, and even more tedious for the watchers. Eventually the weighing was done, the result worked out and the EW (equivalent weight) of copper found. It was just what it should be – 31.7 g.

'What a bore,' I thought at the time. What a fake, I found out later. After I had left school, the lab-steward told me that the two weighings were pretences. They were written on a piece of paper beforehand and kept discretely out of sight.

Another demonstration involved the physics department's apparatus for measuring the expansivity of a steel rod. Again we were nowhere near the apparatus; again we were passive. The teacher took a reading with a micrometer screw gauge, passed steam through a jacket which surrounded the steel rod, and took a second reading. The expansivity was worked out: it came to the right value.

Whether the readings had, like the weighing, been made up in advance I do not know, but I do know that this is no way to *demonstrate* and measure the expansivity of a metal.

Eventually, I worked out a better way. I used six 6 foot lengths of aluminium tube fastened by rubber tubing to make a single tube 11 m long. This fitted diagonally across the lab. Steam was blown in at one end of the tube (Figure 1), which was slightly higher than the other end. The progress of the steam along the tube was followed by *gently* touching the tube for a brief moment. Each pupil announced when it had reached him or her. The progress was timed. Predictions were made as to when the steam would 'get there', i.e. reach the end.

Figure 1

A short length of metre stick had been set up at the far end and a warning issued about keeping faces away from the steam when it emerged. This it did after 4 minutes. The expansion was read off from the stick: no private reading of a micrometer screw gauge on this occasion. The expansion was 2.2 cm, giving an expansivity of 25×10^{-6}/K.

The moment that the steam emerged, the expansion stopped. The water formed by the condensation of the steam was collected in a beaker. The contraction was as fascinating to follow as the expansion. (Why do we measure the expansivity and not the contractivity?)

There are two by-products of the experiment: a value for the specific latent heat of steam and a cooling curve.

Specific heat

The water collected in the beaker had a mass of 23 g. The total mass of the six tubes was 750 g. The room temperature (the starting temperature) was 20 °C.

To raise the temperature of 0.75 kg of aluminium by 80 K required the heat given out by the condensation of 0.023 kg of steam. The specific heat capacity of aluminium is 820 J kg^{-1} K^{-1}. The heat gained by the aluminium was therefore $820 \times 0.75 \times 80$, i.e. 49×10^3 J.

This is the heat lost by 0.023 kg of steam on condensing. Thus the specific latent heat of steam is 49×10^3/0.023, i.e. 2.1 MJ/kg.

Alternatively, of course, the specific latent heat of steam can be assumed and the measurements used to calculate the specific heat capacity of aluminium.

A cooling curve

To help students break the habit of thinking that mercury and mercury alone can measure temperature, the aluminium tube can be used as a thermometer.

In going from 20 °C to 100 °C – a rise of 80 °C – the tube expanded by 2.2 cm. If a clock is started the moment that cooling commences, then from the subsequent contractions the temperatures can be found and a cooling curve drawn. Thus, when the expansion had dropped to 1.1 cm, the temperature on the aluminium scale was $\frac{1}{2}(100 - 20) + 20$, i.e. 60 °C.

But, of course, mercury has been used to read the temperature 20 °C. The use of mercury can be avoided completely if the tube is made ice-cold at the start.

Two aluminium tubes, rather than six, give an expansion of about 7 mm. These can be used in an individual experiment, the expansion being measured with a travelling microscope, and the cooling curve drawn using only an aluminium thermometer.

A thought experiment

Six aluminium tubes with a total length of 11 m expanded 2.2 cm. The size of the lab set a limit to the length of the combined tube and so to the expansion. What about going into the corridor? Here, another limit is set by the heating power of the burner providing the steam.

If the tube is uninsulated, the steam will eventually all be condensed before it gets to the open end. With the bunsen burner I used, I calculated that the steam would go no further than 33 m and that the expansion would then be 6.6 cm.

Some chemical factories have steam pipes longer than 33 m. Dealing with the expansion and contraction of these pipes is something that cannot be neglected.

Aluminium tapes

1 By candlelight

This is an experiment for a junior form: the candles will remind them of birthday celebrations. Cut a strip of aluminium cooking foil about 70 cm long and 1.5 cm wide. Make a rack to hold about 15 birthday candles. Adjust the lengths of the candles so that they anticipate the catenary that is to come. Mount a card with horizontal lines $\frac{1}{2}$ cm apart.

Light the candles, and put the rack in position (Figure 2). I found that a 65 cm strip sagged no less than 3.5 cm when heated by 15 candles. No micrometer screw gauge is needed here: the sag is there for all to see.

Remove the rack – slowly the tape straightens. The sag, of course, is considerably greater than the expansion. A sag of 3.5 cm for a 65 cm span is produced by an expansion of 0.50 cm, as the equation below shows. This corresponds to a rise in temperature of about 400 K.

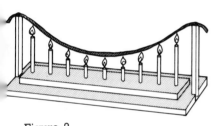

Figure 2

2 By a current

I fixed up a 3 m length of aluminium tape 0.65 cm wide (Figure 3). Strangely enough, at that time, I seem to have been able to get and measure bigger currents than I can now. I applied 20 V, getting a current of 15 A. The sag was as much as 12 cm.

For a catenary, provided that the sag is small in comparison with the span

$$\text{the expansion} = \frac{8}{3} \times \frac{\text{sag}^2}{\text{span}}$$

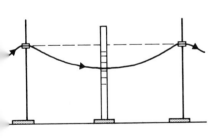

Figure 3

The 12 cm sag in a 3 m span was produced by an expansion of 1.3 cm. (This equation can be used for washing-line calculations!)

On one occasion, after the current had been switched off and we had seen the tape slowly and steadily straighten itself, a pupil (only 12 years old) asked what would happen if the tape was straightened by moving clamps while the current was still flowing. We moved the clamps and straightened the tape. A second question followed: What would happen if we now switched the current off? We did so – nothing visible happened. We now had a longer tape than we had started with. The third question was then inevitable: What would happen if we switched the current on again? There was some expectation that the tape would, so to speak, 'complain' that it had been expanded once and that was enough. The current was switched on. The tape sagged again, and by the same amount as before. In fact, we were able to repeat the procedure many times, with the tape getting longer and longer until it eventually broke.

We teach that metals expand on heating and contract on cooling. This may be true, but it is not the whole truth. The aluminium tape did *not* contract on cooling: it was not free to do so. This brings us to the expansion gap of railway lines.

Clickety-click

In the old days (and still today in some places), railway coaches monotonously repeated 'clickety-click, clickety-click' as they proceeded on their way. (But other people heard 'penny-a-mile, penny-a-mile'.)

I explained to one class that gaps had to be left in the lines to allow for expansion. If there was no room for them to expand, the lines would buckle (there are photographs of such bucklings), and there could be a disaster.

'But sir,' a boy politely asked. 'What about such-and-such a line? No clickety-clicks there, sir!' Once again I had learned from one of my own pupils. If the lines are laid when they are warm and they are firmly bedded down, then they do not contract when cold. Like the aluminium tape, the railway lines are *not allowed* to contract.

Thermal bending

After the First World War there was a shortage of jam jars. Hawkers stood outside the school gates, urging us to go home and collect empty jars. In return, they offered us fascinating 'fish'. These fish – made of some transparent material – came to life, curling up and wriggling restlessly when placed in the palms of our warm, childish hands.

I suppose that the effect was due to thermal bending, though humidity may have had a part to play as well.

The bending of a bimetallic strip when heated is well known. A freezing spray will also bend it – in the opposite direction. The bending is due to the different expansivities of brass and steel: $19 \times 10^{-6} \text{ K}^{-1}$ and $10 \times 10^{-6} \text{ K}^{-1}$ respectively. But thermal bending can take place with a strip of one material only – a monoplastic strip.

Many plastic materials combine big expansivities with low thermal conductivities. If a strip of such a material is placed in the palm of the hand, only the bottom side is warmed and the strip curves round with the convex side below. The transparent windows of income tax envelopes are (or were) made of a suitable plastic. A rectangular strip, 8 cm by 3 cm, placed on a palm which I had warmed by rubbing, curled into a semi-circle in a second or so.

If a hot metal surface is available, e.g. the steam chest from a Lees disc experiment, lay on it strips of paper, cardboard, polythene or perspex. Their bending soon becomes obvious.

Paper is anisotropic. The way in which a paper strip curls depends on the direction in which the paper has been cut. In one direction, the curling takes place across the strip and not along it.

From strips I moved on to circular discs. If a (discarded) gramophone disc is gently warmed on the steam chest, it becomes curved with the convex side below. On being flicked, it will then spin round for a long time.

The behaviour of circular bimetallic discs is very different from that of linear bimetallic strips. The metallic discs now available are rather feeble versions of the old 'thermoflexes' which have gone out of production. These brass–iron discs are warmed between the fingers and pressed so that the brass side is on the outside – the convex side. The disc is then placed on top of a cold surface, with the brass side on the bottom.

Nothing happens for a time and then, suddenly and with a loud click, the disc springs into the air. There is no compromise with these discs: they have to be curved, and either the brass or the iron has to be on the outside. A 'catastrophe' occurs when the change takes place. Sometimes a thermoflex, having been curved by warmth, is reluctant to 'change'. A freezing spray will make it jump.

In a similar way, some items of furniture give out sudden creaks – this is more noticeable with heavy old-fashioned furniture. These are thermal creaks caused by slow temperature changes producing strains which eventually pass some elastic limit.

When I was doing demonstrations of floating, I glued together two thin-walled transparent containers to make a low density vessel (Figure 4). The gluing took place in a cold cellar. I took the vessel to a warm room and was startled by a loud click. I had hardly got over the surprise when it made a second click.

Figure 4

Figure 5

A calculation

To make an estimate of the expansivity of a plastic strip from the extent of curling.

An 8 cm long strip of income tax envelope 'window' curled into a semi-circle when warmed by my hand – a rise in temperature of about 10 K (Figure 5). The thickness t of the strip was roughly 4×10^{-3} cm.

If the length of the inner semi-circle is πr, then that of the outer semi-circle is $\pi(r + t)$. The difference is πt, and so the bottom part of the strip has expanded by a distance πt, i.e. $\pi \times 4 \times 10^{-3}$ cm or 13×10^{-3} cm.

With a 10 K rise in temperature, the 8 cm strip has expanded by 13×10^{-3} cm and so, if e is the expansivity of the material,

$$e = \frac{13 \times 10^{-3}}{10 \times 8}$$

$$= 160 \times 10^{-6}/K$$

A model hot-air engine

The fourth form had reached the subject of heat engines, so I asked the class to bring their model steam engines to the next lesson. A

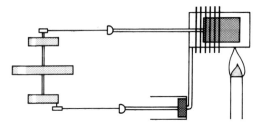

Figure 6

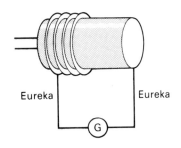

Eureka   Eureka

G

Figure 7

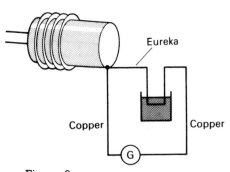

Eureka

Copper   Copper

G

Figure 8

shy boy came up to me at the end of the lesson and asked whether he should bring his model hot-air engine. I had never seen a hot-air engine, but I had read about them in Andrade's *Engines*. Andrade made the obvious point that to develop a useful amount of power hot-air engines have to be very big. A toy one therefore couldn't do much except 'work', in the sense of 'keep going'.

The engine had two cylinders, two pistons and two cranks (Figure 6). One end of the bigger cylinder (8 cm × 2 cm) is heated by a lamp; the other end is kept cool by fins. The displacer piston in this cylinder has to be big, light and loose fitting: it could be made of steel wool.

When the piston is in the left half of the cylinder, the air is heated. It expands and slips past the displacer piston into the second and smaller cylinder (3.5 cm × 1.4 cm), pushing the working piston outwards. The piston rod works a crank which in turn works the flywheel which causes the other piston rod to move to the right. The air is now in the cool half of the big cylinder – it contracts. Atmospheric pressure pushes the working piston back, and the cycle of changes is complete.

Andrade points out that attempts to make commercially successful hot-air engines failed, although small ones were used for stirring liquids or driving fans. Hot-air engines were also scientific curios: one was made so small that it would fit into a matchbox and would work from the heat of a match.

From a teaching point of view, the model had its uses. It showed that just as substances other than mercury can measure temperature so substances other than water–steam can be used as the thermodynamic substance. A class can be asked to suggest ways of improving the efficiency of the engine, which is very low. The need to set the two cranks in quadrature can be shown.

Normally, this model hot-air engine turns heat energy into mechanical energy. But it can be used in the opposite way – as a model refrigerator. If the flywheel is driven round by an external agency, one end of the cylinder can be cooled below room temperature.

Solder one eureka wire to the fins and another to the cylinder (Figure 7). By means of an electric motor, drive the flywheel round in its usual direction. The galvanometer registers a current, for A has become cooler than the fins – a warm finger at A will prove this.

The circuit of Figure 8 can be used to show that A is below room temperature.

Chapter 21
Change of State

A quantity of heat

Before calories had been driven out of the physics lab into the biology lab, there was a simple experiment about them – so simple that it was often overlooked. The calories given out by a burning match were measured by using the match to heat water in a tilted boiling tube and finding the resultant rise in temperature. The rise in temperature multiplied by the mass of water gave the number of calories.

Children liked this experiment. They had to allow the match to burn its full length by holding it at the burned end with wetted fingers. Now calories are out and joules are in. 'Joule' is not a word in common usage, and young children are not very interested in finding the number of joules given out by a burning match. 'Watt' is a commonly used word: facetious children are delighted to find out what is watt.

If, in addition to measuring the mass m of water and the rise r in temperature, we measure the time t taken for the match to burn its full length, we can calculate the wattage of the burning match:

$$\text{wattage} = 4.2 \times m \times \frac{r}{t}$$

'But, please sir, where has the 4.2 come from?'
'You will find that out when you get to the fifth form. You can't learn everything at once.'

Latent heat

There is (or was) a method for finding the specific latent heat of steam which involved passing steam into cold water, and finding the rise in temperature of the water and the gain in weight due to the condensation of the steam. As a class experiment, I found this far too difficult.

Instead, I got the class to find the latent heat by boiling water away. A measured volume of water was put into a treacle tin. A hole was made in the lid of the tin. The water was boiled for 10 minutes. The amount of water that was left was measured and the amount of water that had boiled away was found by deduction. The amount of heat delivered in the 10 minutes was known and so the specific latent heat of steam could be found.

Figure 1

The real steam emerging from the hole is invisible but only for a short distance (Figure 1). It very quickly becomes visible 'steam', i.e. a plume of fine water droplets. ('If you can see it, it can't be real steam.') During the 10 minutes boiling time, the students had nothing in particular to do. To pass the time, they held strips, squares and circles of paper and thin card in the steam jet and observed the consequent curling.

Don't ask me

I was privileged to read some of the questions sent in to the Yorkshire Television popular science programme *Don't ask me*.

A common question was: 'Why is the reflection from the inside of a spoon upside down?'

A better one was: 'Why is it that when you blow on a glowing splint it bursts into flames?'

An absurd one was: 'Why are the colours of the rainbow seen in Australia upside down?'

A thought-provoker came from a six year old: 'Why in books does it look fun to play in snow but in real life it's terrible?'

Evaporation cools

Cover the bulb of a mercury thermometer with cotton wool and fasten the wool in place with a rubber band. Wet the cotton wool with water. Read the temperature. Shake the thermometer vigorously but carefully, to avoid breakage. Read the new temperature – this will be lower by perhaps 2 or 3 °C.

Next wet the bulb with alcohol and shake: the drop in temperature is considerably greater – 10 °C. Water at room temperature is a long way from its boiling point – alcohol not so far, and so its rate of evaporation is greater than that of water.

If ether (boiling point, 36 °C) is used, it evaporates so quickly that more than one dip is required and the mercury will shrink below 0 °C. (The thermometer must be held at arm's length to avoid the vapour.)

The cooling effect of evaporation is used in the water in the wet-and-dry bulb hygrometer.

Other hygrometers depend on the expansion and contraction of fibres with a change in humidity. Pine cones show this effect well and add a touch of nature to a physics lab. When they are dry, they open up; when they are wet, they close down (Figure 2). If cold water is used, the closing down is slow: with hot water, it is much quicker.

The force involved must be quite considerable, as is shown by the Hemlock Stork's Bill. Its seeds are planted by this force. They are attached to the twisted tails of the carpels which fall to the ground. There the tails expand and contract with a change in humidity: carrying the seeds, they screw their way into the ground.

Dry   Wet

Figure 2

Tales from Tura Caves

At Tura on the east bank of the River Nile, there is a range of hills made from white limestone. Great cubes of this limestone were cut out, leaving long tunnels into the hill. They were then transported across the Nile and used as facing stones for the pyramids.

1 Wet-and-dry bulb

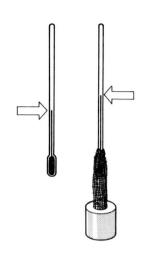

Figure 3

The tunnels known as Tura Caves, being bomb-proof, were used as ordnance stores by the British Army during the 1939–1945 war. As Craftsman Siddons 10542619, I was there from 1942–1944. The shelf-life of dry batteries stored in the caves was disappointingly short. Perhaps (somebody thought) the atmosphere was too dry. A wet-and-dry bulb hygrometer was obtained. Surprise, surprise – the wet bulb showed a higher, not a lower, temperature (Figure 3). Why?

Send for Cfn Siddons – he might know why. I was sent for. I touched the wet bulb with a finger and cautiously tasted it. Acid – dilute sulphuric acid – had somehow got into the wet bulb's water pot. Instead of evaporating and cooling, it was condensing and warming.

2 Hot tea

Another recollection from those MEF days: hot, tired and thirsty, after our day's work, we drank huge mugfuls of scalding hot tea. As soon as the tea entered our mouths, sweat poured from our foreheads. Evaporation (in this case, sweating) cools, some declared. I had reservations. The tea certainly stimulated and refreshed us, but was the cooling from evaporation greater than the heating from the hot tea?

3 Sharp ears

I was classified as a radio-mechanic. My job was to service radio sets but most of my time was spent on non-routine jobs. One such was to obtain the limits of audibility for different groups of people. It was feared that the frequent firing of big guns would affect the hearing range of the gunners. I had to test a group of Palestinian ATS girls. For a fixed output, I had to find the highest frequency at which they could still hear. I was surprised at the high frequencies that the first two or three girls could hear so, unknown to the next girl, I switched off – she also could still hear. I suppose that she was trying to oblige. I redesigned my testing procedure.

4 A camel detector

Cairo had a drugs problem. Metal cans filled with hashish were pushed down the camels' throats. The camels were driven into Egypt across a bridge over the Suez Canal. The animals were then killed and the cans recovered. Could we help? Could we make a drug-carrying-camel detector?

Mine detectors were ruled out – the smugglers would realise what was happening. At one end of the bridge there was a gateway. We rigged up a big coil inside the gate so that it was unnoticeable. It was the inductance of a Hartley oscillator. A listener in a hut heard a note change if a camel going through the coil was stuffed with metal cans.

One or two camels were unjustly put to death. We put it down to acid stomachs.

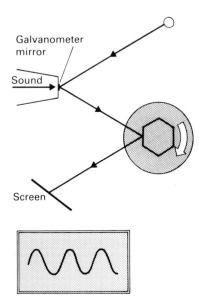

Figure 4

5 The General said 'Oh'

Before the war, I looked forward with eager anticipation to obtaining a cathode-ray oscilloscope for the school lab. I had to be content with a homemade 'phonodeik' (Figure 4).

A rubber membrane was stretched across the end of a tube. A galvanometer mirror was positioned on the membrane. A beam of light reflected from the mirror on to a screen danced up and down when sound fell on to the membrane. On a gramophone turntable, six strips of plane mirror were set up. When the beam of light fell on the rotating mirrors it gave a wave trace: the vowel sound 'O' gave a simple sine curve.

There were no CROs in schools where they would have been used, but there were CROs in Army workshops where they were not used. We had one in Tura Caves.

One day a General was to pay us a visit: Craftsman Siddons was called upon to show him something to impress him, so the CRO was set up. I made Lissajou's figures on the screen with the help of an audio-frequency oscillator. My simple homemade phonodeik had taught me which was the simplest of the vowels trace-wise, so with the help of a microphone I showed patterns on the screen. Daringly I suggested that the General should say 'Oh'. He did, and mercifully for me his trace was every bit as good as mine.

6 Squegging

For a short time our wireless workshop was under the command of a Motor Mech officer. The output of serviced sets dwindled. The officer wanted to know why. With a rebuke at the ready, he approached Cfn Crawley. He chose the wrong man: with a perfectly straight face Cfn Crawley laid the blame on the coils. Because of their low Q value – the manufacturer's fault – the coils were prone to squegging. But if the squegging was cured the superhet oscillated, and so on and so on.

With great self-control those of us who were working nearby also kept perfectly straight faces while Crawley came out with his impromptu rigmarole. We never saw that officer again. There actually is (or was) a word 'squegging' and it had to do with radio, but at the time we thought Crawley had invented it.

7 Some bridge!

The battle of El Alamein having recently been fought and won, an RAOC driver brought a huge Scammel transporter to our radio workshop in Tura Caves. He had come 200 miles from somewhere up the desert. His instructions were to pick up a bridge, a Wheatstone bridge.

'Blimey' was all that he could say when the mistake was pointed out to him. He was given a more modern method of measuring resistance, an ohmmeter. He protested that it was not a Wheatstone bridge – he was not going back without one.

Craftsman Siddons was sent for. I suggested that we should make a wire bridge from brass and mahogany. This we did and embossed the sacred words 'Wheatstone Bridge' on it. The driver was satisfied: he had done what he had been instructed to do.

The passion jug

I saw displayed in an art-and-craft shop a 'passion jug'. I bought one: the box declared that it was a 'love-meter', a 'recreation for a tired business executive'. Held at the base (Figure 5) a stream of liquid shoots up the central tube. The warmer the hand, the more dramatic the effect.

The liquid is volatile, i.e. near its boiling point at room temperature. A small rise in temperature produces a large increase in the saturation vapour pressure of the liquid inside the jug. The 10 K increase from a warm hand is sufficient to produce the fountain.

Figure 6 is a graph of the SVP of water against temperature. The curve is concave: at first, the pressure rises only slowly. Water would be no good for the 'passion jug'.

The fountain can also be produced by cooling the *head* of the jug with freezing spray. Cold hands will also do – the jug should then be called a 'frigidity meter'. The cooling spray is an illustration of evaporation cooling.

The drinking duck

The drinking duck does in fact depend on cooling: the duck needs a cold head, the jug needs a hot bottom. The head of the duck is cold because it is wet – the drop in temperature is not very great as the experiment with the waggled thermometer shows. As the vapour pressure falls at the top end, the volatile liquid creeps up the central tube. The centre of gravity rises above the axis of suspension and the duck tips over, allowing liquid to run down to the bottom again (Figure 7).

It is a fascinating toy – full of physics. Such 'ducks' can be bought in sea-side gift shops. They are not suitable for children, however, since the volatile liquid may be noxious or flammable or both. Every so often – in an 11-year cycle perhaps – they appear in pubs. There is an association of ideas here.

The time between one 'drink' and the next can be measured. It depends on the humidity; the duck can indeed be used as a hygrometer. The drier the room, the greater the rate of evaporation, the greater the cooling and the shorter the time.

Basically the duck is a heat engine. It requires a difference of temperature between top and bottom. It will work with a dry head if it has a hot bottom. A flame must not be used, but sunlight can be directed on to the base with a concave mirror (due attention having been paid to safety). A visitor to an ASE meeting told me of a trick. When the duck was 'drinking' normally, he would bend over to it and, in a loud whisper made with a lot of hot breath, command it to stop: and this it did.

Some years ago the duck got into the papers. Was it not possible to get energy for nothing by fixing up huge models along the banks of rivers and harnessing the kinetic energy of the swings?

If you find a shop that sells drinking ducks, buy two. Ask a class to suggest a method of speeding up the drinking. Eventually somebody may suggest the use of a liquid other than water, a more-volatile liquid. Why not try alcohol?

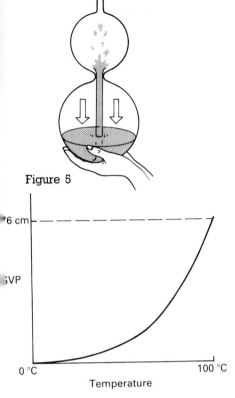

Figure 5

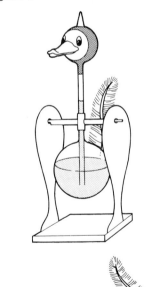

6 cm

SVP

0 °C   100 °C

Temperature

Figure 6

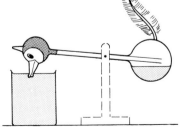

Figure 7

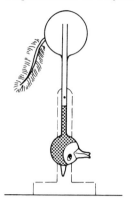

Figure 8

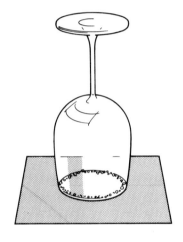

Figure 9

Figure 10

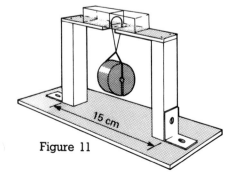

Figure 11

The drunken duck

Put water in one beaker and methylated spirits in another. To start the ducks off, dip their heads into the beakers. The alcoholic duck, having something more interesting to drink, will be much thirstier. The increase in drinking rate can be measured: it is about five times.

It might be argued that this experiment condones alcohol. To answer this, when the duck is thirstily drinking, remove the beaker containing the meths. Deprived of its drink, the duck suffers withdrawal symptoms and comes a cropper (Figure 8).

Kitchen-sink physics

A wine glass is washed and rinsed with hot soapy water and turned upside down to drain (Figure 9). If the draining board has a slope, the glass will gently slide down it. As the hot air trapped inside the glass cools, a line of soap bubbles round the rim can be seen slipping *inside* the glass, slightly lifting the glass as they do so.

This is not the whole story, however. If the glass has been rinsed with very hot water, the bubbles move *outwards* for a time. The hot water inside the glass continues to evaporate and adds its considerable vapour pressure to that of the air trapped in the glass.

Re-gelation

A famous experiment on the melting of ice by pressure is described in John Tyndall's book *Heat, a Mode of Motion* from which Figure 10 is taken. The ice underneath the wire melts and the wire sinks down. The melted ice then freezes again, so the block remains whole. Tyndall said that with the block he used it took 30 minutes for the wire to pass through the block. His block was 10 or 12 inches long and 4 or 5 inches deep: one copper wire was one-twentieth of an inch in thickness; another, one-tenth.

30 minutes is too long for some lesson periods. The bell rings before the climax has been reached. The heavy weights are still held up by the ice, and the children leave the lab still hoping to hear a great bang as the weights hit the bench top. It is therefore an advantage, if not so impressive, to use a smaller block. Blocks 2 cm × 2 cm × 10 cm can be made in the caps of the boxes used for storing colour slides (Figure 11).

The wire must not to be so thin that it breaks under the 1 kg load. Bare 32 swg copper wire will 'work' or 'press' its way through the block in about 2 minutes. The same ice block and the same copper wire can be used repeatedly.

The first time I tried this small block, it took not 2 minutes but 20 minutes. I had not removed the enamel from the copper wire. This was a useful mistake, for it brought out clearly the part that thermal conduction plays in the experiment.

The ice under the wire melts because of the great pressure. Heat energy is required to melt it. Ice is a poor conductor of heat, copper is a good one. The heat to melt the ice flows in from the copper. The water from the melted ice slips round the wire and then, as it is below 0 °C, freezes up again. (How did it come to be called 're-gelation', why not re-freezing?)

Using the Clausius–Clapeyron equation derived from the famous (notorious?) Second Law of Thermodynamics, an equation can be obtained for the time required for the wire to pass through a block of ice (*School Science Review 212*, p.470).

The equation predicts that the time will be proportional to

the square of the breadth of the block
the square of the diameter of the wire

and inversely proportional to

the conductivity of copper
the suspended weight

Neither my time of 2 minutes with the small block nor Tyndall's time of 30 minutes with the big block fitted the prediction: mine was too short, his too long.

To make water boil while it is still cold

If you ask a class to suggest a method of making cold water boil, some facetious pupil will suggest that you try heating it, so you have to add the words 'while it is still cold'. Figure 12 shows how it can be done.

Water is boiled in flask A, borrowed from the chemistry lab. Steam passes into the round-bottomed ½-litre flask B, displacing the air. A pleasant gurgling sound is heard as the air bubbles through the water in the delivery tube C.

Suddenly, the sound changes: harsh clacks replace gentle gurgles – they herald the arrival of steam.

At this point, remove the burner from A and allow B to cool. Water rises in C, slowly at first, going round the two bends and eventually reaching D, the end of the tube. As soon as cold water enters B, pandemonium is let loose, the water rushes into the flask and boils with great vigour. Pupils near the front draw back, expecting something drastic to happen. Nothing does. The large volume of steam has only a small mass. Even though the specific latent heat of steam is high, the first water entering B condenses the steam. This brings about a great and sudden drop in pressure. At the resulting low pressure, the water boils while still cold.

A as well as B fills up with water. The pupils, now re-assured of their safety, ask for a repeat performance which one is pleased to give them. It is easy: simply remove the stopper E. B empties by a siphon action. Then replace the stopper and the burner. In less than a minute, the process can be repeated.

A side-line of this experiment is the invisibility of the steam. This, for some, is hard to believe. When they think of a steam locomotive, they see a great white column emerging from the funnel. If that isn't steam, what is? The repeated filling of B with steam has a cleansing action on its walls. When B is filled with steam – real steam – its invisibility is most convincing.

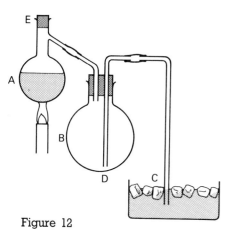

Figure 12

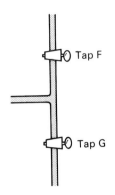

Figure 13

A Savery steam pump

The apparatus shown in Figure 13 is part of a bigger piece described in the *Science Masters Book, Series II, Part I*, p.93. This is a model of an early steam engine, the Savery steam pump. It was invented as long ago as 1698 and was the first commercially successful steam engine.

In place of the single delivery tube C there is a T-piece (Figure 13) and two delivery tubes provided with clips F and G.

Water was raised from the bottom of the mine in two stages. First, with tap G open, tap F closed and the heat turned off, water was raised by atmospheric pressure to fill the vessel B by the procedure already described. The vessel B therefore had to be less than 32 ft (1 km) above the bottom of the mine. Tap G was then closed, tap F was opened, the heat was turned on again and steam was raised. The pressure of the steam forced water to the top of the mine. A limit was set to the height raised in Savery's day by the inability of the boilers to withstand high pressures without bursting (the limit was about 8 atmospheres or 250 ft (8 km)).

In the lab model the heat can be turned off by removing the bunsen. Savery could not do this: he solved the problem by having two vessels B. The steam was led into each one in turn. Andrade in his book *Engines* says that the pump was no great success in mines but was 'extensively used for raising water for gentleman's seats'. In the physics lab, when I had raised the water, I led it out of the top window, having made sure that there was no window-cleaner down below.